ECONOMIC CAREERS

It is only during the twentieth century that it has become possible to pursue a career as an economist. The dramatic expansion of higher education and the growing numbers of economists in public service and in the private sector have created a demand for a thoroughly professional economics. In *Economic Careers*, thirteen senior economists describe their early introduction to the study of economics and their contribution to the development of academic economics in Britain.

With experience covering a period stretching from the mid-1920s to the late 1960s, many of the contributors not only provide an insight into the role of university disciplines in the education system, but describe their experiences in wartime administration, or as government advisers. The interview format of the work makes for accessibility and readability in a sometimes arcane area of work.

In addition to the thirteen economists, Sir Albert Sloman, the founding vice-chancellor of Essex University describes the inspiration and planning behind the creation of one of the most successful of the post-war universities. Throughout the interviews the themes of career paths, academic institutions and the development of economics intertwine. The result is a fascinating picture of the changing shape and role of economics in the twentieth century.

Keith Tribe is Reader in Economics at Keele University. This publication is part of a research project upon which he has been engaged for the last ten years, tracing the development of economics in Britain as an academic discipline. He has previously published related studies on Germany (*Governing Economy*, CUP, 1988 and *Strategies of Economic Order*, CUP, 1995).

ROUTLEDGE STUDIES IN THE
HISTORY OF ECONOMICS

ECONOMIC CAREERS

Economics and economists in Britain 1930–1970

Edited by Keith Tribe

London and New York

First published 1997
by Routledge
11 New Fetter Lane, London EC4P 4EE

Simultaneously published in the USA and Canada
by Routledge
29 West 35th Street, New York, NY 10001

Typeset in Garamond by M Rules
Printed and bound in Great Britain by
Mackays of Chatham PLC, Chatham, Kent

British Library Cataloguing in Publication Data
A catalogue record for this book is available from the British Library

Library of Congress Cataloging in Publication Data
Economic careers : economics and economists in Britain, 1930–1970 /
edited by Keith Tribe.
p.   cm.
Includes bibliographical references and index.
1. Government economists – Great Britain – Biography.
2. Economists – Great Britain – Biography.   3. Economics –
Great Britain – History – 20th century.   I. Tribe, Keith.
HB103.A3E28   1997
330′.092′241 dc21   97–10405
CIP

ISBN 0–415–14708–5

CONTENTS

ACKNOWLEDGEMENTS

My first debt in this book is to the interviewees who co-operated in the task of recording, correcting and revising an interview, which then led to the exchange of many letters and requests on my part for details of matters mentioned in passing. All were unfailingly helpful and constructive throughout this lengthy process, which has made my work on this book a rare pleasure, despite the months I have spent buried in the transcription and editing of the words of others.

I would like to thank the British Academy for providing some initial support for travel and transcription costs during 1994 and early 1995. Recording equipment was provided for me by the Department of Economics at Keele, which also underwrote the costs of interviews during the latter half of 1995 and throughout 1996.

Initial transcription of the tapes was womanfully carried out by Barbara Bowers, the accuracy of whose work demonstrated to me that the conversation of articulate and coherent speakers has to be heavily edited if the printed word is to convey their meaning. If oral historians really did observe rigorous conventions of authenticity, then the enterprise would close overnight.

Final thanks to Lin for encouraging me as I struggled for day after day at the keyboard trying to convert a true record of the spoken word into readable continuous prose. On balance, I'd rather eat mangelwurzels.

Keith Tribe
Worcester
10 February 1997

1

INTRODUCTION

As members of a discipline whose principles, theorems and style are rigorously impersonal, the practitioners of economics have long shown an inordinate interest in biography. From its foundation in 1891 the *Economic Journal* has always included obituary notices, by the 1920s extending to carefully crafted essays on the lives of the modern founding fathers, such as J. Bonar's 'Memories of F.Y. Edgeworth',[1] and of course Keynes' obituary of Marshall, later included in his *Essays in Biography* alongside appreciations of Malthus, Jevons, and Foxwell.[2] Keynes' approach here to his subjects is courteous and appreciative – not what one might have expected from a friend of Lytton Strachey, whose *Eminent Victorians*[3] set the modern style for the critical re-evaluation of public figures through biographical essay.[4] Autobiography as a significant genre has developed much more recently – only natural in a young discipline which has had to wait for its young adepts to become senior scholars and public figures. This newer phase can perhaps be dated from Lionel Robbins' own reminiscences,[5] although there are personal memoirs dating from the 1940s that have remained unpublished.[6] Many of those who played a part in the establishment of modern economics died in the course of the 1980s, sharpening our appreciation of the contributions made by individual economists and promoting both biographical obituaries[7] and the autobiographical essay. Since

---

[1] *Economic Journal*, vol. 36 (1926), pp. 648–53; Bonar also contributed over the years obituaries on Friedrich Engels (1895), Henry George (1897), John Ruskin (1900), Herbert Spencer (1904), and Böhm-Bawerk (1914).

[2] J.M. Keynes, *Essays in Biography, Collected Writings*, vol. X, Macmillan, London, 1972; first published in 1933, an augmented edition was prepared in 1951.

[3] First published in 1918.

[4] There is, of course, an irony here, since Keynes' highly influential essay on Marshall, relying on family sources for his social background, has been shown to be seriously misleading in this respect; see Ronald Coase, 'Alfred Marshall's Family and Ancestry', in R. McWilliams-Tullberg (ed.) *Alfred Marshall in Retrospect*, Edward Elgar, Aldershot, 1990, pp. 9–27.

[5] *Autobiography of an Economist*, Macmillan, London, 1971.

[6] Sydney Chapman, 'Some Memories and Reflections', unpublished manuscript, c.1944 (Manchester Rylands Library); L.L. Price, 'Memories and Notes on British Economists 1881–1947', unpublished manuscript, 1946 (Brotherton Library, University of Leeds).

[7] Geoff Harcourt's recent appointment as Obituaries' Editor of the *Economic Journal* demonstrates the continuing strong interest in reflection upon the history of economic analysis on the part of a major journal.

1979 the *Banca Nazionale del Lavoro Quarterly Review* has regularly carried such essays by prominent economists looking back on their careers,[8] the number of contributions to date being well on the way to forty. Szenberg's *Eminent Economists*, a collection based on the 'life philosophies' of leading economists, was simultaneously published in both hardback and paperback, reflecting a surprising confidence in this market on the part of a traditionally cautious publisher.[9] Geoff Harcourt's own personal contributions to the genre have also been published in a collection.[10] And, finally, Keynes himself now accounts for at least three major biographies, in which he has undergone a dubious kind of Stracheyian revisionism.[11]

Biography is therefore very definitely in vogue, and the interviews collected here add to an already growing literature. In this case, the initial impulse to approach senior British economists arose in connection with my own research on the development of economics as a discipline. This provides a focus to this collection, but it could well be objected that the interview format, with its inherent spontaneity as well as its silences, is ill-suited as a major source for the understanding of a newly emergent discipline. Can we in fact learn anything useful about the development of a modern science from the recollections of participants who, in many cases here, are looking back over sixty years to their own youth? How reliable is such oral history?

There are two separate issues that require discussion here. First, there is the technical question of what one recalls and the authenticity of such memories. It is important to understand the functioning of memory if we are to employ oral evidence in the construction of a historical narrative. This issue will be dealt with below, but there is another more general point: that of the status of oral evidence alongside other sources. Oral historical research is more usually associated with the new social history of ordinary people's lives, where written sources are either absent or confined to impersonal legal and administrative records. Applied to members of an intelligentsia who by definition write and speak on and off the record, the deficiencies of this approach become conspicuous: memory of persons and events is selective, whether consciously or not; precision is difficult to achieve; and compared to, for

---

[8] The series began with John Hicks' 'The Formation of an Economist', *BNL Quarterly Review*, vol. 32 (1979), pp. 195–204; Jan Kregel has gathered a selection of these essays into two volumes of *Recollections of Eminent Economists*, Macmillan, Basingstoke, 1988 and 1989.

[9] Cambridge University Press, Cambridge, 1992.

[10] G.C. Harcourt, *Post-Keynesian Essays in Biography: Portraits of Twentieth Century Political Economists*, Macmillan, Basingstoke, 1993.

[11] Roy Harrod's original biography (Macmillan, London, 1951) combined personal history and intellectual evaluation; R. Skidelsky's first volume (Macmillan, London, 1983) was self-consciously 'post-Holroydian' in his criticism of Harrod's silences and especially in the way he drew attention to Keynes' bisexuality. This volume added little to our understanding of Keynes as a person or as an economist; in fact, the most revealing sections of the book deal with Keynes' father, Neville Keynes. Fortunately the second volume (Macmillan, London, 1992) of Skidelsky's projected three-volume cycle is a distinct improvement. Don Moggridge has also produced a short (Macmillan, London, 1976) and a long (Routledge, London, 1993) intellectual biography.

example, the examination of private and official correspondence oral historical research is both immensely time-consuming while at the same time yielding a comparatively poor return. In some cases material thus gathered is of very poor quality indeed. Given the choice, a historian would use oral histories as supplementary sources of data, but not as primary sources.

What counts as a primary source depends, however, on the object of study; there is no fixed hierarchy of historical evidence in which the manuscript source occupies a privileged position. The history of economics typically deals with the evolution of concepts and theories; the principal source is the printed book and article, supplemented perhaps by the unpublished papers of individual economists. Little attention is paid to intellectual, social, cultural or political contexts. In this the history of economics is little different to the history of science as practised twenty-five or thirty years ago when the debate on 'internal' versus 'external' history was only just beginning. Since then, argument among historians of the sciences has moved forward to a new contextualist synthesis in which the creation and transmission of knowledge are understood as a social process, albeit one involving complex ideas and principles. Important here is an appreciation that the context relevant to the development of a particular science is not necessarily self-evident and has to be laboriously constructed by the historian.

The focus of the research for which these interviews form a part is the development of the discipline of economics in Britain. This statement requires some elaboration. As previous work has shown,[12] economics emerged as an independent university discipline towards the end of the nineteenth century. This is a virtually simultaneous international phenomenon; earlier models of diffusion from 'early starters', in particular, France and Britain, have been shown to be without foundation. 'Economics' has of course been around in one form or other for three hundred years or so, and in the early nineteenth century underwent a thorough systematisation that brought its basic principles into line with those espoused today. However, it remained a subject that for the most part attracted the attention of a small number of scholars who, although they were widely read by their contemporaries, neither could live from their writing nor saw themselves as pursuing a career as a 'political economist'. If anything, the 'marginal revolution' during the last third of the nineteenth century was 'marginal' in more ways than one, since this new approach to the classical problem of value was less accessible to an educated public and furthermore had less obvious practical applications than the classical theory. It was only the development of advanced teaching in the subject which provided a new audience for 'economics', as it now became, marking the transition of its principles from public property to academic training.

---

[12] A. Kadish and K. Tribe (eds) *The Market for Political Economy*, Routledge, London, 1993; see in particular the prefatory remarks outlining the international study of the institutionalisation of economics of which this volume forms a part.

This transition occurred at much the same time in a number of key countries, and the key variable which brought about this international movement was the formation of what we can term the modern university. This can be defined as an institution incorporating new technical and vocationally oriented subjects whose teachers were required to be specialists in their field and to engage in the development of their subject. A university discipline therefore became defined by the research activity which shaped and developed it, its proponents being recruited on the basis primarily of their commitment to a career dedicated to research in their chosen subject. The recurring complaint that status in academia rests upon a research and not a teaching reputation arises therefore from a simple misunderstanding of the characteristics of the modern university, an institutional form which is however today, with few exceptions, giving way to a more routinised apparatus for the conferral of credentials.

Economics had a special place in the modern university, since it laid claim to its position both on grounds of vocational relevance and of theoretical rigour. The former argument was everywhere advanced by exponents bent on securing the future of economics as a leading university discipline: that it was the key 'modern' subject for the effective education of the increasing number of managers and public administrators, who have indeed formed an increasingly significant part of the labour force in twentieth-century industrial economies. Mostly, however, such arguments were premature and reflected an aspiration which first began to be fulfilled in mid-century, not before. With few exceptions, it was only after 1945 that a formal training as an economist began to be recognised by employers as involving specialised skills. This is apparent from the personal histories included here: before the war Terence Hutchison with his First from Cambridge, but without the patronage of Keynes enjoyed by Hans Singer or Brian Reddaway,[13] could find no suitable opening and simply became an English-language teacher. By contrast, after his return from the war he quickly found an academic post because the rapid expansion of students wishing to study economics had altered the prospects of university employment beyond recognition.

This pattern is evident in many of the interviews below: that the sustained increase in the market for trained economists after the Second World War was induced within universities by student demand, and not at first by a marked increase in external demand from industrial or administrative employers. Once these cohorts of students had graduated, they of course found employment, in part in business and in administration, but also as teachers elsewhere in the education system where the demand for 'modern subjects' was also on the increase. In some respects, therefore, the market upon which the post-war expansion of university economics rested was self-sustaining, fed by a general

[13] Hutchison had studied Classics for Part I and did not distinguish himself in the second-year examinations. He did not therefore come to the notice of Keynes and was not invited, as promising undergraduates were, to the Monday night seminars. See p. 130, and p. 62 for Singer and p. 74 for Reddaway.

but non-specialised public interest in economics and related social science sub-jects which gave employment at lower levels in the educational structure to teachers versed in these skills by virtue of having a university degree in the sub-ject. The same phenomenon is evident in the outcome of formal commercial training at university level earlier in the century: a large proportion of B.Com. graduates found their way not into industry, as had been intended by those who had designed their courses, but into teaching in technical and commer-cial colleges. Central government employment for anything but a handful of economists was very slow to develop; in Britain this only began to change in the latter half of the 1960s, and there is little to indicate that large employers in industry were much in advance of this trend.

Tracing in any detail the linkage between institutional constraints, labour market demand, and the elaboration of economics as a university discipline requires that one particular case be studied. This does not exclude considera-tion of international developments, indeed, in the latter half of this century economics has become an international discipline; but given the centrality assigned to institutional factors, the case study has much to recommend it over the comparative approach. Modern economics is first and foremost a cre-ation of university specialisation and research. The manner in which this first came about and developed requires close study of a range of sources and a familiarity with the cultural and social significance of individual institutions and networks. It is these institutions and networks that are the proper context for an understanding of economics: not 'British elite culture', nor 'industrial society'. Modern economics is a creation of the modern, research-based uni-versity; its specific national dynamics derive from the peculiarities and character of an evolving set of national institutions, together with the charac-teristics and proclivities of those individuals who built the discipline.

This establishes the outlines of a research programme. First we must study the institutions, and then use this context to revise prevailing views of the development of economics based upon an older history of ideas tradition and the conventional wisdom embedded in some key sources.[14] We must start therefore with sources that can provide insight into the foundation and devel-opment of this or that university: its purpose, funding, the recruitment of staff and students, the evolution of its teaching plan. The first problem encountered is that university archives typically contain a great deal of material relating to their early years, but the amount and utility of this material rapidly diminish as the institution becomes more established. So for instance, there are reports and correspondence on the early years of the Faculties of Commerce in Birmingham and Manchester, but little dating from about 1920 onwards. More critical still is the fact that very little material now exists at departmental or university level

---

[14] Such as for example G.L.S. Shackle's *The Years of High Theory: Invention and Tradition in Economic Thought 1926–1939*, Cambridge University Press, Cambridge, 1967 which presents a very misleading account of inter-war British economics.

for the post-war period, exactly the critical period of consolidation and development in economics and the social sciences in general.[15] There is, however, a more useful source of information that we can turn to in the form of the University Calendar, which during the early part of the century typically carried course outlines and reading lists, staffing details, student numbers, names and degree of graduates, examination papers, and even in some cases attendances per class. These calendars are, despite their ephemeral character, in fact the prime source from which the history of individual departments can be reconstructed, reinforcing the point made above concerning the manner in which the object of analysis dictates the order of relevance for sources, rather than the reverse.

However, in most institutions – the exceptions are LSE, Oxford and Cambridge – calendars or other internal publications were not printed during the war years and when publication resumed, sometimes in the late 1940s, they usually assumed a much reduced form from which only the most general impression of institutional development can be gained. This is of course a serious difficulty, given what has already been said about the holdings of manuscript sources and correspondence in university archives, and in view of the importance of the post-war period for the development of economics. It was for these reasons that I turned to students and staff of the period for their oral histories: for these individuals, most of very advanced years, are in many instances the sole source of information remaining on important phases in the evolution of the British university system, let alone the development of the discipline of economics.

The focus on Britain meant that interview subjects were not necessarily British, but had spent a good part of their student and working lives in Britain. By 1994, when the series of interviews began, many important figures were either already dead or too unwell to interview; priority was therefore given to the very oldest, whose student and working lives reached typically from the 1930s to the 1970s. Those reproduced here have been selected for the manner in which they cover institutions and phases of development in economics. There is no claim to completeness; but it is hoped that the range of testimony will extend and revise the accustomed image of the development of economics in Britain. But how reliable is this testimony? It is time to return to the technical issue of memory broached above.

Some of the subjects interviewed here have become used to recounting their early intellectual biographies and tend to repeat familiar stories: Boulding

---

[15] For example, when the University of Birmingham constructed the Muirhead Tower in the 1960s and moved in the social science departments it appears that non-current department records were weeded out and simply discarded. In Manchester the situation is slightly better: they still possess in the Faculty Office a run of prospectuses for Economic and Social Studies going back to the early 1950s. In London University there are no central students records other than the printed degree lists, which themselves are bound by year and unindexed. When Bernard Corry sought disaggregated student examination results over the period 1960–90 for Queen Mary College he found that these data were held neither by College nor University.

actually does this in print, since his contributions to Szenberg and the *BNL Quarterly Review* are virtually the same, including the same little stories. It has long been recognised by psychologists that once a subject begins recounting a story in one particular way, that subject tends to adhere to this form when repeating it. Economists such as those assembled here present a particular problem: having participated in the development of a branch of modern economics, it is sometimes difficult for them to disentangle later accretions, originating with themselves or with others, from their original insights. This is a familiar problem: once one has understood something properly it is difficult to recall, or even imagine, what it felt like not to understand it. Asking one of these subjects today what they thought in the 1930s or in the 1940s is unlikely to elicit a reliable or an interesting response: in fact, one could suggest that the clearer the response, the more unreliable it is as a personal memory, as distinct to one suggested by subsequent discussions.

This does not mean that memory is completely unreliable. Rather, it directs attention to the patterns of memory. Bartlett's research in the 1920s has endured as a comprehensive treatment of the phenomenon of human recall:

> Remembering is a function of daily life, and must have developed so as to meet the demands of daily life. So our memories are constantly mingled with our constructions, are perhaps themselves to be treated as constructive in character. It is true that they claim the confirmation of past, perceptual, personal experience; but the claim must not, psychologically speaking, be taken too seriously, whatever may be the logic of the matter.[16]

Remembering criticises previous experimental studies of memory on the grounds that the techniques for standardisation between subjects, such as giving them nonsense words to memorise or applying statistical methods, eliminated the object of study: how and what subjects recalled, and equally, what they forgot or reconstructed. Bartlett's experiments included the use of a folk tale taken from the anthropologist Franz Boas, which subjects read and subsequently, at set intervals, were asked to recall. The same tale was used in a serial experiment, in which subjects were asked to memorise the narrative and then pass it on orally to another subject, who then repeated it to a third, and so on. Some of his major findings were as follows:[17]

1 Accuracy of reproduction is the rare exception, not the rule.
2 In a series of reproductions from the same individual the general form is remarkably persistent once the first version has been established.
3 With frequent reproduction the form and items of remembered detail very quickly become stereotyped and thereafter undergo little change.

---

[16] F.C. Bartlett, *Remembering: A Study in Experimental and Social Psychology*, Cambridge University Press, London, 1932, p. 16.
[17] Bartlett, *Remembering*, pp. 93–4.

4 With infrequent reproduction omissions of detail, simplification of events and structure, and transformation of items into more familiar detail may go on almost indefinitely, or so long as unaided recall is possible.

5 In long-distance remembering, elaboration becomes rather more common in some cases; there may be increasing importation, or invention aided by the use of visual images.

7 Long-distance remembering is of two types:
   (a) the general setting and outstanding detail persist, the memory process being strongly constructive, with much use of inference;
   (b) isolated but striking details are retained.

8 In all successive remembering, rationalisation, reduction of material to a form that can be 'satisfyingly' dealt with is very prominent.

Memory is therefore neither completely arbitrary, nor uniformly unreliable. Of especial interest here is the phenomenon of long-distance memory, since one might assume in a simplistic way that a subject's 'memory bank' is richest for the recent past and fades progressively back through the years, leaving a few isolated elements. Bartlett established that memory does not operate in this passive way – remembering is an active process of association and recall, not a passive summoning-up of given images and events. More recent research has also rejected what is termed 'a monotonically decreasing retention function', and pointed to an interesting phenomenon: reminiscences are for older people strongest for their years between 10 and 30, and not from a fixed period of elapsed time, for example, forty years ago. Further, at 50 the strength of such reminiscence increases, whereas at 30 years of age it does diminish in the simplified manner outlined above.[18] At its most extreme this is apparent in the phenomenon of an elderly person have perfectly clear and accurate[19] recall of events several decades previous while being very forgetful in the present.[20]

Asking elderly subjects what and how they thought several decades ago is clearly fraught with difficulty: quite apart from the problems of recall, memory has been subjected to 'hardening' and is overlaid with subsequent developments that make it very difficult, if not impossible, for subjects to disentangle a number of layers of meaning. But this does not apply to their more direct career experiences, for these are marked by very clear and memorable turning points – going to university, meeting new friends, taking examinations, being interviewed for posts, changing jobs – that are not so easily confused. Furthermore, in many cases below the interviewees have not recounted this particular story before to a stranger; Henry Hardman's struggle to remember

---

[18] D.C. Rubin, S.E. Wetzler and R.D. Nebes, 'Autobiographical Memory across the Lifespan', in D.C. Rubin (ed.) *Autobiographical Memory*, Cambridge University Press, Cambridge, 1986, pp. 212–13.

[19] I.e. verifiable from a range of alternative sources.

[20] One interviewee, who gave a perfectly lucid account of his work in the 1930s, could not later recall that I had visited him at home to conduct the interview and had spent an afternoon with him and his wife. Elderly people tend to put this down to their failing memory, but although this example might be extreme, it indicates an alteration in the functioning of memory, not its general failure.

whether Henry Clay taught him on Tuesdays and Thursdays in the mid-1920s[21] is a sign of his memory working well, rather than the reverse. In many cases I was able to show interviewees photocopies of reading lists and other documentation from the time that they were students, which served to prompt reactions and as a support to recall. These interviews are, however, less effective precisely for that period which provided their initial impulse: the 1950s and 1960s, when many were already in their forties and memory is less precise. Accounts of the 1920s, 1930s and 1940s are by contrast more vivid.

In all of these interviews a definite strategy was adopted of questioning subjects on concrete aspects of their emergent careers, in the belief that the questions did not touch on controversial or confidential matters, that they did not involve opinion, nor did they require the subject to adopt a position with respect to some distant theoretical dispute. In so far as confidential matter arose in the course of the conversation, the subject was offered the opportunity of reviewing, editing and if necessary correcting the transcript. Amusing stories did get lost along the way as a result, but a successful interview is founded upon trust and this is a natural part of academic etiquette.

What follows is therefore some distance removed from a pure transcript of an interview.[22] In some cases quite severe recasting has been necessary to render readable the recorded spoken word; in many cases useful clarifications and additions were subsequently made by interviewees. At first I resisted this trend, since I believed that the transcripts should reflect as closely as possible a given interview. As work progressed I abandoned this principle, and increasingly made editorial interventions of my own for the sake of coherence and readability. This of course violates key principles of oral historiography;[23] but it is nevertheless true that whatever appears below as the utterance of an interviewee might not have been said in quite that way at the time of the interview, but has subsequently been endorsed as reflecting what they would have liked to have said.

Only in a few cases are interviews printed complete.[24] This was dictated as much by considerations of space as by a wish to provide a clear focus on the interaction of individual careers and institutional formation. Subjects were usually given a general idea of the purpose of the interview beforehand, but there was no rigid agenda for individual interviews. It is in the nature of such events that subjects touch on unanticipated matters, or fail to respond satisfactorily to prepared points. The course that an interview would take could not therefore be easily predicted; the concentration required of interviewer and

---

[21] Interview with Sir Henry Hardman, p. 16.

[22] I intend to deposit the tapes of these interviews with the Economic and Social Research Council Data Archive when my research in this area is complete.

[23] See, for example, discussion of problems similar to those outlined here in A. Seldon and J. Pappworth, *By Word of Mouth. 'Élite' Oral History*, Methuen, London, 1983; more generally see P. Thompson, *The Voice of the Past*, second edition, Oxford University Press, Oxford, 1988.

[24] As a consequence, few end in a tidy manner, since to have made them do so would have gone beyond even the relaxed principles of authenticity applied here.

interviewee alike meant that the experience could be quite taxing, for interviews generally ranged in length from two to four hours. Given that the interviewees are for the most part retired, interviews took place in their homes, lending them an informality often reinforced by a pleasant lunch beforehand.[25] In fact, throughout the course of this programme of interviews I have been struck by the courtesy and promptness with which subjects responded to the initial contact and then made arrangements for the interview itself. In very few cases has there been no response to the initial approach, and where respondents demurred this was always on the grounds of failing health or illness.

The interviews reproduced here are in roughly chronological order, beginning with Henry Hardman's account of Manchester in the 1920s and ending with Albert Sloman's description of the foundation and early years of the University of Essex.[26] They provide an overview of the relationship between the development of Economics as a discipline and the emergent careers of those who formed this discipline. Inevitably, Cambridge and LSE figure large; Oxford and the PPE (Philosophy, Politics and Economics), for a number of reasons, is less well represented.[27] Due emphasis is given to a number of provincial institutions, especially Manchester, which remained a major institution into the 1960s and which contributed a large number of staff to wartime economic administration. The cycles of recruitment and retirement have followed a definite pattern in Britain; for example, a number of senior positions were vacated in the mid-1940s, and many of those in the dominant age group here retired in the late 1960s and early 1970s. This coincided with a general shift in the nature of economics towards a more abstract and econometric approach, a shift which in the 1980s accelerated as desktop computers became widely available. Many of the interviewees here deplore this change in the character of the science that they did so much to develop; but they are not themselves in a position to provide detailed insights into it.

Several features emerge strongly from these and other interviews conducted as part of the research project upon which I have been engaged. For one thing, the assumption that, before the 1950s, study at university was generally open only to those from a privileged background is shown to be at best partial. The new discipline of Economics recruited many of its most eminent practitioners from students whose social backgrounds were relatively humble.

---

[25] In a more intensive programme of interviews where interviews follow closely upon one another this can be something of a mixed blessing; one researcher is said to have declared an allergy to cream buns so that she might politely decline the food offered to her.

[26] Although I have a personal interest in this (I was an undergraduate at Essex from 1968 to 1971) my interview with the founding Vice-Chancellor of Essex was prompted by Dick Lipsey. The interview has been included here since the early history of Essex exemplifies the institutional conditions under which Economics has developed since the 1970s.

[27] Death and illness prevented interviews with some economists who had studied and taught in Oxford during the 1930s; other interviews which were completed were for various reasons unsuitable for inclusion. Although this presents a problem of balance for this collection, there is a great deal of relevant material that can be found in W. Young and F.S. Lee, *Oxford Economics and Oxford Economists*, Macmillan, Basingstoke, 1993.

This was of course in part because it was a new discipline without an established cultural identity; but the personal histories of social mobility recounted here are not untypical for the system as a whole. The London colleges and the new provincial redbrick universities were founded in the nineteenth century with the aim of extending access to university education, and the practice of sitting London degree examinations as external candidates unattached to any specific institution was common up to mid-twentieth century. University education might have been the preserve of a select few, but this was largely an intellectual, rather than a social, elite.[28] Higher education was in certain respects more open at the beginning of the twentieth century than it is at its close, for the university system itself was less differentiated.

Second, personal contacts and an emergent academic network were crucial throughout this period for promotion and recruitment. Not until the 1950s was qualification as an economist generally recognised as a definite asset in academic and commercial labour markets. Even then, recruitment to senior academic positions continued to be effected through patronage and personal knowledge. Qualifications assumed the function of a complementary sufficient condition to the necessary role of patronage in placing candidates. And so this remains; the appointment of candidates to positions of responsibility requiring the exercise of individual initiative cannot reliably be effected through the examination of paper credentials alone. Wishing things were otherwise, or simply extending the range and quantity of credentials, will not change this basic fact of social organisation.

Third, these interviews have confirmed the chronology for the development of economics which has emerged in the course of my research: that the discipline assumed its modern guise first in the course of the 1950s, and that a major turning point arrived in the 1970s with the adoption of an increasingly formalised style, intensified in the 1980s by enhanced access to computing facilities. These substantive developments coincided with a third generational changeover:[29] the generation educated in the 1930s, which had in large measure created the modern discipline, began to reach retiring age in the late 1960s. This coincided with a general expansion in university posts resulting from the simultaneous impact of the expansion of the university system and the high status enjoyed by economics during the late 1960s. Career paths shortened as a result: bright young graduate students quickly assumed senior positions and reshaped the discipline. Unfortunately, this younger cohort of economists was brought up on the certainties of the 1950s, rather than the

---

[28] Those who took London external degrees in science and engineering, for example, were overwhelmingly students of provincial technical colleges.

[29] The first general shift occurred in the 1920s with Macgregor's accession to the Drummond Chair in Oxford, the death of Cannan and his replacement first with Young and then Robbins, and the deaths of Marshall, Edgeworth and Ashley. The second took place in the 1940s, when Robertson replaced Pigou in Cambridge, Henderson replaced Macgregor in Oxford, and a number of new appointments were made.

social and political uncertainties of the 1930s which had been such a formative and disturbing experience for many of the interviewees included here. For them, economics had been a discipline that could play an important role in moderating the social and political strife that led up to a World War in which many did in fact play an important role as professional economists.[30] For those trained in the 1950s and 1960s, however, this was all in the past; economics became a discipline geared to the management of growth and the optimisation of domestic welfare. It is unfortunate that this new generation assumed control at the very point when the long post-war boom, which they had grown to take for granted, turned sour. The world economy has, of course, never staged a complete or lasting recovery. It is not surprising, therefore, that economists have suffered a bad press over the past twenty years, since they have been confronted with economic and political conditions which belonged, they had always assumed, to a darker, past age. Among the present generation of senior economists there are very few with the intellectual reflexes of their predecessors; they are the present-day equivalents of Keynes' dentists, which just goes to show how misguided Keynes was in thinking that such an evolutionary development was something to be welcomed. Their capacity to respond creatively to the many challenges posed by the political and economic instabilities of the world economy since the 1970s is strictly limited, which has itself contributed to a decline in the public repute of academic economics.

[30] In the case of Henry Phelps Brown, when asked what had prompted his interest in economics, he replied that it was the depression of 1921 (interview conducted 14 November 1994, Oxford).

2

SIR HENRY HARDMAN

Henry Hardman was born in December 1905 and studied for a Commerce degree at Manchester University, graduating in 1927. He taught for the Workers' Educational Association from 1929 to 1934, and then as an extra-mural Economics Tutor for Leeds University. He was seconded voluntarily to the Ministry of Food in 1940, where he was assigned to general administrative duties. Shortly after the end of the war he was promoted to Deputy Head of the British Food Mission to North America, and went on to work in the UK delegation to NATO and the OEEC. During the 1950s in the Ministry of Agriculture, Fisheries and Food (MAFF) he became involved in the provision of agricultural subsidies and later in British membership of the European Economic Community. In 1961 he was appointed Permanent Secretary at the Ministry of Aviation, and from 1963 to 1966 was Permanent Under-Secretary of State at the Ministry of Defence.

The following is based upon an interview conducted on 9 June 1994 at Sir Henry's home in Brighton. When sent the transcript he added substantially to it in the areas dealing with his Civil Service experiences of the 1940s and 1950s, and these additions have been retained in their entirety.

HARDMAN: I knew the University of Manchester in the 1920s, and in those days it was struggling after the war to re-establish a place among redbricks, with the sciences and medicine as well as history and philosophy making big contributions. The Faculty of Commerce and Economics was facing the problem of numbers, how to get activity and resources, and they did that in part by organising an evening degree. So it was possible to get an Ordinary degree by evening attendance, a Bachelor of Commerce, as it was first called, in those days. But it was also concerned to attract full-time students of quality, willing to go on to do research. At that time this tradition was upheld in economic history rather than in economics, because George Unwin was the real academic and contributor to economic ideas.[1] He was overthrowing notions,

---

[1] George Unwin (1870–1925) worked first as an office boy in his native Stockport before gaining a scholarship to study at University College, Cardiff in 1890. He then gained a scholarship to Lincoln College,

13

created by the Hammonds, of nineteenth-century economic history: the history of the Industrial Revolution as a clear-cut affair, horrible for the workers without mitigation and all the rest. Unwin wrote studies like that on *Samuel Oldknow and the Arkwrights*,[2] very different from the harsh black-and-white of the Hammonds. George Unwin was the outstanding economic historian. But Daniels,[3] in so far as he made any academic contribution, did it in a small book he wrote on economic history.[4] And Ashton,[5] who taught economics, went on to be a very considerable economic historian at LSE.

TRIBE: When did you graduate?

HARDMAN: I got a B.A. in Commerce in 1927.

TRIBE: So you were one of the first B.A.s when they changed from B.Com. to B.A.Com.?

HARDMAN: Yes. Having matriculated at 15, I had to leave school and got a local education authority job which required part-time day studies to continue for two or three years. I began at the University in 1922, when the degree was B.Com., attending both daytime and evening classes, and ended my daytime studies in 1925. After that I took German at evening classes for my degree, as well as reading in economics on my own, to graduate in 1927. The value of the evening course was not academic quality: it was bringing funds in and creating an interest. And at the same time you had the desire to improve quality; and that really came with the appointment of Henry Clay to the Jevons Chair.[6] I think people like E.D. Simon – who was a distinguished industrialist, very

---

Oxford, graduating in 1897 with a First in Lit. Hum. He spent the following year in Berlin attending lectures by Schmoller and Wagner, returning to teach Economic History at the LSE and act as Leonard Courtney's secretary. In 1908 he was appointed Lecturer in Economic History at Edinburgh, and then to the first British chair in Economic History at Manchester in 1910. His first book, *Industrial Organisation in the Sixteenth and Seventeenth Centuries* (1904) is marked by its comparative treatment of European economic development.

[2] G. Unwin (with A. Hulme and G. Taylor), *Samuel Oldknow and the Arkwrights*, Manchester University Press, Manchester, 1924.

[3] G.W. Daniels trained originally as an electrician before taking a degree and joining the staff at Manchester as an Assistant Lecturer in Economics in 1912. In 1921 he was appointed to the new Chair of Commerce and Administration, before in 1927 succeeding Henry Clay as Stanley Jevons Professor of Political Economy. See obituaries in *Manchester Guardian*, 18 December 1937; *Manchester School*, vol. 9 (1938), pp. 67–77.

[4] G.W. Daniels, *The Early English Cotton Industry*, Manchester University Press, Manchester, 1920. George Unwin contributed to this volume an introduction (pp. xix–xxxi) which placed the development of the English cotton industry in a wider European context.

[5] T.S. Ashton's reputation was as an economic historian, but until his appointment to the Chair of Economic History at LSE in 1944 he had taught Economics. Appointed as a Lecturer in Economics at Manchester in 1921, he was promoted in 1927 to a Readership in Currency and Finance, the post which he held until moving to LSE.

[6] Henry Clay (1883–1954) read Greats at Oxford, graduating in 1906. Between 1909 and 1917 he lectured for the WEA, and joined the Ministry of Labour towards the end of the First World War. He was a Fellow of New College, Oxford from 1919 before moving to Manchester 1922, as successor to D.H. Macgregor, who had been appointed Drummond Professor in Oxford. From 1930 he worked in the Bank of England, and then he became in 1944 Warden of Nuffield College, Oxford, a position which he held until 1949. See J.R. Hicks, *Oxford Magazine*, vol. LXXIII, no. 1 (14 October 1954), pp. 8–10; *Dictionary of National Biography* 1951–60, pp. 227–9 (J. and S. Jewkes).

important also in the activities in Manchester where he was Lord Mayor for a time and wrote a book about it – were helpful in making the University academically important, with people like Clay, as well as in terms of getting some revenue. The work for an ordinary degree was in many ways a very odd arrangement. You had to cover all kinds of activities for the degree, like Law for example, and French and German of course. The French course was produced by the French Department and so you read Maupassant; and the German was by the German Department, and so you read *Minna von Barnhelm*; when, after it all, I got a First in the final exam in German, I didn't know what the German word *Steuer* meant, the word for tax!

TRIBE: So commercial correspondence in foreign languages, which had been an element in the original Manchester commerce degree, practical German, had already faded out by the time you did it in the mid-1920s?

HARDMAN: Certainly. My German illustration must have been in 1926 I suppose. 1926–27.

TRIBE: So there was no commercial correspondence, commercial German, commercial French, whatsoever then?

HARDMAN: Maybe you were told to look at a book, the title of which was mentioned. But the teachers were interested in the Department of German where they came from to do this course for Commerce students, as they were rather slightingly called. They were interested in, well as I say it was *Minna von Barnhelm* that we read, or *Weh'Dem, Der Lügt* or *Jörn Uhl*, and you were called upon to know about that. In economic terminology there was never any guidance from teachers. No examination certainly.

TRIBE: How long did you take, when did you start studying for the commerce degree?

HARDMAN: The first year was 1922–23.

TRIBE: So then you took five years to complete?

HARDMAN: Yes. My work as a university student was arranged without guidance and in some ways foolishly. For example, I discovered that if B.Com. candidates qualified in a Science, it would serve for the degree, so I chose to do Physics (though I passed the exams, it turned out, alas, to be no help to me, either in terms of qualification for the degree or of what I learned!). For a year I enjoyed Bragg's lectures each week and I managed the practical work. But it would have been much wiser, of course, for a would-be economist to do maths. At the end of two years I had satisfied all the requirements for an ordinary degree, save for German. However, I had heard of a daytime-only course for 1924–25, to be run by Professor Clay, which would involve attendance every morning in the week. So I arranged a timetable with my employers and applied for entry, to be accepted. For a time at the beginning of the academic year I worked at German as well. But when I realised that if I went on I could not do justice to the additional course, I decided to leave it for a later year.

TRIBE: Were there many other people doing it in the same combination?

HARDMAN: For the ordinary degree the numbers at evening sessions could be large – up to a hundred for first year 'Pol.Econ.': as it was called, or Modern History – but varying with subjects and perhaps no more than about thirty doing German. Numbers at daytime classes were much smaller. The evening students were mainly concerned to secure an extra qualification as school-teachers or, later, local government officers, rather than being interested in the subjects studied and they therefore differed markedly from the daytime ones, most of whom had come straight from school. The 1924–25 group for day students – Hons.Econs students as they were called – numbered no more than five. There were two M.A. students, or who hoped to get M.A.s; one student who disappeared very early in the course; then Leonard Cohen who became a businessman in Manchester, and myself. Henry Clay used to lecture four mornings a week. On Mondays and Wednesdays we had 'History of Economic Thought' which was chiefly Marshall, but a first term on Adam Smith. Clay used to come in and lecture formally to four of us and there was no discussion. On Tuesdays and Thursdays, was it Tuesdays and Thursdays? My memory is obviously not as good as all that. We worked on a 'Special Subject' as it was called. In 1924–25 it was the distribution of property ownership, a topic neglected by Marshallians mainly concerned with the price mechanism. On Fridays T.S. Ashton lectured on Banking and Finance and, as I recall, there were also occasional seminars with him for discussion of a contributed paper. Our 'Special Subject' introduced us to the work of Bowley and Stamp, who were pioneering in statistical enquiry into ownership.[7] But that was no more than one of the ways in which Clay showed awareness of issues that were ignored by most economists. In my first year I went to the introductory 'Pol.Econ.' course which Clay took that year. He began by talking for several sessions about quantitative economic assessments – the national income and its constituents. The fact that these were topics not mentioned in any textbook made it for schoolboys somewhat baffling at first! And there were other topics, later to become of major interest, to the study of which he contributed. I saw recently in the appendix to the second volume of Skidelsky's book on Keynes some reference to Henry Clay's ideas at the time of the *Manchester Guardian Supplements*, which will mean something to you I think, and how he had ideas which Keynes later adopted.[8] He was very much a pioneer and I have always felt he was under-rated.

TRIBE: So you see Clay very strongly as a major figure at that time? You mentioned Daniels. What was his role?

---

[7] A.L. Bowley and J.C. Stamp published their important book *The National Income, 1924* (Oxford University Press) in 1927, although both had been working for many years on the problems of compiling a reliable statistical estimate of the level of economic activity: see A.L. Bowley, 'The Census of Production and the National Dividend', *Economic Journal*, vol. 23 (1913), pp. 53–61; and Stamp's 1920–21 Newmarch Lectures, *Wealth and Taxable Capacity*, P.S. King & Son, London, 1922.

[8] Sir Henry is thinking of the entry for Henry Clay in 'Dramatis Personae', R. Skidelsky, *John Maynard Keynes vol. 2. The Economist as Saviour 1920–1937*, Macmillan, London, 1992, p. 691.

HARDMAN: With the arrogance of young students, I am afraid we regarded him almost with contempt. After I had graduated, A.P. Wadsworth – he was the editor of the *Guardian* later on, and Labour Correspondent in those days – and his wife asked me to dinner with the Clays, and Clay at one point said, 'But Daniels is so appallingly slow!' His contribution was very inferior, I thought. He gave a miserable course of lectures to second-year economics students based on Marshall's *Industry and Trade*, a very inferior volume anyhow, that was dreary in the extreme. And his only academic contribution was the book that Unwin really inspired and helped with, I think.[9] The intellectual force was in economic history. As I said already, that was Ashton in his research, as well as Unwin.

TRIBE: Ashton was lecturer in economics wasn't he? He came in 1924, or earlier.

HARDMAN: Yes. In Hons.Econs, we had seminars with Ashton, but I can't recall much. When I was a civil servant I was once infuriated because the man who was appointed to the Agricultural Department as Permanent Secretary when I was a Deputy Secretary, and after my departure took over agricultural price negotiations, was criticising economists and saying, 'I can't see how in their eyes prices ever change; if demand increases then obviously prices go up, and then if prices go up demand falls so prices go back.' I can remember discussing that elementary topic with Ashton in one of the Friday morning seminars.

TRIBE: There was a striking contrast in commerce between Manchester and Birmingham. Birmingham had the first Faculty of Commerce in Britain, but they did very little economics and they had no-one who could teach the kinds of things you are referring to. What has impressed me about Manchester is the way that, within the broad commerce curriculum, they managed very quickly to appoint a number of characters who later became prominent economists in their own right. Henry Clay is part of a series which includes Bickerdike, Hallsworth, Forrester, Macgregor, Chapman. What other courses did you do as part of the ordinary degree of the B.Com., which then became the B.A.Com. degree?

HARDMAN: Oh, well, about ten subjects. Pol.Econ. and then Industry and Trade. Economic History with Unwin. Modern History with the History Department. Accounting. French and German. Law; the absurdity of the course: the lecturer simply read his notes at dictation speed. Eastwood was the name of the lecturer: he read his notes and you copied them down. Attendance was compulsory; it was registered, and if you didn't get regular marks you couldn't qualify. I was fortunate in that I broke a leg playing rugby football and so I was off for a term! I borrowed somebody else's notes and I had no difficulty at all. And it was a good excuse that you were in hospital.

---

[9] G.W. Daniels, *The Early English Cotton Industry*, with an introductory chapter by George Unwin, Manchester University Press, Manchester, 1920.

17

TRIBE: Was this Commercial Law then? It was geared more to your requirements than the language was?

HARDMAN: True. The course in Modern History was very good. I was greatly interested in nineteenth-century history; in my view, economists these days don't pay sufficient attention to it. But it was political history, of course, above all.

TRIBE: Did you do Transport, for instance?

HARDMAN: No.

TRIBE: Economic Geography?

HARDMAN: Geography, yes.

TRIBE: What would be covered in that?

HARDMAN: Nominally it was geography of the whole world I think, but in 1923 that meant principally Europe. Lithuania I can still remember learning about! How many subjects is that? I think that another subject might have been Taxation with Ashton, but haven't I mentioned that as part of the course for the four students who were doing further work in economics?

TRIBE: I have noticed that the new B.A.Admin. took away immediately a third to a half of the students from the Old B.Com., which indicates that about half of the old commerce students were . . .

HARDMAN: Administrative.

TRIBE: Would you have seen yourself in that kind of mould? You came from local government.

HARDMAN: No. Partly because Henry Clay had spent some of his time, when he was at Oxford I suppose, as an extra-mural lecturer; and therefore I became interested in extra-mural education and in the WEA particularly.[10] I went to Summer Schools, and related activities. I used to give the odd lecture before I was involved professionally in teaching. Mary Stocks – does she mean anything to you?

TRIBE: Yes.

HARDMAN: She lived in Manchester and had a WEA class in economics: they asked me to lecture as she was on holiday – it was in the summer – and so I gave a lecture to the WEA Branch on the return to the Gold Standard. I became much more interested in WEA activity and working-class education than in university activity. That was at the beginning of my association. No doubt my interest in economics and adult education was not lessened when, after a year as a graduate, I reminded my employers that I was still on the job which I had begun at 15. But it was then made clear that, as I had no qualification as a 'trained teacher', there were no prospects for me save minor promotion over many years in the safe job which I was doing (and on

---

[10] The Workers' Education Association followed on from the University Extension movement of the late nineteenth century, forming alongside university extra-mural departments and, as is evident here, sharing tutors with them.

which I continued for another year). In the evenings therefore I was willing to volunteer for any adult teaching related to my studies.

TRIBE: But actually that was adult education with a university which co-operated with the WEA.

HARDMAN: That came later for me when I took a WEA job for Leeds. Until then my links in Manchester were with fringe bodies (including Strangeways Prison!). The WEA was, perhaps in Manchester and certainly in Leeds, the only significant body. The University there wasn't really interested in collaboration with anyone else, I would say. That was a complicated area, with big differences between universities. Leeds was dominated for a long time by a man who had been a student of Henry Clay's in one of his earlier WEA classes – a man called G.H. Thompson – who ran the University activities. The University Registrar was supposed to be his equal number, sharing the job, but he wasn't interested. Manchester was quite different. At Manchester the University people were much more involved in adult education but I don't really know much about Manchester and the WEA. I turned down a University Adult Education job at Manchester because I wanted to get away from it. In the two years between the end of my university course and my move to North Yorkshire, I went on working at my local authority job but lived in the University Settlement and took part in its activities. They ranged for me from odd talks at Settlement Clubs and participation in a residents' study group on ethics to amateur dramatics (for example, the Settlement organised a performance of Shaw's *Saint Joan* in which John Stocks was 'The Inquisitor' and Kingsley Martin,[11] 'Brother Stogumber'. I played the part of Dunois). I began research then into juvenile unemployment in Manchester and collected data for it through the Employment Bureaux. But I busied myself also with lecturing to adult education groups at a local authority college and several courses in Strangeways, the local prison.

TRIBE: Were these in effect recreational courses, or were they geared towards some long-term objective, gaining a diploma or some . . .?

HARDMAN: Recreational ones, and in the prison relatively short courses. I talked about economic history, I think, there. But it is over sixty years ago and all rather vague now.

TRIBE: What sort of economic history did you talk about?

HARDMAN: The nineteenth century. As I recall, I devoted one or two courses to biographies – Cobbett, *The Tailor of Charing Cross*, Edwin Chadwick, J.S. Mill – and others to aspects of the Industrial Revolution, including developments in the Poor Law and public health as well as industry. The prison work was fascinating; only an hour's lecture, and I objected to

---

[11] Kingsley Martin (1897–1969) was Editor of *The New Statesman and Nation* from 1930 to 1960; from 1923 to 1927 he was an Assistant Lecturer in Political Science at LSE, and from 1927 to 1931 on the staff of the *Manchester Guardian*.

having a warder in, and so I was locked in the prison cell: the prisoners used to talk to me occasionally after the lecture. I remember them stealing money from me and returning it just to show how easy it was to pick pockets!

TRIBE: How many would you normally lecture to there?

HARDMAN: Perhaps twenty. It was all away from the University, save in the links provided by the Settlement. In adult education John and Mary Stocks were very much concerned with the Settlement and with the WEA too, so they brought a different flavour from Leeds. The history of adult education in England is of very different patterns in different areas. In Yorkshire the contrast between the University of Leeds and the University College of Hull was striking. For several years nine-tenths of the latter's activities were in adult education and the adult education department was very important in the University College. In Leeds it was insignificant: in Manchester marginally less so.

TRIBE: So when you worked in Leeds as a WEA lecturer what area would you have covered?

HARDMAN: Well, mainly the North East coast. I lived in Middlesborough for a time. Indeed, I met my wife in Middlesborough, because she was on the staff of the University College of Hull and I was taking classes for the University of Leeds.

TRIBE: Can you give me an idea of the kinds of work you would have done at that time?

HARDMAN: In adult education?

TRIBE: Yes.

HARDMAN: My first year, I can remember, was mainly on the North East coast. I had one class in economics – the whole of economic theory in twenty-four lectures: it was absurd, but the group had been led to expect it. Another in 'social' economics – population changes, poverty, the distribution of wealth. One class was in nineteenth-century economic history, and another in local government. Finally, as I had evinced interest in literature, I was invited to speak for twelve, and then for another twelve weeks, to a rural group about the novel. I had five classes and five different topics; it was hard going.

TRIBE: What text did you use for the economic theory in twenty-four lectures?

HARDMAN: A tiny sixpenny pamphlet produced by one of the enterprising publishers, Ernest Benn, I think. The students could afford it, though sixpence was a lot of money in those days.

TRIBE: What materials would you use to prepare your lectures?

HARDMAN: Mainly what I had acquired as a student of course, basing it on what I had learnt in my activities. What text would I use? Good gracious. Partly of course what was reported in the newspapers every day: but I was anxious to have economic theory as the basis of what I had to say . . . I objected to having to lecture about isolated incidents alone because that seemed to me to be of no value at all: they had to be related to background theory. I suppose

Henry Clay's *Economics for the General Reader*. Henderson's *Supply and Demand*, D.H. Robertson for the better students.[12]

TRIBE: The Cambridge Economic Handbooks.

HARDMAN: Yes. Marshall of course, for me.

TRIBE: Ah, that was what I was fishing for.

HARDMAN: Marshall certainly.

TRIBE: Which Marshall? *Principles* or *Economics of Industry?*

HARDMAN: Oh *Principles*. *Economics of Industry*[13] was, as I know now, scandalously undervalued, and I used to look at it because it was a brief introduction to Marshall's ideas; but I didn't appreciate it as much as *Principles*, partly because for a whole year, an academic year, I had been working at the *Principles*. That is why I found subsequent Keynesian ideas so difficult to absorb. And I still find myself saying 'Thank God Keynes isn't quite so important as he was!' It isn't only macroeconomics, but also microeconomics that matter nowadays. Perhaps it was partly because, especially for outsiders, economics was so confusing in the 1930s, when you didn't know whether people from Cambridge were saying 'saving and investment are equal' or 'saving and investment are not equal': It was the *Treatise* or the *General Theory*, depending on to whom you had been talking the day before, or the night before.

TRIBE: It has been suggested that the second edition of *Economics of Industry* was a device for propagating Marshallian economics; and although it does not seem to have much practical success in this direction, it did succeed in displacing the first edition, which was an entirely different book.

HARDMAN: Well that was because Marshall wanted it: he really was an unpleasant character. Mary Marshall was a marvellous woman and I am sure contributed, but he finally took the credit: it wasn't produced by the two of them; it was produced by Alfred Marshall only. I can remember a story which interested me very much of the Webbs going to a meal in Cambridge with Mary Marshall and Alfred Marshall; and of Beatrice Webb talking about how interesting it was that there were brought together four people working in two couples, in each case both having contributed. And that was during drinks before they went into the lunch. When they were going into the meal Mary Marshall said to Beatrice Webb, 'Don't talk about Alfred and I having done this, it upsets him so much.' Marshall was a great economist, I think, but a stinker of a man.

TRIBE: You moved over to become an economics tutor in the University of Leeds in 1934? What did that involve?

HARDMAN: It meant that I did work in the University as well as carrying on the work with the WEA. After a year as a WEA tutor I was asked in 1930 to

---

[12] Henry Clay, *Economics for the General Reader*, Macmillan, London, 1916, H. Henderson, *Supply and Demand*, Nisbet, London, 1922 and D.H. Robertson, *Banking Policy and the Price Level*, P.S. King, London 1926.

[13] Sir Henry clearly has in mind here the original *Economics of Industry* which Marshall wrote in collaboration with Mary Paley Marshall, not the 1891 summary of the *Principles* that masqueraded as a 'second edition' but which was in fact an entirely different book.

take some classes sponsored by the University Extra-Mural Department (with substantial support from the Board of Education, as it then was). The classes were organised by the WEA but financed by the University and required from those who enrolled a commitment to study for a period, normally of three years. So far as I was concerned, the University was committed only to the individual classes and to that extent the job was, from my point of view, precarious. But in the 1930s one did not cavil about a job. And in 1934 I was made a member of the University Staff in what served as the Extra-Mural Department as tutor in economics. I went on with economics for WEA students, but after a time began to teach also undergraduates in the Economics Department. For many years there had been a tradition in economics at Leeds of links with the WEA. Among others Henry Clay, Arthur Greenwood,[14] and Arnold Shimmin[15] had been WEA tutors (Clay had sided with strikers and against the Vice-Chancellor in a Leeds tramway strike about 1913 and gained great kudos among WEA students). I was concerned to revive the tradition and pleased when J.H. Jones,[16] who was Professor of Economics, wanted me to teach in the Department.

TRIBE: Yes. It seems that what you were doing was more systematic than what was going on in Leeds at the time.

HARDMAN: Perhaps. I remember lecturing one year to first-year students and trying to persuade them not to take down everything I said; but to 'bring their knitting', and then tried to persuade them to comment on elementary, yet vital, economic ideas such as 'productive work', 'comparative cost' and 'opportunity cost', and that in economic affairs bygones are bygones, which in my experience students find difficult to absorb.

TRIBE: What would you have counted at that time as 'recent ideas in economics'? You have already expressed your reservations about Keynes.

HARDMAN: In 1937 or 1938 I talked to third-year students about the ideas of different economists on the causes of the trade cycle. I would take perhaps eight or nine different analyses. Though I tried to link these ideas with what I could glean and understand on the Keynesian revolution, I doubt whether I was able to get much across. Naturally, I suppose, I was impressed by the doubts even in Cambridge of critics (e.g. Pigou and Robertson) and could not see how with the application of Keynesian ideas inflation could be avoided. But undergraduate teaching was only a small part of my job in the University, which was tutorial class work. I should add that under J.H. Jones the teaching of economics was poor. He wrote a weekly article for *The*

---

[14] Arthur Greenwood (1880–1954) was active in adult education in Leeds after graduating from Yorkshire College in 1905. He entered Parliament in 1922 and became Deputy Leader of the Labour Party in 1935.

[15] Shimmin had been Assistant Lecturer in Economics in Manchester 1913–15 before moving to Leeds, where he was Lecturer in Economics, until 1945, when he was promoted to the Chair of Social Science.

[16] J. Harry Jones had been an Assistant Lecturer in Liverpool before his appointment in 1919 to the Chair of Economics in Leeds, which he held until 1945.

Accountant and on press day he often wouldn't turn up for students. I knew some of them as contemporaries, and when I was working in Leeds they used to tell me how little they got from Jones. The other Professor was a man called Richardson, J.H. Richardson, who was at one time a Civil servant in Geneva; he produced descriptions of events with no economic analysis whatever. The only really competent economic intellectuals were H.D. Dickinson and, after 1936, Donald MacDougall.[17] It was with Dickinson that I interested one of the best groups of my WEA students, and it was from contact with those WEA students that Dickinson wrote his book on *The Economics of Socialism*, a book which for a time was revered until the later Hayekian developments rather destroyed it. Who was the man in Poland who produced a similar book?

TRIBE: Lange?

HARDMAN: Lange, yes. Oscar Lange.

TRIBE: So a lot of the teaching was fairly old-fashioned, or fairly casual. Richardson was anyway Professor of Industrial Relations so he wasn't really meant to teach economics . . .

HARDMAN: Let me go back to my teaching of economics to WEA students, which was the major part of my university work. Standards varied considerably, both between and within classes. At one extreme, theories could be described and discussed only in the simplest of terms, and with plenty of examples, as illustration of the working of economic principles. Most classes had students with firmly held views about how the economy ought to be organised and were convinced that 'workers were exploited' by employers. But they were willing to consider economists' analyses and their ideas about scarcity, distribution of wealth, the price mechanism, international trade and comparative advantage, etc. In a few cases standards in tutorial classes were at least as good as those in university ones, especially in the third year when no more than half a dozen students would justify a class. One group which I took in Thornaby-on-Tees, where I used to travel each week from Leeds, included three students, one of whom, R.B. Cant, went on later to LSE: he became a staff tutor at the University of Keele and later MP for Stoke-on-Trent. Two others, unemployed, became enthusiastic Hayekists: perhaps my doubts about Keynesian ideas influenced them unduly! Both secured extra-mural scholarships at Cambridge: one, a pupil of Richard Kahn, died soon after he graduated but the other became a lecturer in the University of Dublin. But of course I did not regard the preparation of University teachers as a main part of my job: that was rather the education of potential leaders in working-class movements.

TRIBE: You also spent some time in Kiel in 1936?

---

[17] See the comments about Dickinson made by Ronald Tress, who worked with him at Bristol. MacDougall, an Oxford graduate who worked with Harrod and Lindemann during the war, mentions Sir Henry in passing in relation to his time in Leeds in his biography, *Don and Mandarin: Memoirs of an Economist*, John Murray, London, 1987, p. 15.

HARDMAN: I am afraid my interest there was more in political happenings in Germany than in the development of economic ideas. From the second half of the 1920s I had spent some time each year in Germany or Austria, at first on holidays from my job and, after 1929, for longer periods. Gradually I grew concerned about the crumbling of the Weimar regime and the rise of the Nazis: from incredulity that their ideas would be taken seriously, I became alarmed at their growing acceptance. In 1933 I spent some time with John Edwards, who spoke no German, trying to assess their significance (he was appointed to the University staff when I was and later went into politics). In 1935 I stayed in Leipzig for a month or two with the Jewish family of the sociologist Arno Schirokauer and in 1936 in Kiel with Walther Hoffman, editor of the quarterly journal, *Weltwirtschaftliches Archiv*. Of course I talked with Hoffman and some of his colleagues in the *Institut*[18] about ideas in economics. I was fascinated, for example, by a study being made of 'protectionism in Ireland' which enabled some anti-Nazis to criticise Nazi economic policy through the analysis of that of the Free State! But it was with German politics rather than aspects of economic thought in which I was primarily interested.

TRIBE: You were an academic economics tutor; did you apply for lectureships or did you not have an interest in becoming an academic, as you were much interested in adult education, in a more educational side of it?

HARDMAN: Yes, I suppose I was. If I had gone back to Leeds after the war, when I was urged to, I suspect I would have been made Professor of Adult Education. Not the job that I wanted: but anyhow having had four or five years in the Civil Service I decided I would like to stay.

TRIBE: How did that transition come about from being in Leeds to joining the Ministry of Food?

HARDMAN: Well, because by way of preparations for the war all academics were put on the 'Academic Register'. When Departments wanted staff, one way was to consult the Register and get into touch directly with people who might meet their needs. I was telegraphed fairly early in the war from the Ministry of Food offering a job, but at low salary. The University refused to allow me to accept it unless I resigned my post on the grounds that, at the time, with the possibilities of Forces' education on the far horizon, my university job was more important than the job offered. I could count upon no other resources than my salary, thought that I had something to offer and wanted to exert some influence, so in the end I decided to wait. But that was in the period of the 'Phoney War'. Some time towards the end of 1940 and after the Blitzkrieg had begun, I was offered, and accepted, a more important job in the Ministry of Food. By then of course, after the Allied collapse in Continental Europe, the whole situation had changed.

The Academic Register was very important, but of course it was by no

---

[18] The Institute for World Economics.

means the only way in which people were recruited as 'temporaries' to the Civil Service. I suppose that the single most important source was based upon social class – families, schools and colleges, London clubs, etc. – but professional links as with economists were also significant. From then on I had to realise that because I was enrolled as an administrator – a 'generalist' – and not as an economist, my future in the wartime organisation was likely to be as a civil servant. I was constantly grateful for my economic training and increasingly made aware of the scope for economists that was neglected. But that was never a view shared by more than a handful of 'established' civil servants.

TRIBE: What kind of work did you do?

HARDMAN: I was first appointed to 'Establishments' to succeed a classical scholar who had been transferred to the 'Holy of Holies' as Private Secretary to the Minister, Lord Woolton. The Establishment Department was responsible for all aspects of the staffing of the Ministry. But, with the worsening of the war, new problems demanded staff even from Establishments and, after a short spell, I was transferred to 'Emergency Services'. Two problems there demanded most of my attention: a third arising from the salvage of foodstuffs after air-raids was, I am afraid, largely ignored. But a growing fear of the use of poison gas by the enemy demanded collaboration with experts among scientists, precautions by local authorities that had to be organised as well as financed, and the provision of protective equipment. The other responsibility was the rapid development of the dehydration of foodstuffs in all its possible forms to secure reductions in the demand for shipping space. Dried eggs proved to be edible (if barely so). Surpluses of potatoes in the first years of the war demanded research into the possibilities of incorporating dried potato into bread. Unfortunately the potato flour produced by known methods turned out to be unsuitable for bread: and when the thirty-six satisfactory drying factories hastily put up in Northern Ireland were ready for production, there were no surpluses of potatoes until after the end of the war. Dried vegetables proved to be more promising and an effective team was recruited from Cambridge: but the outcome in terms of satisfactory supplies came long after the end of the war. After nearly two years I was moved to 'Wartime Meals' to support the Director, a Liverpool businessman. The Department was mainly concerned initially with making snack meals available after air-raids but moved gradually, with the increasing employment of women in industry, to organising the provision of regular, cheap meals to fill the gap. Two years later I was made responsible for the collection and presentation to the Treasury of the Ministry's import programme, for debate and defence before other importing Departments. Then, after nearly another year, I was sent to Washington as Deputy to the Head of the Food Mission, representing the UK in the allocation after the end of the war of inadequate supplies by an International Emergency Food Council.

TRIBE: So did you find there was a difference between you doing that work and your colleagues doing similar work?

HARDMAN: The Ministry of Food was a ragbag of Departments, with old civil servants, academics, business people, all thrown together. The heads of all the Commodity Divisions had been recruited from the food trades and were accustomed to think in business terms, which made the Department exceptional in Whitehall. Yet even there I learnt that economists through their training have advantages in many ways. I can remember in the Ministry of Food going to a meeting after the war because the Foreign Office were pressing that the UK had to buy some barley from Iraq because that would save the ruling regime, instead of American barley or some other that was available. I talked to our experts in cereals and found out what the cost of the exchange would be. The Foreign Office said, 'It is absolutely vital we must do this'; so I said, 'Well the Ministry of Food is very willing to collaborate and this will cost £Xm. Can the Foreign Office take that on their vote?' Their total vote wasn't £Xm. They were absolutely flummoxed. And Eddie Playfair from the Treasury said, 'Well, I think Henry has won this battle, we needn't go on any longer.' That illustrates the kind of odd ideas that civil servants had in the days before economic activity was part of government concern. Of course, the activities of government before the Second World War were relatively slight by comparison with today, and certainly by comparison when we had all-out war.

TRIBE: Through your career in the Civil Service did you notice a shift towards a definite attempt to recruit academics who had some kind of systematic economic background?

HARDMAN: If I may comment first on the pre-war situation, one of the few Whitehall Departments which employed economists was the Ministry of Agriculture, mainly as a relic of the Empire Marketing Board of the 1920s. They were used in the 1930s with the development of the Agricultural Marketing Boards (milk, pigs, bacon, etc.), but given no scope in the working out of agricultural policy, either then or later. Of course the war and the return to peace caused dramatic changes in the need and place for agricultural production. But that should have made the case for sound economic advice the stronger. It was sad that the economists in the Ministry of Agriculture tended to become collectors of statistics and spokesmen for agriculture, rather than Government Economists, and kept in separate categories from economists. It took a long time to secure acceptance of the notion that there were agricultural economists who were of some merit as economists and not mere voices for the Ministry of Agriculture. But Alec Cairncross and Donald MacDougall both helped, I think, to change that; and economists today for the Ministry of Agriculture come from the general pool of economists. But that of course is all relatively recent.

TRIBE: Is this the 1960s and the 1970s, or would you put it any earlier than that?

HARDMAN: I suppose, with Alec Cairncross: I would have said perhaps the 1960s. But that is a long digression. So far as concerns economists more generally during my time in the Civil Service, as you will well know, the adoption of Keynesian ideas, even before the outbreak of war, made for an enormous expansion in their potential role. With the war, the Economic Section of the Cabinet Office with the Central Statistical Office was a major driving force for the provision of economic information. But its contribution, as well as that of a good many other economists, was by no means restricted to encouraging the provision of quantitative data: perhaps not less important was securing the application of relatively simple economic ideas. In the Ministry of Food, for example, there were difficulties about the individual rationing of the many miscellaneous foodstuffs which could be made available. Yet a solution in the introduction of 'points rationing' was regarded with great suspicion: the personal allowance of supplies was to be expressed in 'points' and the 'points values' of individual items moved up and down in reflection of the availability of supplies. The objections of Commodity Directors were overcome in part by a brilliant exposition from Lionel Robbins of how the price mechanism worked.[19] In economics, as in physics, simple principles can be of immense use in practical problems. Again the businessmen selected on the eve of the outbreak of war, often by their fellows, one for each of the competitive food trades, were nominally guided by permanent civil servants as their deputies. They tended to be over-impressed by the convenience for administration of treating the UK as a unit and consequently to ignore or under-estimate the influence of distance upon economic costs. Only when a uniform encouragement to egg production resulted in a vast expansion of production in remote areas, at its greatest proportionately in the Orkneys, were they persuaded that the need for zones urged by the economists had a point.

But with the end of the war there was an exodus from the public service of pre-war professional economists (or, as in the Ministry of Food, of business people with economic expertise). Some incoming Ministers like Dalton and Strachey were expert in economics. But the new Labour Government relied mainly upon the regular Civil Service for economic advice and made no attempt to replace those who had left. Even those who remained in government service, like Eric Roll in the Ministry of Food, were regarded and employed as career civil servants. If their knowledge and influence plus the legacy of economic education among regular civil servants from the war years had some effect upon Whitehall, it was for a time a limited one, varying in its effects from department to department. The Ministry of Food was exceptional, not only in the retention of trained economists like George Bishop and John Wall, but in that its permanent secretaries, Percival Liesching and especially Frank Lee, had worked closely with economists during and immediately after the war. However, with the series of economic crises for the UK from 1947, the need for people with economic training became more pressing,

---

[19] The relation of points rationing to the price mechanism and Robbins' role in winning acceptance for the new system is discussed in A. Booth, 'Economists and Points Rationing in the Second World War', *Journal of European Economic History*, vol. 14 (1985), pp. 297–317.

first for service with the Economic Planning Staff when it was set up and then, more important, for work on preparations leading to the Marshall Plan and the establishment of the OEEC. Western European countries looked to the UK to lead with the United States in the allocation of American funds and the techniques adopted for the division of aid, which involved assessing national incomes, for example, demanded more and more of the expertise of trained economists. Staff in the Treasury bore most of the burden, but economically literate career civil servants were pulled out from other departments. During these years the stock of the UK in Western Europe stood high and other countries tended to take its pre-eminence for granted. However, debate about macroeconomic data, national incomes and the like was looked upon almost with disdain by many career civil servants, not least in the Foreign Office, and with the exhaustion of American aid to Europe, the Civil Service demand for experts in economics abated. Continental Europe looked in vain for further leadership from the UK and the Foreign Office was encouraged by Ministers to develop the fantasies of the UK as the centre of the three over-lapping concentric circles of North America, Europe and the Commonwealth. Economists recruited as career civil servants who had served with OEEC tended to move back into general administrative work with the posts which they had filled sometimes reverting to 'regulars' without economic background. At the end of those years there was, of course, incomparably more economic awareness in Whitehall than had existed before. But the substantial recruitment of professional economists came more slowly. Robert Hall was at the centre as the government's economic expert from 1947, but my impression is that trained economists were not recruited in any numbers until well into the 1950s and that the big expansion came under Cairncross and, later, MacDougall, in the 1960s.

The Ministry of Food, absorbed within the Ministry of Agriculture in 1955, was again exceptional in that it retained substantial involvement in economic activities long after the end of the war. The annual agricultural price review was the determinant of much farming enterprise until UK entry in the European Community in 1973. It would not, I think, be too much to say that the wartime recruits trained in economics who came from the Ministry of Food into the combined Ministry brought a new attitude towards support for farming (though it is difficult to maintain that Ministers were much affected). Long-term contracts and agreements, entered into by the UK for many overseas products over varying periods, continued well into the 1950s – for wheat with Canada, meat with Australia, dairy products with New Zealand, bacon with Denmark, sugar with the West Indies, etc. They involved the UK in negotiations which demanded economic understanding and expertise. And rationing of supplies for the consumer as with meat, for example, continued until 1954.

The policy of the incoming Labour Government on home agriculture immediately after the end of the war was determined mainly in the Ministry of Agriculture, with the Treasury and other central economic staffs: the Ministry of Food having relatively little influence upon it. The major contribution from the Ministry of Agriculture took the form of what became the Agriculture Act, 1947, upon which claims for continued and increasing support from the National Farmers' Union (NFU) were based for many years. The decision from the Treasury to finance the agricultural expansion programme of 1947 was justified on the grounds that it could save imports and lessen the worsening of the terms of trade that was regarded as inevitable given the permanent dollar shortage which was forecast.

The creation of the combined Ministry of Agriculture, Food and Fisheries (MAFF) in 1955 was in part a consequence of the change which had occurred in the potential availability of food supplies in the world after 1950. Ministry of Food officials, and not least the economically literate among them, had always been critical of what has been described as the 'cosy' relationship between the Ministry of Agriculture officials and the Farmers' Union. With more food coming on to world markets, it became easier to demand that increased home production must be at a lower cost, and not at any cost. As a Deputy Secretary in the combined department, I was Chairman of the annual price review negotiations with representatives of the Farmers' Union from 1954 until I was transferred to the Ministry of Aviation in 1960. Since I believed that the scale of agricultural support was excessive and could not be justified on economic grounds, I was not disappointed that, against all precedents, the price review settlement of 1956 was approved by Ministers in spite of, for the first time, the objections of the Farmers' Union. But officials overestimated the scope for a change in policy which Ministers would impose and stick to. The outrage of farmers and the campaign which the Farmers' Union organised throughout the country so alarmed the government that the Minister, Heathcoat Amory, insisted and embarked upon further negotiations in 1956 which led to an additional government commitment in the 'Long-Term Assurances' to farmers: limits were set to the scope for changes in prices at Annual Reviews over periods of years. As it turned out, however, the continuing fall in the value of money meant that the assurances were of little practical significance. But the experience did make Ministers in subsequent years more chary about agreeing to price proposals which might be regarded by farmers as unduly harsh.

But that is more than enough about Food and Agriculture. Of other departments in the years to 1960 I know much less and can only say that, apart from exceptions like the Board of Trade, within the Civil Service generally there was never, of course, universal agreement that more professional economists were called for. Those inside, like those outside, were not always sufficiently modest about – nor mindful of the limitations of – their understanding of the real world. Denis Healey's later criticism as Chancellor of the reliability of economists' estimates and his gibe that economists had acquired a spurious respectability through the use of numbers had been heard many times before, along with views of them as 'number-crunchers' who assumed that the immediate future would reproduce exactly the recent past. The number of major policy decisions taken by Ministers from the 1940s on the basis of statistics which turned out to be erroneous is a lengthy one. But decisions cannot always be postponed. And perhaps on the desks of more forecasters there ought to be the reminder 'Economics is more like medicine than physics'.

TRIBE: Earlier you mentioned that there were Summer Schools during this period organised by Austin Robinson?

HARDMAN: What I had in mind were various conferences or weekend schools on agricultural policy, to one of which, financed by ICI early in the 1950s, Austin Robinson and Ronnie Tress came. Austin expounded, along the lines which with other Cambridge economists he had urged for some years, his gloomy analysis of how UK trade would be forced to develop and concluded that expansion of agricultural production ought to be encouraged. As the wits have it, 'Forecasting is always difficult, especially about the future', and, short of providing alternative forecasts, so is criticism of detailed estimates for it. Tress was duly sceptical, but the hosts of course were delighted. As it turned out, Austin's forecasts for exports proved to be far too gloomy. From 1947, however, they were extremely influential in the determination of subsidies for agriculture. About the wisdom of such subsidies there is, I accept, room for two views: the case for them in 1947 was much stronger then, when there were substantial world food shortages, than after 1950 when their disappearance was not difficult to foresee. If then comparative costs had been allowed much greater scope to shape the pattern of agricultural development, who can say what the outcome would have been? But I doubt if Britain would have become a significant exporter of cereals as it is today. A defence of UK agricultural policy immediately after the end of the war would, I suppose, put great stress on the political constraints – the memory of wartime and the reality of post-war food shortages, the existence of machinery for rationing and allocation, and extensive trade restriction. But I suspect that it would also imply a rejection of the assumptions of a free marketeer.

TRIBE: What was your view then around the mid-1950s concerning the impending formation of the European Economic Community, and its likely concentration for the first few years of its operation on the development of a Common Agricultural Policy?

HARDMAN: Well, that of course is a much bigger question, involving as it does not only agricultural policy but UK economic activity generally, and indeed the responsibilities of a civil servant to his Minister. But first let me try to deal with the specific question. Of course I thought that the CAP was indefensible economically. But I was equally sure that, without at least some of it, UK entry into the Community would never be agreed. Moreover, so far as I could see, no other realistic policy was open to the UK. I have already indicated what I thought of the mirage of the UK as a world power at 'the centre of concentric circles'. Given that American concern about Europe was likely to diminish with increasing interest in the Pacific plus the possibilities of growing isolationism, any continuation of the 'special relationship' with the USA was improbable. All the UK efforts to organise a European Free Trade Association had come to nothing of significance. A Western European organisation without the UK would almost certainly be protectionist and therefore more harmful to the UK than one of which it was part. Consequently, I thought the UK ought to accept the CAP but, once inside, work for its reform. Fortunately farming opinion in the UK (not least the NFU) was in favour of entry. So effort from those aware of economic realities could concentrate upon ensuring that the negotiating teams included at least some good economists. I still hold that the view which I took in the mid-1950s was the right one and that then a great opportunity for the UK in Europe was missed. Recent years have seen some recognition of economic realities in Europe, supported by the UK, with the acceptance, for example, of the GATT and some sensible dents have been made in the CAP, which I applaud. But the scope for them is, alas, much restricted. Meanwhile deep divisions over Europe in both main political parties persist with critics of European collaboration offering no alternative indication of UK policy than a Micawberish waiting for something to turn up. And if the UK showed greater willingness to collaborate in the European Union, I believe the contribution which British pragmatism could make to the solution of problems arising with Central and Eastern Europe from the collapse of Communism would be welcomed.

TRIBE: The drift of what you are saying then is that decision making in the 1950s and the 1960s was driven simply by political considerations . . .

HARDMAN: Your comment suggests a misunderstanding of the role in government not of an economics specialist but of a 'generalist', which is what I was. If a Minister, his economists and regular civil servants, are all agreed on the policy which ought to be followed, that can be much benefit. In the late 1940s John Strachey at Food, encouraged by his officials, agreed with Stafford Cripps as Chancellor of the Exchequer that consumer subsidies on food, then very considerable and rising fast, were undesirable economically and within two or three years had secured their elimination. If after the end of the war Ministers in Housing Departments could have been served by persuasive economists and civil servants with economic understanding, the sorry tale of UK housing policy over the years since then might have been very different. But agreement on public policy is seldom so wisely and speedily achieved as it was with post-war food subsidies.

In the Ministry of Agriculture after the amalgamation with Food, I thought that the agricultural policy of Ministers was a mistake and that some of the resources provided to farmers could with gain be better directed to other activities. But of course I accepted that my personal views were irrelevant. More important was that both main political parties supported substantial and continuing aid for agriculture: and despite the considerable costs involved, alike as consumers and tax-payers, there was little or no public support for cutting down. Most important was that, as a civil servant, I was employed to serve Ministers: to oppose *à l'outrance* their policies would properly be an invitation to be shown the door! The sensible course must be to help Ministers to carry out their policies in what one hoped would be the least harmful way. And of course, where economic realities were being ignored, one must attempt to make Ministers aware of them. I recall one day shocking Heathcoat Amory as Minister of Agriculture by expressing satisfaction that the figures for employment in agriculture about to be announced were significantly down. My impression was that he had never previously appreciated that since, with increasing incomes, a declining proportion would be spent on food then, particularly with increasing agricultural production from research and development, there would be reduced demand for labour in agriculture. Some of the satire in *Yes, Minister* is very near the mark!

One final and perhaps obvious comment from what I have said already is that, outside a few central departments like the Treasury, a departmental official must recognise that government policy will emerge from the bringing together of policy recommendations from many departments and that proposals from this may have to be sacrificed for what Ministers look upon as the more important claims of others. In my view it is because of this burden upon Ministers that politics in a democracy demands (but alas does not often get) the service of the ablest in society.

TRIBE: As a new generation of politicians came through – Harold Wilson in a sense represents part of this because he had read PPE in Oxford – did you in the 1960s begin to notice a difference in the attitudes of the politicians?

HARDMAN: Of course they brought more awareness of economic realities. But, equally, the decisions they had to make affected far more activities than in the pre-war generation of politicians. Much more important was that they recognised their primary job was as politicians and not as economists. Gaitskell was widely regarded as the worst post-war Chancellor of the Exchequer because his interest in the economics of problems prevented the proper performance of his political and ministerial responsibilities.

TRIBE: You would seek to bring in economics from outside or on a temporary basis into the various kinds of departments you were working in. Did you look to any particular group of economists, or any particular contacts that you had? Was it people from the LSE particularly or . . .?

HARDMAN: In the Ministry of Agriculture before the amalgamation with Food, economists were employed on work for the Annual Price Review. When I took over responsibility for them, I tried to extend economic awareness in more of the new Ministries by widening economists' assignments to include food as well as agriculture rather than by recruiting additional staff. In the Ministry of Aviation, where I found one solitary statistician and no economists, I recruited for part-time and short-term jobs outsiders, beginning with Ely Devons from LSE whom I knew, and gradually adding a few more. But the technical complexities of the topics to which they gave attention were enormous and I cannot say that their intervention yielded any outstanding benefit. In the Ministry of Defence therefore I looked to the guidance and training which US economists concerned with programme budgeting under Charles Hitch gave to the full-time UK career civil servants who worked for a time with them and this was much more successful. My experience of the difficulties of securing worthwhile but part-time and occasional guidance from outside economists tended to be confirmed after I left the Civil Service. For about ten years I served as Chairman both of the Covent Garden Market Authority and the Home-Grown Cereals Authority and at each of them I set up an Advisory Panel of economists recruited from universities along with one or two able businessmen. Though meetings were always agreeable occasions, and the comments from the panels on the problems put to them were often helpful, it is difficult looking back to be sure that with more than one or two exceptions they justified the costs incurred in securing them. Much more successful in the Home-Grown Cereals Authority was the commissioning soon after the Authority was set up of a team of economists under Denis Britton, then at the University of Nottingham, to produce over two years a study of the UK cereals industry. The report on production, marketing and utilisation not only proved to be a most useful guide but led to some significant changes in the organisation of price support for cereals.

TRIBE: Did you ever feel tempted yourself to switch over from being a civil servant to becoming a politician?

HARDMAN: No. I had friends who did. John Edwards, who was at Leeds when I was, went into politics and was a Minister in the first post-war Labour Government. He died about twenty years ago I suppose. But I had absolutely no desire whatever. My interest in the Civil Service and economics overcame any interest in political activity.

TRIBE: So did you see yourself as an economist then through your . . .?

HARDMAN: All my friends who are economists think I am a civil servant and all my friends who are civil servants think I am an economist: that is why I managed to get away with so much!

TRIBE: In the later 1940s and early 1950s, if one thinks of public sector economics one usually means macroeconomics. You had a strong allegiance to a microeconomic tradition, and never really took macroeconomics completely on board. Do you see there a distinction within government, that in fact the majority of the economists would be identified as macroeconomists?

HARDMAN: I do, yes. I was interested in David Henderson, later of OECD, whom I recruited to the Ministry of Aviation, saying not long ago that he was more interested now than he had been ten years ago in microeconomics; he thought microeconomics was far more important than he had earlier appreciated. And I would have thought that was true of most economists: there has been a very considerable revival of interest in microeconomics in the last few years. I feel they are just coming nearer to the views in which I was brought up, though of course in a much more sophisticated form.

TRIBE: Arthur Brown, for instance, when I asked him a similar question about the way in which they taught economics, made it clear that by the late 1940s and early 1950s what was thought to be elementary economics was primarily macroeconomics.

HARDMAN: Yes. Much earlier Joan Robinson's introductory book and later James Meade's text-book were important influences. But that is very different from Clay's *Economics: An Introduction for the General Reader*, or from Henderson's *Supply and Demand*, or the kind of thing that had been basic undergraduate reading in my day.[20]

TRIBE: From the time that you were in government service, can you see any other changes that have occurred in the last, say, twenty years, apart from this change towards microeconomics?

HARDMAN: You must recall that I was never a 'government economist'. Though I was in touch with some of them, I was not sufficiently and continuously close enough to be aware of changes to their focus of attention in economic theory. Whether my views on changes even in government service over the past twenty years, if that is what you mean, are of much value, I beg leave to doubt. After all, I retired as a civil servant in 1966 and have been free of all public responsibility for almost twenty years. But, as I see it, not only has the volume but the quality of macroeconomic data made available increased steadily year by year. Far more full-time economists are now employed: moreover, they work not only in the Treasury and the departments close to it but in more and more other departments. Their full-time employment offers substantial benefit. As I said earlier, in the Ministry of Aviation I recruited academic economists (e.g. Ely Devons, Maurice Peston) for part-time help: subsequently with the Covent Garden Market Authority and the Home-Grown Cereals Authority, I set up panels of academic economists with government economists and one or two businessmen whose advice was sought regularly. But inevitably the interest of economists was peripheral to their main work and was sometimes, I suspect, of more value to their teaching than to their part-time employer. In the Ministry of Defence, again to repeat myself, in the collaboration which was begun in the mid-1960s with C.J. Hitch in the Pentagon and his Rand associates over 'Programme Budgeting' and quantification of defence policy objectives, the work was entrusted with better results to civil servants who were guided and helped by American economists. A third change has been brought about by the creation of parliamentary committees. Before the reforms introduced by St John Stevas (as then he was), and the Public Accounts Committee always apart, the

---

[20] Joan Robinson, *Economics is a Serious Subject*, W. Heffer, Cambridge, 1932; James Meade, *Introduction to Economic Analysis and Policy*, Oxford University Press, London, 1936; Henry Clay, *Economics. An Introduction for the General Reader*, Macmillan, London, 1916; Hubert Henderson, *Supply and Demand*, Nisbet, London, 1922.

committees were of slight significance and imposed no heavy burden of work on the Civil Service. But their extension, coupled with the increased importance of radio and television as sources of news and publicity, must now make for a substantial load, not least because MPs can nowadays employ outside experts (including economists) to provide material as a basis for cross-examination of Civil Service witnesses. Some MPs seem to use their opportunities to admirable effect. But, alas the number of Frank Fields among back-benchers is very limited and much of the effort expended, not least by outside experts, seems to be wasted in the securing of short-term publicity for individual MPs.

I was quite exceptional, alike in my training and in the course I took, and it was only because I was able to start so young. You couldn't go to university before you were 16 and as soon as I was 16 I went to the University. But you see, there were only four honours students listening to Henry Clay. I was spoilt. I can remember being asked by A.R. Prest, Professor at Manchester, about 1968, to give a talk to the Economics Department. Well, I went to give this lecture, and people came pouring into the lecture room, so I said, 'I thought this was for academic staff?'; the reply was 'Well it is'. And I thought of Henry Clay and his four students in 1925 or whenever it was; incredible change.

3

SIR ALEC CAIRNCROSS

Alec Cairncross began his university studies in Glasgow in 1928 before, in 1932, moving to Cambridge, where he was among the first group of students to pursue graduate work with a view to the award of a Ph.D. Returning to Glasgow, he taught for a time before joining the fledgling Economic Section in the Cabinet Office, moving later to the Ministry of Aircraft Production, where he rose to the post of Director of Programmes. After a brief spell in Berlin he was made Economic Adviser to the Board of Trade in 1946, moving in 1949 for a year to the OEEC. During the 1950s he played an important role in the development of teaching in economics and management in Glasgow, and was made Economic Adviser to the government in 1961. In 1964 he was made Head of the Government Economic Service, a post which he held until 1969. His experience of government, industry and university life has been extensive, and he has over the years written several books and articles in which personal experience and historical research are combined. Chief among these are *The Economic Section 1939–61, A Study in Economic Advising* (with Nita Watts) and *Planning in Wartime, Aircraft Production in Britain, Germany and the USA*. He also published in 1944 his textbook, *Introduction to Economics*, which has gone through several editions and was especially influential during the 1950s and 1960s. His contribution to the series of memoirs published in the *Banco Nazionale del Lavoro Quarterly* appeared in 1992.[1] The following is based upon an interview conducted at Sir Alec's Oxford home on 18 July 1994.

CAIRNCROSS: When I went to Glasgow in 1928 I went intending to cut two years off my apprenticeship as an accountant; because you could become a chartered accountant with a degree and limit yourself to a three-year apprenticeship, instead of a five-year apprenticeship. When I got there I took Political Economy precisely because that was a subject that seemed to be part of the curriculum leading to an accounting qualification. Now at Glasgow the

---

[1] A. Cairncross, 'From Theory to Policy-Making: Economics as a Profession', *Banco Nazionale del Lavoro Quarterly*, vol. 45 (1992), pp. 3–20.

main degrees then were 'Pass' degrees – that is three-year degrees – but there were a lot of four-year degrees in which you took Honours. But Honours almost invariably was in two subjects. In some cases this was rather a fiction, because if you took Honours in History you could take Honours in History and some other form of history, e.g. Constitutional History. If you took Honours in Economics you took Honours in Economics and perhaps Political Philosophy, or Philosophy or Maths. I took Economics and Politics which was the most common of the options. There was a thesis, there was a paper on Economic History, there were three papers on Economics and three papers on Politics.

The classes were quite large in economics, because many people intending to compete for, say, Civil Service employment thought it would be useful. If they were taking Honours, they thought this was one avenue of employment. This was in 1928–32, a period in which it was rather difficult to find a job. There were a number of people ahead of me who did move into government. Stewart Bates went over to Canada and ultimately became the head of the Canadian Central Mortgage and Housing Corporation. Two at least moved into Whitehall – Sir Matthew Stevenson, who was the head of the Ministry of Fuel and Power for a while, and Sir William Strath who was on the Planning staff under Plowden. There were no doubt others as well. That was one avenue of employment, and one reason why people were interested in economics. They liked, if they were taking a degree in some other subject, to mix in a little economics, so that the Ordinary Class, the first-year class, was quite a large class, about two hundred or perhaps even more. There was in economics a first year, second year and third year, but no fourth year; although it was a four-year degree. So I took in my first year History, English and Political Economy. In my second year I took Moral Philosophy, Logic, Political Philosophy and Economics a second time.

TRIBE: You would have had four lectures a day? That is quite a number of hours per week.

CAIRNCROSS: I should think in Political Economy it was Monday, Tuesday, and Friday but I am not quite sure about that. I think on Thursday there might be an additional lecture given, say, by Macfie on the theory of value; because in those days price was always called value and you were led to believe that economics was a branch of philosophy. I don't remember the Professor ever mentioning a single figure from start to finish, except when he happened to mention there was something called the national income, which he thought was worth about four thousand million pounds, or whatever it was. The subject was entirely non-quantitative as taught in Glasgow.

TRIBE: I did notice with the Ordinary Class from the late 1920s that one of the assigned books is Marshall's *Elements of Economics*, the 1891 primer, which is quite unusual . . .

CAIRNCROSS: That was the assigned book. Quite unreadable. If only we had read the *Economics of Industry* I think it would have been much better, but we were also asked to read Smart's *Theory of Value*, and Smart was very much in fashion there – he translated Böhm-Bawerk. I don't think I learned any economics to speak of in the whole of my four years at Glasgow. When I went to Cambridge I might as well have had no economics at all. I did do a lot of work, on my own, on international trade. I think I was probably as well-posted on the theory of international trade as anybody in Cambridge when I got there because I had read all the books. It was a wearisome business, looking back on it now. I marvel that I had the patience to read the theory of international trade, which seemed to me to have jolly little to do with international trade (apart from the idea of comparative costs). But I had done it, and I did a thesis (as part of the course in my final year) on the transfer problem[2] essentially – on capital exports and the terms of trade. This was the time when Keynes and Ohlin were debating this subject; but I approached it much more from the angle of Taussig, who had published his book on international trade and purported to show that a movement of capital from A to B turned the terms of trade against A. The reparations problem raised much the same issue, and there were articles by some of the Cambridge economists – though none of them had written extensively on international trade – on the transfer problem from one angle or another. Pigou had also written on the subject. At any rate, I did a thesis. That thesis I sent to Cambridge in case there was any prospect that it might win me a scholarship at either King's or Trinity. In fact in the end I plumped for Trinity, and I was successful in getting what was an unimaginable amount now, £300 a year. That was for three years, and allowed me to take my doctorate.

TRIBE: That was quite unusual at the time, wasn't it, since the Cambridge Ph.D. had only started in the 1920s, and together with Hans Singer and Rao you were, in effect, the first Cambridge economics doctorates? There was no doctoral programme, so it was not a normal move to go to Cambridge to read for a doctorate.

CAIRNCROSS: No, there wasn't a doctoral programme. You were out in the cold. There had been one doctorate in economics, and that was G.T. Jones, who wrote on increasing returns. He was run down by a bus and killed. When I went up, nobody had a Cambridge doctorate. Many of the staff didn't even have a degree in economics. I don't think Keynes had a degree in economics. He never sat an exam in economics in his life, except for the Civil Service. There had been two research students when I went up in 1932: Ronald Walker, an Australian who took a Ph.D. in 1933, and P.H. Asher who was awarded a Master's degree. When Ronald Walker got his Ph.D. the other graduate students gave him a dinner, because he showed it could be done. I think I was next, submitting in 1935. Hans Singer was next in 1936, and then V.K.R.V. Rao, followed by Brian Tew. In 1939 there weren't more than about five Ph.D.s in all.

---

[2] The 'transfer problem' was a major issue in the 1920s because of the impact on the international economy of German war reparations made under the terms of the Treaty of Versailles.

TRIBE: Pigou was nominally your supervisor, but did you in fact have much contact with him?

CAIRNCROSS: Yes, I went to Pigou as my supervisor but I had some difficulty. I got a postcard from him summoning me, but I couldn't make out the date, or the signature, or the message. Finally, I noticed it was stamped King's College, and that was some help; and I saw it was signed 'A.C.P.' and that was a help; and then I managed to make out that it was either Tuesday or Thursday and the time I could make out. So I went on Tuesday at four o'clock, and he didn't seem to be at all surprised. But after going to Pigou for one term I decided I had better get somebody else, and go to Colin Clark. I went to Colin Clark, as we were working in the same field: he was studying capital investment, I was studying capital investment, so we worked together.

Hans Singer when he came up was put under my protection. He came from Istanbul. He had been working under Schumpeter and Spiethoff in Bonn. He didn't do the housing problem in Britain, although he did write on the subject. He did a thesis on land values, if I remember rightly. Lorie Tarshis, who died very recently, came from Canada. He did stay on, I think, to do a doctorate, but I don't think he stayed quite as long as that. Bob Bryce more or less ran Canada for a time. He was at the top of the Civil Service. He knew what it was all about. A great crowd of Canadians came over in 1932.

At first I was supervised by Pigou, but I was really under the care of Dennis Robertson. Dennis looked after me. He might read some of my stuff. Kahn read some of my stuff because it was critical of Kahn. Pigou said to me, when I wrote a piece that was rather critical of him on capital transfer, 'You ought', he said, 'to have a positive thesis, you shouldn't just go round criticising people all the time. Have a definite thesis. What you need is a vice.' I was a bit startled by that, but it became apparent that what he meant by 'a vice' was something to hold the argument together and advance it. I think Colin was the chap who really inspired most of the research workers at the time. He was a hopeless lecturer. Facing the blackboard all of the time and muttering, so that you hadn't a clue what he was talking about except what he wrote up on the board, that gave us some idea; but as a supervisor it was a different story. He could be very useful, he would tell you what to read and so on.

TRIBE: You attended undergraduate lectures as well?

CAIRNCROSS: Oh, yes. As I say, I knew no economics to speak of. I had been reading books on economics but they were all behind the times. I don't think that Scott ever mentioned Keynes or Pigou. He lectured on the life of Adam Smith mainly.

TRIBE: So on the whole it would have been difficult to learn economics in Glasgow, with the syllabus or with teaching as it was organised when you were there as a student?

CAIRNCROSS: There are different views. Alexander Werth, who was one of the leading journalists of his day, travelled all the way from London to hear Scott. I thought Scott gave a lecture in the form of a single sentence, because if you tried to take it down, you didn't know where to put the point; and I can remember that I sometimes stopped and then Scott would lean over benevolently towards me and repeat what he had said, assuming that I hadn't heard.

TRIBE: In Edinburgh there are three sets of students' notes on the lectures of Shield Nicholson: one set with a doubtful date, one from the early 1890s and one set from about 1900. And the two which are about ten years apart are almost identical, certainly the way that they start out – it seems that from year to year his lectures not only did not change in substance, the form of delivery was very similar too.

CAIRNCROSS: That could happen. There was one professor I know of in History who was a very splendid lecturer; but somebody who got all his notes to deputise for him found a note saying, 'Please remember to tell the boys there is a holiday on Monday, as it is the Queen's birthday', and that wasn't the present Queen. That would be about 1930. Scott came into the room with a large black folio under his arm which he put on the desk and then never looked at. When I came to lecture I got access to his room and could look at this mysterious book, and I found that it was essentially Marshallian, quite sensible, quite illuminating. But his lectures bore no relation to it. If he had dictated what was in that I couldn't have complained, but what I did hear, especially in the Honours classes, was lecture after lecture on the life of Adam Smith. He was doing research on Adam Smith for a book on the subject, and he would tell us all about that. In the Ordinary Class it would be elementary stuff about the Physiocrats and the Mercantilists, what I would think of as pre-first-year stuff rather than even first-year stuff. No rigorous theory of any kind. Scott was a most distinguished figure; he was Treasurer of the British Academy for one thing. A very distinguished economic historian. His famous three-volume work on the joint-stock company we never looked at. But his predecessor Smart, who wrote books on Böhm-Bawerk, was I think much more to the point.

TRIBE: What has struck me looking at the Glasgow *Calendar* and the syllabus is that the rough outline of the Ordinary Class remained the same from the later days of Smart's reign through Scott's, and then started to change only in the late 1940s and 1950s. It seemed that Scott didn't bother to change the rubric . . .

CAIRNCROSS: I think the first-year class was the same. He wouldn't change it very much. What came out verbally might differ because he wasn't really reading his lectures out, as so many professors did in those days. There was only one Honours class because the second and third year were amalgamated, and you went to it two years running, that was all. They had only two classes in economics, and you took them both. You did get a different picture when Macfie or Nisbet appeared. Nisbet was later professor at St Andrews. Macfie was later professor at Glasgow.[3] Macfie was interested in the philosophic side

---

[3] Alec Macfie (1898–1980) was appointed Assistant Lecturer in Political Economy at Glasgow in 1929, was promoted to Lecturer in 1933, and to Professor in 1945. He retired in 1958.

of things, and he was very helpful and very much to the point. I valued what he had to say. Nisbet was a brisker character who turned out *laissez-faire* economists by the dozen, some of whom are now in rather important positions.[4] If you really want to know about the IEA I would start with J.W. Nisbet. But these two were only let loose once a week.

TRIBE: If you look at Nisbet's work, or you look at the kind of teaching he did, it is not immediately apparent what the basis of his undoubted influence was.

CAIRNCROSS: Well he was very much *laissez-faire*. He believed in the market. He didn't put it that way; I mean the market was not talked about, but *laissez-faire* was talked about. He really did think that things should take their course; and he did a book called *A Case for Laissez Faire*.[5] Indeed, the whole atmosphere in Glasgow meant you had to work on your own. I developed a theory of bad lectures as a very useful spur to reading. I maintained in my farewell lecture at Glasgow that what students really needed was a set of *bad* lectures, to oblige them to read the subject. If you went to really *good* lectures such as we had in Moral Philosophy, which were wonderful, you felt you could never compete, you would never want to pursue the subject. If you listened to these lectures in economics you felt, 'I think I could do better than that.' You were encouraged to go on with the subject. It was a four-year degree with only two classes to occupy you, so you had freedom to range over the whole subject. I had intended to do mathematics as well so as to cover absolutely the lot – History and Mathematics, Philosophy, Logic, English, anything. But I didn't get round to the maths; I had to teach myself calculus for that purpose. Duncan Black was a contemporary of mine. There were four Firsts in my year. And, I think, well-deserved Firsts. Jim Chapman who became very senior in Colemans and associated firms. Died unexpectedly in a mountaineering accident. Charles Wilson, who became Vice-Chancellor of Glasgow. Duncan Black has now been written up very extensively as an important economist.[6]

TRIBE: Black graduated in the same subjects as you?

CAIRNCROSS: He was senior to me. The Logan Medal, for the best Arts graduate, was shared between Duncan Black and myself. Much to my astonishment, I may say. Duncan hardly opened his mouth so I didn't know what potential he had, but he clearly was very bright. He had taken mathematics

[4] James Nisbet (1903–74) was Assistant to Scott at Glasgow from 1926 to 1931, then Lecturer at St Andrews 1935–39, when he was promoted to a Readership. He became Professor in 1947 and retired in 1970.

[5] P.S. King, London, 1929.

[6] Duncan Black (1908–91) taught economics with Ronald Coase at the Dundee School of Economics 1932–34, was briefly Lecturer in Economics at Queen's, Belfast before moving to University College, Bangor, where he was first Lecturer and then Professor of Economics. Like Coase, he had a slow start to his career since the originality of his early work went largely unrecognised; his single most influential publication is probably *The Theory of Committees and Elections*, Cambridge University Press, London, 1958.

already. Firsts came in a bunch: you had a cycle. About every fourth year you got three or four Firsts. There had been another good crop some way further back. I think too, when you get people who are good together, they do egg one another on.

TRIBE: You said that you had gone to Glasgow because of this relationship to the accountancy qualifications. Later on you taught with Macfie in the accountancy class, didn't you?

CAIRNCROSS: Oh yes.

TRIBE: When they introduced that course for students in accountancy in the early 1930s it was, according to the syllabus,[7] an accounting course, but by the time it came round to you it had become an economics course. Do you know anything about the reason for that change?

CAIRNCROSS: I have no knowledge of that. There was of course a separate University class in Accountancy (later under a Professor). When I got there in 1935 I found that there were forty lectures to be delivered twice a year to the accountants, and I was to split these lectures with Macfie. Instead Macfie took ill every time it was his turn, for four successive years, and I delivered to every accountant who ever passed through Glasgow in those years a course in economics lasting ten weeks. That is where I learned how to lecture. When I started I barely knew how to fill the hour by talking to them and I wondered how you could spin out a lecture to last an hour; by the time I had got halfway through the first course my question was how I could get it all into the time. What I did in the end was to say to them, 'Look, don't try and take down what I am saying. I can see from your exam answers that you don't really understand. Or at least the notes you take are not such as to make you understand it. I will give you notes printed out which will be a better summary of what I say than anything you can take down, and then you might concentrate on what I am saying and give up taking notes.' And at the end of that – this is the origin of the textbook – at the end of two or three years, in 1937 I think, the Glasgow School of Accountancy asked if I would do a textbook for them. I said, 'No, I have got my Ph.D. thesis to publish. I just haven't got the time.' And they said, 'Would you like to see what we are using now?' and I said, 'Yes, I would be very interested.' So they handed me Crew, *Economics for Commercial Students*[8] and some other book (not Silverman, they weren't even up to Silverman at that stage),[9] which I looked at with utter horror. It was badly written, badly illustrated. Wrong, absolutely wrong here and there. And gave you no conception

---

[7] 'Syllabus of Economics Class for Students in Accountancy', *Glasgow University Calendar for the Year 1932–33*, pp. 136–7.

[8] A. Crew, *Economics for Commercial Students*, Jordan and Sons, London, 1921. By 1936 this book had reached its twelfth edition, and it was finally republished in a thirteenth edition in 1950. Crew wrote several books, chiefly on law and procedure, for commercial students; see for example *The Law and Practice Relating to Dentists and Dentistry*, J. Bale, Sons and Danielsson, London, 1926.

[9] H.A. Silverman wrote a number of introductory texts on economics: for example, his *The Substance of Economics*, Sir Isaac Pitman, London, 1922, reached its thirteenth edition in 1950, while *The Groundwork of Economics*, Sir Isaac Pitman, London, 1926, reached its fourth edition in 1953.

of a consistent body of theory. Absolutely terrible. I thought, 'Something has got to be done.' I said, 'All right, I'll have a go.' And I started in 1938, was interrupted by Munich in the vacation, and a lot of other things I had to get on with. It was nearly finished when the war broke out; and I managed in the course of the war to write the odd chapter or two that was still needed, and got it out. But James Meade had already come out with his book.[10] If I had known that that was there I would have said, 'What is the point?' The same was true of Benham, which came out about the same time.[11] In 1937 there was no adequate textbook. Nothing worth reading in 1937. You were told to read Marshall, but it was unreadable. Henry Clay was the nearest.[12] And Henry Clay wasn't all that hot, he had never heard of Keynes at that point of course. There was nothing about Keynes. Nothing about Joan Robinson – imperfect competition, unemployment, statistics. None of them. And Pigou, welfare economics, nothing there. Absolutely nothing.

TRIBE: In the accountancy classes, according to the Calendar again, the textbooks in 1936–37 were Jones, *Economics of Private Enterprise,*[13] and Mills on *Money.* Did Jones' book have any influence on the structure of your textbook?

CAIRNCROSS: I don't think I have read him. I thought to myself, 'What do I start with? Do I start as James Meade starts it, or do I start with the simple things?[14] And my hunch was that, if you are teaching economics, people understand running a shop, but they don't understand running a country. And therefore I started with the microeconomics and brought in the macroeconomics later. That seemed to me to be sensible. It is not the accepted view now. But at that time I was satisfied that if I were going to get anywhere, my students in Glasgow, whatever they were, would understand the micro problems, but might have considerable difficulty with the macro.

TRIBE: It is interesting that you put it in terms of micro and macro, because that distinction wasn't named in that way at the time. Why I said it is rather like Jones is because, once you get past initial definitions and the introductory material, you then move into production. You deal with production and then with consumption and demand. If you look at a later book, Samuelson's *Economics,* this has a straightforward national income framework; or then again Eastham's book, based on his Dundee lectures from the 1930s, has price formation and consumption first;[15] more consumption-orientated than production-orientated, unlike your book.

CAIRNCROSS: I thought that I had been put in touch with the Home University Library as publishers, but I was wrong, it was Butterworth. There

[10] James Meade, *Introduction to Economic Analysis and Policy,* Oxford University Press, London, 1936.
[11] Frederic Benham, *Economics: A General Textbook for Students,* Sir Isaac Pitman, London, 1938.
[12] Henry Clay, *Economics: An Introduction for the General Reader,* Macmillan, London, 1916.
[13] J.H. Jones, *The Economics of Private Enterprise,* Sir Isaac Pitman & Sons, London, 1926.
[14] Meade began his book with a section on unemployment which recapitulated elements of Keynesian theory.
[15] J.K. Eastham, *An Introduction to Economic Analysis,* English Universities Press, London, 1950.

was a firm called Thornton Butterworth which published the Home University Library, a highly respected series of volumes, and I thought it was the same firm. When I went to see this publisher it turned out that the idea of publishing my book went back to the then director and chairman of the company, who wanted to turn Butterworths into a McGraw-Hill, was going to start with economics, and this was the first book. They were a legal and medical publisher, and very enterprising. Very enterprising. But the chairman died in 1942–43. The fellow handling my book had just come back from India and when I went to see him he said, 'Nobody will want to read economics after the war.' And I asked, 'How many copies are you going to print?' He said, 'Two thousand.' 'Two thousand?' I said, 'you have missed out a digit.' In the end, after a bit of argument he said, 'All right, I will make it four thousand.' I said, 'What is the most you have ever published?' 'Oh', he said, 'there was a book on bankruptcy that did very well, very well.' 'How many did you sell of that?' 'I think we got up to fifteen thousand', he said. 'Well', I said, 'you have got a digit wrong somewhere, I can tell you that.' And when it came to the second edition, I dictated the format, the type, everything, they did exactly as I told them. The first edition. Oh dear, if you had seen the very first copies they turned out, they had to start all over again. It was very unreadable. It used a type that was just hopeless.

TRIBE: Was that simply to do with the war restrictions on paper or . . .?

CAIRNCROSS: Well, it had to this extent, that if there had been no restrictions on paper I would have gone to another publisher there and then; but I thought if they are committing paper to my book I can't afford to drop that, so I let them go ahead. They did bring the book out in next to no time. I didn't know it was out. It took me months to find out it had been published. So that when they really got down to doing the job they did it pretty well. It was a great pity. I should have had an American edition before Samuelson got out, and I had somebody in mind but it didn't really come off.

TRIBE: What was the run of the second edition? How many were printed?

CAIRNCROSS: Oh, I have no idea. I know that in total it was well up over 100,000 and probably about 150,000 or something like that. It wasn't enormous but for economics a lot, given the time, taking all the editions together. It is still in print. I believe it still *sells* in India.

TRIBE: It was a very popular book through the 1940s and 1950s.

CAIRNCROSS: Oh, I know that. I would give lifts to people in my car and they would say to me, 'You are Cairncross? Who wrote that book?' All kinds of unknown characters would talk to me. Very odd. Chiefly because in England there wasn't very much competition. Benham was the chief competition. But Benham hadn't got some aspects of it right.

TRIBE: Well, Hicks said about Benham in his review that it had bits of everything but not enough of anything, that it was too general.[16]

---

[16] J.R. Hicks, review of Benham, *Economics, Manchester School*, vol. 9 (1938), pp. 184–6.

CAIRNCROSS: It was too general I think. It was agony writing mine. Mind you, teaching accountants was a great help, because for the first part I could draw on examination answers for illustrations. They taught me a lot about specific things about industry. I learned a great deal in other parts of my career about industry, but they did give me very good illustrations, so I was indebted to them. They were quite a good bunch, these boys. There were usually about forty or fifty. The main job of a young assistant in the University of Glasgow was correcting, correcting, correcting. You might do a little lecturing now and again when you got a chance, but you had to correct essays, you had to correct exam papers, you had to keep at it all the time. The essays might be extremely long and some of them got very enthusiastic. I can remember John Gunn who stood first in my class in his year but was later Professor of Physics, doing an essay of eighty pages, and big pages, on monopoly. And if you went through a lot of essays like that and had to comment on page after page of them, it really took quite a lot of time. Some 200 essays twice a year, plus exam papers. That was the real thing. The Professor never did a thing of that kind, it was left to the lecturers and since Macfie was ill it was left to me pretty well.

TRIBE: When you went from Cambridge to Glasgow, was anyone else at the time interested in taking the job? Was it difficult to get the job?

CAIRNCROSS: Nobody was asked. It was mine for the taking! They knew me. I had just almost completed my Ph.D. and it was almost automatically offered to me, I think. I am sure they didn't consider anybody else.

TRIBE: So when you were in Glasgow in the later part of the 1930s did you have any regular contacts with people in Edinburgh or Dundee?

CAIRNCROSS: To some extent. Dundee particularly. Yes, I was in touch with them: I knew Eastham, Marian Bowley and, of course, Duncan Black, but we rarely met. I was in touch with Aberdeen, because Glasgow and Aberdeen were always very close together. I was in touch with Fraser Noble more through the International Student Service, or what is now WUS, as I was Scottish Secretary. Not with Lindley Fraser in Aberdeen.[17] Through ISS Paul Streeten went to Aberdeen.[18] He was going to come to Glasgow, but we had more money and we took Kurt Rothschild and his wife,[19] sending Paul Streeten up to Aberdeen; and about four or five others. I made contact with people in Aberdeen in that sort of way, and with Edinburgh and St Andrews. I remember, East–West Conferences at Easter, where Boulding appeared for instance, about 1938, from Edinburgh. He didn't find much favour with Edinburgh because he stammered a bit. The Professor, Alexander Gray, who was otherwise a marvellous man, felt Boulding was not what they needed,

---

[17] Lindley Fraser was Fellow and Lecturer in Economics at Queen's College, Oxford from 1928–35, then Professor of Economics at Aberdeen from 1935 to 1946.

[18] See Paul Streeten, 'Aerial Roots', *Banco Nazionale del Lavoro Quarterly*, vol. 39 (1986), pp. 135–60, reprinted in J.A. Kregel (ed.), *Recollections of Eminent Economists*, vol. 2, Macmillan, Basingstoke, 1989.

[19] See Kurt Rothschild's account of how he came to Glasgow in late 1938 in his 'Glimpses of a Non-Linear Biography', *Banco Nazionale del Lavoro Quarterly*, vol. 44 (1991) pp. 6–7.

and he went off to America.[20] I was in touch with these people, but I don't know that I saw a great deal of them, because I had quite a lot to occupy me. I had a book on migration practically ready, but it all got thrown away in the war.

TRIBE: The view from Dundee of the Scottish universities is of the separateness of Dundee from the rest of Scottish economics.

CAIRNCROSS: Well, they were all quite separate, except that economists might meet, and did meet, although rarely. I don't recall, now you mention it, that any of the Dundee economists came to the East–West Conference or anything of that kind. We later ran, after the war, a series of conferences annually for Scottish economists, in the 1950s at the Burn, in September, and that was very successful in uniting people wherever they were. The East–West Conference was not on economics; it was a meeting of students from Glasgow and Edinburgh who came from the less-developed countries and were being assembled as a group. They talked about economics to some extent, that is why I was there, and why Boulding was there. I knew the head of the International Club at Glasgow – Aaron, an Indian, who induced me to take part.

TRIBE: It is evident from the Calendars that when Gray was replaced in Edinburgh in 1956 by Alan Peacock there had been little change in the organisation of teaching since the 1920s.[21] In fact, the Ordinary Class list starts off with Adam Smith, goes through Ricardo, Mill, List, Marx and up to Marshall; and gradually, later material is added on. And then when Peacock comes in it is all thrown out and his text is Samuelson; there is a major shift in the teaching. Would that be to do with that relationship between the lecturing and the professor, on the one hand, and the teaching of the staff at that time, on the other?

CAIRNCROSS: I think it sounds very likely to me. Certainly with Scott. I mean if I had been appointed professor after the war it would have been on the basis of my textbook. I might not have started with macroeconomics, but I would have certainly got round to that. So there would have been something like a revolution. The tendency was to start with the development of economics, to go right back to the Physiocrats, and I can remember that that was how Scott began, and worked forward. Of course this was combined with another class in Politics taken by A.K. White. Now that had a big effect. I think Duncan Black again was chiefly interested in what White was saying, more than in the economics. That would not have been true of Jim Chapman. We two were much more interested in economics than in politics. But he had a quite different style, you see. White would suddenly read you bits from Gladstone. What did Gladstone think about politics? What was the moment

---

[20] See Boulding's own account of this in his contribution to M. Szenberg, *Eminent Economists: Their Life Philosophies*, Cambridge University Press, Cambridge, 1992, p. 72.

[21] See *Edinburgh University Calendar, 1957–58*, pp. 379–85 where the Honours course rubric has been completely recast.

at which you should act? It would be very important to him, something the textbooks never mentioned. Gladstone had given a lot of thought to it: when was the time *ripe*? And he would go through different writers in that way, and show great interest in them, including American writers, which was more than ever happened in economics. I talked about Taussig, but he was not mentioned in class, I don't think anybody mentioned Taussig, or any American. So that Politics was in a sense a corrective to Economics. As in all courses, the two things were side by side and never brought to bear on the other. Nothing that was said in economics was suggested to you as a matter of politics. Nothing in politics suggested to you that it was involved with economics. Dotty. Absolutely dotty. But that was the way it was done, and continued to be done after the war.

TRIBE: When did you leave Glasgow for London?

CAIRNCROSS: 5 January 1940.

TRIBE: How did that come about?

CAIRNCROSS: In December 1939 I was approached, it must have been very early in the month or even in November, by Nicol McNiven, who was in the Scottish Office, and who told me that his Minister wanted to set up a special economic information service of some kind. To produce the necessary statistics at a moment's notice; and also run a kind of one-man, a one-man-*directed*, pub crawl over Scotland eliciting what the mood of the public was, and what the state of morale in the pubs was. I was to be in charge of this pub crawl, and at the same time supply figures. But just at that point, I think it must have been about the 24th of December, just before Christmas, I think, Austin Robinson rang me up and said that he and John Jewkes were now doing a job at the Cabinet Office or about to undertake it, and they had decided they needed help, and would I be prepared to join them? I said yes. It was like going into the Ark [two by two]. They had first approached Stamp, the busiest man they could find, the poohbah of British industry, and said to him, 'Would you like to conduct an enquiry into the plans for the war effort?' That was in July 1939, when war was imminent. Stamp after a month or two said to himself, 'I can't do this myself, I must get hold of two more.' So he got hold of Henry Clay and Hubert Henderson. In time Hubert Henderson and Henry Clay said to themselves, 'This is just too much for us, we can't do it all, we will get two more,' and they got John Jewkes and Austin Robinson – and Harry Campion – and when they thought about it they quickly came to the conclusion they too would need some help. I think I was the first man to be approached and Ely Devons the second; so by the time it got to March we had begun to get a kind of group, and then in May and June of course there was an enormous surge when Lionel Robbins and James Meade and all sorts of other people came in to join us. That is how I joined.

TRIBE: Did the Academic Register play a role in this?

CAIRNCROSS: No influence on any of these. It may have had an influence on Franks. It may be that Franks was picked on for that reason when he was

Professor of Moral Philosophy at Glasgow, because he went early. But I don't think that Austin was.[22]

I would swear that a very large number of the recruits were individually selected; once somebody got in he then said, 'Why not get the others?'; and it was done by word of mouth. I couldn't say that of all fifty or sixty who were in. There must have been at least fifty or sixty. There would be others who came in differently, but the chaps I knew in the Economic Section were all recruited individually, and that was a dozen or so. Right through Norman Chester, or even the new boys like Ronnie Tress, or Nita Watts. Nita Watts was recruited from the Bank of England, and so on. But they were all really I think recruited quite separately. The Register was a hopeless thing. The only thing where I think it may have been used was in Beveridge's Manpower Survey. There was some survey and there are papers in the PRO that bear on this which I only dipped into, and saw that a whole lot of names were there of economists that I was surprised to find. They had been working in 1940 and I didn't know they had been doing anything. Mainly on manpower. Of course, you know the story on manpower: when Harold Wilson and John Jewkes went together up to Lytham-St-Annes to say, 'Look, how can we fight a war without manpower statistics?' The government had suspended all manpower statistics, virtually. 'Without manpower statistics how can we do the job?' And the Under-Secretary looked at them pityingly, stood it for a while and then said, 'Don't you chaps realise there is a war on?' No good at all![23]

TRIBE: Was that interest in statistics widespread? Looking at it from the Manchester angle there are Harry Campion and John Jewkes, both of them ended up in statistical work, Harry Campion particularly, and also Jack Stafford later.

CAIRNCROSS: Well, Devons was the man. I mean Devons, you can forget the others. It was all really done by Devons.[24] He never got credit for it. Harry Campion was hopeless from that point of view. Very slow-moving, very deliberate, wanted to be quite sure of his ground all the time.[25] Devons was prepared to take a chance. Series A, Series B, Series C, Series D, Series E, Series F, Series G were *all* Devons' work, and they survived in the post-war period in the form of the *Monthly Digest* and all the other things. The selection of Gill Sans type was not I think exclusively Devons' work. I think that

---

[22] See A. Cairncross, *Austin Robinson: The Life of an Economic Adviser*, Macmillan, Basingstoke, 1993, pp. 78ff. for detail on this period.

[23] For a summary overview of the role of economists in wartime administration, see Sir Alec's 'Economists in Wartime', *Contemporary European History*, vol. 4 (1994), pp. 19–36.

[24] Ely Devons (1913–67) was from 1935 to 1940 Economic Assistant to the Joint Committee of the Cotton Trades Organisation in Manchester, and then joined the Ministry of Supply in Cotton Control. During the war he was, with Campion, instrumental in the foundation of the Central Statistical Office, and then worked in the Ministry of Aircraft Production to 1945. After the war he was first Reader, then Professor, of Economics at Manchester, moving to the Chair of Commerce at LSE in 1959.

[25] Harry Campion gained an M.A. in Commerce in Manchester in 1928 and was appointed Lecturer in Statistics in 1931.

Harry Campion may have had a hand in it. And Harry may have been more involved than I have given credit for. But I can only say that in my dealings with Harry both in 1940 and 1941, and later, when I went back in 1961, Harry was a very slow-moving character and rather difficult to get going. The driving force was unquestionably Devons. And it was the same at MAP. When it came to MAP, Jewkes took him with him. Jewkes[26] was very able, much abler than people thought, because while he didn't believe in planning, as so often happens, the people who don't believe in planning know what they are up against and do a much better job than the people who *do* believe in planning, who simply make a mess of things. But Ely was the chap who really got the figures in order and unless you had the figures in order you couldn't really do planning. MAP in 1942 was just a mess.

TRIBE: You carried on in government service after the war until 1951 . . .

CAIRNCROSS: My immediate reaction at the end of the war was to say, 'I will now opt for the private sector'. I agreed to go to *The Economist*. But before I ever got to *The Economist* I was persuaded to go out to Berlin and work there, to take over from Austin Robinson and Donald MacDougall. So I spent six very hectic months in Berlin on the plan for the level of German industry which we all agreed, but about which in the end nothing came, fortunately.[27] When I came back I went straight into *The Economist*, but almost as soon as I was on *The Economist* the Board of Trade got after me to join the Wool Working Party. So I spent Sunday night, Monday, Tuesday on the Wool Working Party. We went to press on Thursday. So I had Wednesday in which to do anything I did for *The Economist*. And when after six months John Henry Woods asked if I would come back into the Board of Trade because Austin had gone, again, I followed Austin the second time, or perhaps the third time, and went into the Board of Trade. I had been assured by John Henry that, of course, it is all very well writing articles in *The Economist*, that doesn't necessarily have any influence on Ministers. 'You can come into the department and speak to Cripps directly.' I soon found when I got in that (a) that Cripps wasn't there, or that (b) he had no time, or (c) more probably that he was busy reading *The Economist* so I didn't really get very far that way. But at any rate, I soon established that I was not advising the Minister, I was advising the Permanent Secretary, and I remained for three years, fundamentally as John Henry Woods' adviser. And doing what I could to do some co-ordination in the department, because it was a very unco-ordinated department.

TRIBE: What was the stimulus for the move to the OEEC in Paris then?

---

[26] John Jewkes (1903–88) gained a B.Com. in Manchester in 1923 and an M.Com. in 1924. He was appointed Lecturer in Commerce at Manchester in 1927, and promoted to the Chair of Social Economics in 1936, switching in 1947 to the Stanley Jevons Chair in 1947 before being appointed Professor of Economic Organisation at Oxford in 1948. After the war he became a staunch opponent of planning, as can be seen from his book *Ordeal by Planning*, Macmillan, London, 1948.

[27] This episode is documented in his book *A Country to Play With*, Colin Smythe, Gerrards Cross, 1987.

CAIRNCROSS: Well, in 1949 after devaluation was over and I thought things were taking the right turn, Cripps called me and asked me if I would go to Paris, to succeed Donald MacDougall this time. They needed somebody to prepare the approach to the Americans, the Second Report of the OEEC, the bid for aid, and I agreed to go. As in many other cases, I said no, and then in the end I thought, 'Well, I suppose I had better do it.' When I was asked to go, Cripps said, 'It will only take you six weeks', but I said, 'If I am going, I will go for six months'; and I did, and at the end of six months assumed that my job was finished. But in practice they hadn't found a successor as they should have done, and I stayed for another six months and then found my own successor in the person of Reddaway. It was a wonderful time. 1950 was *the* year when everything seemed to blossom.

TRIBE: Didn't you regret leaving it then to go Glasgow?

CAIRNCROSS: No, I left to go to Glasgow in 1951. I came back to Glasgow through the snow in January 1951. Just at the end of the year and stayed there for a bit.

TRIBE: It seems that there was some competition between academic departments in resuming work after the war, and trying to get people back out of government service; with the possibility that many of those economists who had been in government service might have preferred that to returning to an academic environment.

CAIRNCROSS: Very few wanted to stay.

TRIBE: So why would that have been?

CAIRNCROSS: They wanted to get back to academic life. They had had six years away, and that is a long time; I think they felt, 'This is all very well in wartime.' You could make your own way in wartime. You could really make your own career. But in peacetime you were going to be part of a solid structure, and unless you get in the right post to begin with you may find it very difficult. Nearly all the Economic Section disappeared and went back to their universities. Lionel Robbins wasn't going to stay on, and James Meade wasn't going to stay on. James did stay on in fact to be Head of the Section but he got fed up, and partly ill and partly because of Dalton – he left. No, it was a great problem finding anybody for *any* of these jobs in the immediate post-war period. I had some assistance. I got assistance from Polly Hill, Keynes' niece. That is the only period in my career I have never written up, the Board of Trade. I still have quite a lot of the papers. They destroyed the papers. They destroyed all my papers. They destroyed my papers in Berlin. They destroyed my papers in the Cabinet Office and they destroyed my papers in the Board of Trade. You look in vain for them. The things you find are the things you keep. MAP was the worst case of all. *All* the policy papers, all the things that would have mattered to MAP.

I think it is important that if you take something like planning, you are dealing with choices, and economists have an instinctive feel that there *is* a choice, where other people may not see it as a choice at all. There are people whose response to any dilemma is to say, 'Let's have both', when they can't have both. In drawing up programmes in aircraft production particularly it was quite clear that choices were inescapable. Moreover, economists have a sense of what are the key points in the economy. When I joined at the beginning of 1940 I had read Arthur Salter pretty widely,[28] and I knew from what Arthur Salter was saying after the First World War, that the whole future of our defence rested on maintaining imports. That if we couldn't get the stuff in through the ports to the points where they were to be distributed to and maintain a stock of them, we were done for. And when I went in I fastened on that point. I looked to see whether we could be sure we had enough shipping, or if anything was being done about shipping. Whether the ports, if they were bombed, would still be able to handle the goods. Whether goods were not cluttering up the ports and could be moved through and on to satisfactory centres. I was involved in inland sorting centres and all that kind of thing. So that you had a clue as to what were the points, the weak points in the economy and the strong points in the economy. And the same with manpower. If you looked at manpower, it was the currency of planning in those days. So there were things which economists were peculiarly fitted to do, and I think that the Second World War, if it was a much better conducted affair than the First, was so because there were far more economists involved in key positions. In the First World War there were rather few. You can mention Henderson, Layton, Keynes, Beveridge and that is about it. Maybe one or two others, but not very many. Not in the key positions.

TRIBE: What happened then in the 1950s and 1960s?

CAIRNCROSS: They had forgotten. They assembled people who knew nothing about planning. Donald had never done planning. He was running the Department of Economic Affairs (DEA). If they had really understood economic planning they would have said, 'We must (a) have a forecasting staff; (b) we must have charge of the budget; (c) we must have charge of the rate of exchange', and so on. It had none of these things. *All* the things that really mattered remained in the Treasury. And they were given Incomes Policy and things of that kind. And then they drew up a Plan. What the devil was the Plan? Did it assume devaluation or did it not assume devaluation? The chaps who were in DEA thought there would be a devaluation, but they couldn't say so. We were saying, we have no authority to assume devaluation. So, your plan has to be on the basis of the current rate of exchange. But it wasn't.

TRIBE: In a sense, your description just there is rather like your description of the early period in the MAP that you describe in *Planning in Wartime*, where the programme was set, and your task was to somehow either make it work or . . .

---

[28] See J.A. Salter, *Allied Shipping Controls*, Economic and Social History of the World War, Oxford University Press, London, 1921; and his *Security. Can we Retrieve it?*, Macmillan, London, 1939.

CAIRNCROSS: Oh no, that was not our task. No, not at all. We went into MAP when they had a programme which ran at twice the level of output. Twice the level of output. It didn't matter. Nobody paid the least attention to it. Why should they? That was the way we ran things. We said we are going to produce 600 heavy bombers a month, and produced 100 heavy bombers, or something of that kind. It was just chaos. The beginnings were when you assembled the statistics. When I went in there were 300 Wellingtons on the beach at Blackpool, without propellers, and I was asked to find propellers. Where were the statistics of propellers? What was the output of propellers? Nobody knew. They knew the numbers that had been supplied against contract A, against contract B, against contract C in the past week. But they had not totted them up. They had no sense of a time trend at all. None. I am talking of only one department, but the whole thing was like that. And when you said, 'Is your output of engines in line with your output of aircraft? Is it in line with the future output of aircraft, and have you thought of how the engines are going to change in design, and the aircraft are going to change in design?' The answer is no. They had done some thinking before the war because they had a kind of plan, but all plans become obsolete inside a very short period of time, so that the only thing that really matters is not planning but re-planning. Re-doing it. You are always re-programming. And we had to face a department which thought that making programmes was their business. And if you said to them, 'How do you co-ordinate one programme with another? Are you going to take responsibility for making sure the engines and aircraft match?' – they had no answer. But they still went on saying, 'We are responsible for propeller planning. The hell with you!' I had a long, long struggle to get agreement that I should do the propeller planning, and, my God, it had no connection with things. And when I went to the firms, the firms had no idea of planning. When I went to one of the two main firms I said, 'Can I see your plan?' they produced a document which they had just received from the Ministry, telling them what they wanted. I said, 'How many did you produce last week?' British industry was hopeless really. They had no conception of planning. Very, very few firms that you could really have entrusted with a major job, Shell, ICI and one or two others, but when it came to handling the atomic bomb or anything of that sort they weren't geared up to it at all. They were really very primitive. It wasn't just economics that was primitive. *Business* was primitive.

TRIBE: Did that improve after the war as far as you know?

CAIRNCROSS: Slowly. Slowly.

TRIBE: Why was that then?

CAIRNCROSS: Well, it has improved a lot I think since they began to go to university and take courses in subjects. Most businessmen in 1945 had not gone to university, particularly the chaps a little further down. And in fact, if you see how British industry is dominated by accountants, you will see what I mean. They have got to get somebody who has really done some professional training in something. If it were engineers it would have been much better. The Germans at least knew that you went through the design and said, 'Let's make sure it is easy to manufacture.' In Britain there was no attempt to go through things. The prima donnas were the designers, and they said that is what it is to be like. Even when it was hell to make.

TRIBE: Well, the Americans had got better ideas . . .

CAIRNCROSS: The Americans were rather better. We *could* design. I mean we had the best fighter aircraft in the war. The one we didn't make, the Americans made, was a British design. The Mustang was ahead of any of the others. It was a British design. It was engined with a British engine. The designers were all right. I mean when I saw the muddle the Germans made I could see why we won. They were much worse. The muddle in Germany was the ministers. The muddle in Britain was the officials.

TRIBE: Coming back to Glasgow. You were in Paris and you came to Glasgow in January 1951. Did you go there because it was a research job, or were you equally interested in a teaching or research job?

CAIRNCROSS: Normally when I was asked to do a job that I knew nothing about I said 'No', and then when I thought about it I said, 'Well, perhaps.' I think I have probably refused every job I subsequently took. I expected to do teaching as well as research, and I did. It was a new Department of Social and Economic Research, and I was Professor of Applied Economics within it. I had no lecturing duties, but of course, you can't really do research without lecturing, at least not in my experience. So I did lecturing whenever I got a chance. Whenever I could agree with Macfie that perhaps I could take on this or that. The idea was that we should build it up . . . I don't know if it was ever made very explicit, I think it was left to my judgement, but it was intended, I would think, to be a department dealing with industry and trade and labour problems in the Glasgow area, with perhaps a bit of social economics as well. Concentrating on industry and trade, not on the macro stuff. I thought this was appropriate to a university like Glasgow. Within about a year or perhaps two years after I got there, the Professor of Accountancy came to me to say, 'We must do something for industry. We must do something for business. Teaching young managers. Really it is indispensable. Something has got to be done.' So I said, 'I know nothing about management. I don't know what to do. If I teach them straight economics that may be not what they want at all.' So we started off with a series of lectures. I gave five lectures, I remember, of which the sixth was economics and development. I gave 'Economics and Trade'. Economics and this, Economics and that . . . and after the first year they kept coming back and coming back and coming back while I developed the course. It didn't cost the University a penny. We all lectured free. We collected from them some £5 or £10 a time, and the University made a profit. The only thing they ever made a profit on, I am sure! On a management course. And then we started to take them through to St Andrews for a weekend, talking to everybody. What these chaps wanted, as managers, was to feel they were still in touch with the University. To feel that somebody could understand their problems and discuss them. Their problems were essentially problems of human relations, not economics particularly. Accountancy was not what they wanted particularly. We did limit the courses we ultimately gave to economics and industrial relations. But it was the industrial relations that really got them. Hooked them. There were many people there who had degrees, some from Cambridge even. But as young managers they were really in trouble. They wondered what their responsibilities were, what their rights were in relation to the boss and to the labour force. What they most needed was a philosophy. From my point of view, if I was going to run a research department of the kind I had in mind, the more contacts we had in industry in the neighbourhood the better, because we could get them in time to come and share their problems with us, and we would really be working as a group. I mean, we would almost enter into it. I don't know that that happened in the end, but we did do quite a lot with different firms in the area. But the later boys I think, and other universities see it quite differently, they see training managers as a rather technical issue. You give them lectures. You teach them techniques, and so on. That is not really what they were after. They were really feeling lost in a new world in which they had major responsibilities, and they didn't really know the limits of these responsibilities. They needed a philosophy. And it is the philosophy young managers want more than anything.

TRIBE: Was that also linked to the development in the University, that you must have had more students through in the 1950s, so there would have been a general expansion of staff . . .?

CAIRNCROSS: There was an expansion. Hector Hetherington was very sympathetic. He said, 'You are one of the few really rapidly growing areas. This is going to grow fast.' And he could see possibilities in different ways. He could see all that. So he was quite supportive. We had no problem there. But we didn't need money. That was the last thing we needed. We wanted people's time. But we were giving them time in doing a thing from which they were learning. If you are lecturing to managers you are in an area where you find you are developing a different aspect of the subject, and you are getting to grips with something quite different. And very realistically. So I thought it paid off.

TRIBE: You went to Washington in 1955–56. Was that back to an organisation similar to the OEEC?

CAIRNCROSS: Eighteen months. I went in 1954 to the World Bank to prepare a report for them, on the possibility of some kind of training institute for people from the less-developed countries. I did the report, and they almost inevitably said, as people do, 'Why don't you come and do it?' And I said, 'No, I have got my University to look after.' And they said, 'Well, make a start.' And I thought, 'Well, two years, I should be able to get somewhere. I went to Hetherington, the Principal, and he said, "My boy, you are not going for two years."' So that was that. He was quite firm. But we discussed it and eventually he agreed to eighteen months. In eighteen months I got the Economic Development Institute launched, quite successfully. The first course was complete, the second course in progress, profiting from experience of the first course, and so on a very different basis, and things were going pretty well by the time I came away. And I still kept in touch. I used to go out to the EDI at intervals of a year or two, and tried to get the Bank to establish an annual lecture on economic development. In 1966 I gave what I thought was going to be the first of a series of annual lectures on planning and all that. It was very successful, but they didn't do it again the next year, and I thought that a great pity. They needed more contact with academic life, and I kept telling them, 'Look, you have got to get into closer relationship with academia, and this is one way you can begin.' They did in the end get somewhere, because they appointed a kind of economic adviser. They appointed a lot of economists. More than they had to. When I was there there were very few.

TRIBE: What made you leave Glasgow, and go back into government service as Chief Economic Adviser?

CAIRNCROSS: If you're asked to be Chief Economic Adviser to the government you don't turn that down. I think that is very hard to turn down.

TRIBE: How did that come about?

CAIRNCROSS: Well, I expect Robert Hall must have said something; and Frank Lee must have said something. Frank Lee was Permanent Secretary. Robert Hall was the Economic Adviser. I knew them both very well. I had been in very close touch with both of them; Frank Lee during the war. Robert Hall particularly over devaluation in 1949. And at other times I kept in touch with them. I think they knew it was either Donald MacDougall or me; and they had to make up their minds. If I had said no, it would have been Donald. And I just didn't think I could say no. Then I found of course I was being put in an awkward position when there were far too many senior economists around, all expecting to be consulted on every damn thing. It was just a jumble. It changed after 1968; indeed, even 1968 wasn't so bad, but 1964–67 was just a muddle. Terrible business.[29]

---

[29] Sir Alec has been working on his diaries for the period when he was Chief Economic Adviser, and he has recently published *The Wilson Years, 1964–69.*

4

SIR HANS SINGER

Hans Singer was born in 1910 and studied economics at Bonn University, where he was taught by Joseph Schumpeter among others. When the National Socialists came to power in 1933 he broke off his doctoral studies and left Germany, ending up in Istanbul along with Wilhelm Röpke. Through his connection with Schumpeter he was able to move to Cambridge, where he completed a Ph.D. He then joined the Pilgrim Trust Survey of unemployment, which led him to Manchester where he subsequently became a Lecturer, teaching there together with John Hicks through the war. The interview covers the period up to the time that he went to the University of Glasgow. Hans Singer has contributed a biographical essay on his work related to economic development at the UN and the ILO to P. Arestis and M. Sawyer (eds), *A Biographical Dictionary of Dissenting Economists*, Edward Elgar, Aldershot, 1992, pp. 526–32. The following extract is from an interview conducted in Sir Hans' office at the Institute of Development Studies, University of Sussex, 8 June 1994.

SINGER: I was born in Germany, in fact very close to Bonn in the Rhineland and so it was almost natural that I should study in Bonn. My father was a doctor and he wanted me to study medicine, but within a week or two of my arrival I was at a Schumpeter lecture; and I was so intrigued that, against the wishes of my father, I switched over to economics. So I studied under Schumpeter in Bonn and I took my first degree there, but in Germany the first degree after three years' study was called a diploma, an economic diploma. That was in 1931. I started then on a dissertation on urban land values. And then Schumpeter left for Harvard. Schumpeter left in 1932. Many people think Schumpeter left Germany because of Hitler, but that's not correct. Hitler only came to power in 1933. Schumpeter left before for quite different reasons. He was not a victim of the Nazis, he was, you might say, a victim of the Social Democrats. Because in 1932 the Chair of Economics in Berlin, at Berlin University, became vacant, when Werner Sombart retired; and Schumpeter was by far the best-known, certainly the nationally best-known economist in Germany at that time. We all expected that Schumpeter would be offered this post, but the allocation of the University Chairs, especially of important Chairs like this, was a matter of politics. It was in the hands of the regional government, the Government of Prussia. The Prussian Minister of Education in 1932 was a Social Democrat, a man called Becker (not connected with the tennis player), and this man Becker, or the government of which he was a member, said of Schumpeter – who was, of course, a sort of liberal, slightly right-of-centre man – 'We have already too many of these damned liberals in chairs of Economics, we want a solid Social Democrat in this Chair.' So the Chair was given to a man called Emil Lederer, quite a reputable economist but not comparable to Schumpeter.[1] And Schumpeter was so disgusted by this, he had a standing invitation from Taussig in Harvard to come to Harvard, and he accepted this. By the way an ironical postscript to this: Emil Lederer, when Hitler came to power, had to emigrate and it was Schumpeter who got Lederer a job in New York with what was then called the University in Exile, later the New School for Social Research, which Alvin Johnson had started for refugees. But, anyway, there I was in 1932, in Bonn, Schumpeter left, so I switched my allegiance to the other Professor at Bonn. That was Professor Spiethoff. Also a reputable economist, a great expert on trade cycles although to me he was nothing as exciting as Schumpeter. But still I continued on my dissertation and then Hitler came; and I had to leave Germany in a considerable hurry, so I went to Istanbul, to Turkey. There was a whole group of economists who had worked under Schumpeter which included Wolfgang Stolper, August Lösch, a well-known man, he became very famous later; and this whole group was very strongly anti-Nazi, some were Jewish, some were not Jewish, but all were anti-Nazi, and the whole group had to emigrate. I had to get out quickly, so I first went to Switzerland, because Wolfgang Stolper was not married then, but he was already engaged to a Swiss girl; so I stayed with her family for a bit and then I went to Istanbul. Kemal Pasha was very keen to build up Istanbul as a modern western-type university and therefore was very generous in inviting refugee scholars.

TRIBE: Röpke was there too, wasn't he?[2]

SINGER: Exactly yes; the man whom I knew there was Wilhelm Röpke; and he said to me when I contacted him from Switzerland, 'Well, if you come here, I will see what I can do for you.' Of course, the Turks didn't want young students or research assistant types, they wanted established scholars to teach Turkish students, and Turkish young economists, understandably. So I went

---

[1] Emil Lederer (1882–1939) studied law and economics in Vienna from 1901 to 1905, and was a member of the Seminar led by Böhm-Bawerk and von Wieser; he completed his *Habilitation* in Heidelberg in 1912. In the same year he published his analysis of the 'salaried proletariat', *Die Privatangestellten in der modernen Wirtschaftsentwicklung*, representing a line of thinking which was to have a great influence at the New School in the late 1930s and thence on American sociologists like C. Wright Mills. See, for example, his *Technical Progress and Unemployment. An Enquiry into the Obstacles to Economic Expansion*, International Labour Office, Studies and reports, Series C, no. 22, 1938.

[2] Wilhelm Röpke was an important figure in the development of social market economics. During the late 1930s he worked in Geneva and then moved to Ankara.

there not with any great prospects. In fact, my plan was to open a bookshop at the university because the thought was, if they want a modern university they must also have access to books.

TRIBE: Was the teaching in German there? Or was it in English? Because if there was so many Germans . . .

SINGER: Well, that I don't remember, but we were expected to learn Turkish pretty quickly. But I had only been for a few weeks in Istanbul when I got a letter from Richard Kahn, from Cambridge, to tell me that Schumpeter had written to Keynes about me, and King's College, Cambridge was offering a scholarship for a young refugee economist from Germany. My name had been mentioned by Schumpeter to Keynes and on the strength of that letter they invited me to come for an interview. Well, obviously, you can imagine that I didn't lose any time. I had nothing to lose in Istanbul. No prospects. So I came for the interview, and I got the scholarship.

TRIBE: Who interviewed you there? Can you remember?

SINGER: Yes. Among the interviewers, apart from Richard Kahn himself, was Austin Robinson. I think Clapham, who was Professor of Economic History, was one of the interviewers. It was, in fact, a very informal interview. My recollection is that it was not a single interview with a panel of interviewers, but I had to go round from one person to another. What was his name, the socialist, Marxist economist?

TRIBE: Maurice Dobb.

SINGER: Yes, Maurice Dobb. Shove. Those are the people I remember. And I think they had already decided before I came, I would imagine, that I should get it because I was not aware of anyone else being interviewed. So at any rate after the interviews I got the scholarship for two years.

TRIBE: That was from King's College?

SINGER: At King's College, yes. I moved from hell in Hitler's Germany to the Cambridge paradise, King's College, Cambridge! With Keynes and Pigou there. The wildest dream come true for a young student. The scholarship was, if I remember correctly, first £150 a year, plus meals in college; and then it was even increased in the second year to £200 a year. On the strength of that I married. I had already been engaged more or less, and moved to Cambridge. And of course my plan was to use the two years to get a Ph.D., that was obvious. I continued to work on my dissertation, which was connected with land values, and of course the man who was particularly interested in this was Colin Clark, who became my supervisor. There were three of us that were starting our dissertations at the same time. The dissertation, by the way, at Cambridge at that time was not taken as seriously as it would be today. You were judged more on your performance in the Keynes Club, the people who knew you, your supervisor's report. You were supposed to publish one or two articles while you were writing the dissertation, which I think all the three people involved amply did. My own dissertation would probably not be accepted today, because it was very scrappy. I later developed it into a book, but when I submitted the manuscript it was not very highly organised. There were three of us starting out at the same time, more or less racing each other for the Ph.D. The three were Alec Cairncross; V.K.R.V. Rao, the Indian economist – we used to call him 'Alphabet Rao', because of his four initials – and me. Alec won the race; he got his Ph.D. first. I think I got mine four weeks after him and four weeks before Rao. We were closely bunched together in getting our Ph.D.s, and that was the first group of Cambridge Ph.D.s in economics except for one man. There was one man who had taken the Ph.D. well before us. A man called Jones. I forget his initials now. His dissertation which was published as a book was on Increasing Returns. He took his Ph.D. well before us, as soon as it was possible to get a Ph.D. in economics. But this man Jones wrote a brilliant dissertation and then published it as a book called *Increasing Returns*.[3] Then after he took his degree, after the graduation ceremony in Cambridge he went for a holiday in Germany and the day after, on his first day of the holiday in Germany, the day after taking his degree, he was run over by a tram and killed in Darmstadt. So if you count him out, because he died immediately after taking his degree, the three of us were the first generation of Cambridge Ph.D.s.

TRIBE: Among the names of graduate students from the *Cambridge University Reporter* in 1936 there were only thirteen economic students listed;[4] you are among them, but the other ones who obviously must have come after you, or started after you were Bode, Bryce, Daly, Tarshis and then . . .

SINGER: They came after me. Daly was an American. Rao developed his dissertation on the Indian National Income, also under Colin Clark. If you look at Colin Clark's book *National Income and Outlay*, and his subsequent books, he quotes amply from V.K.R.V. Rao, and he also quotes amply from my dissertation. The sections that deal with land values and urbanisation in Colin Clark's book, they are all taken over from my dissertation, with full acknowledgement, with full, very generous acknowledgement, all taken over.[5] So we worked more or less almost, you might say, as a team under Colin Clark, inspired by this then-new idea of national income, and of course very much encouraged by Keynes. Because Keynes wanted a statistical equivalent of his concept of aggregate demand for the *General Theory*. And then, by the way, jumping forward a bit, my dissertation on urban land values led me directly in 1945 into the Ministry of Town and Country Planning under the Attlee Government. The Labour Party had won the election on a manifesto which included the nationalisation of development rights in urban land, with compensation. Not expropriation, but nationalisation with compensation, and therefore they needed an economist, or a statistician, somebody who could calculate on various assumptions the sums that might be appropriate, or might

---

[3] G.T. Jones, *Increasing Returns*, ed. C. Clark, Cambridge University Press, Cambridge, 1932.

[4] *Cambridge University Reporter*, vol. LXVI, no. 31 (21 April 1936), Annual Report of the Board of Research Studies, pp. 870ff.

[5] C. Clark, *National Income and Outlay*, Macmillan, London, 1937, p. 98.

be needed, for compensation. And at that point Keynes, who was then Chief Economic Adviser to the Government, remembered my Cambridge dissertation and simply shifted me – Keynes was in a position simply to shift people around – into the Ministry of Town and Country Planning as Chief Economist.

TRIBE: Was Colin Clark your supervisor for the whole period, the two years you were there?

SINGER: Yes. Practically yes. In fact I had hoped that Keynes would be my supervisor, since I was also in his college and Keynes had agreed. Keynes was invariably very extremely kind to me. But then at that point, this was Summer 1934, not only was he very much involved with the writing of the *General Theory*, but he fell ill at that time and that is why I was switched to Colin Clark, or he switched me to Colin Clark and I was very happy with Colin Clark. It was a very different Colin Clark from the later Colin Clark, very different yes.[6] He was then a bachelor. He was an ardent non-religious person living in great disorder in a room on the spot in Cambridge, it was later demolished to make room for the Arts Theatre that Keynes had inspired in Cambridge after he married Lydia Lopokova. Colin Clark lived in this room in terrible disorder. More or less like my room here! I remember when I turned up for my tutorial, he never made me read my essays, he talked, which was for me much more interesting. I mean, he took my essays and read them and commented, but in the tutorials, he did most of the talking; and my vivid recollection is I would turn up in his room on the top floor of this old building, and every chair was covered with books and papers, and Colin would simply take one of chairs, turn it upside down, dump everything on the floor so that I could sit down. It was a very informal setting for the tutorials! I owe him a great deal, he was a wonderfully inspiring man.

TRIBE: You described them as tutorials then; so how often did you have to write essays for him?

SINGER: Well, he was not very strict on that. He left it to me. Strictly speaking I didn't write any essays. When I had a bit ready for my dissertation, he read it and gave comments to me, you could call it an essay, he discussed it, gave me comments and that helped me to develop it for my dissertation.

TRIBE: You also said that in the process of being a graduate student the Keynes Club was important, and other kinds of meetings and discussions.

SINGER: Keynes' lectures in Mill Lane were always eagerly expected. Well, it was called the Circus around Keynes, which included younger Faculty members, graduate students, but also the brighter undergraduates. This was a time

---

[6] Clark had stood as a Labour candidate in the 1929 General Election; but by the 1950s he had become a critic of the welfare state and, during the 1960s, was a strong supporter of the Pope's opposition to birth control. His views on public and private welfare and pension provision coincide in large part with the tax and welfare reforms introduced in New Zealand in the late 1980s. See the entry by H.W. Arndt in *International Encyclopedia of the Social Sciences*, vol. 18, Biographical Supplement, Free Press, New York, 1979, pp. 121–4.

when people like Brian Reddaway, or David Bensusan-Butt were there; there was a very bright generation of undergraduates also. The brightest undergraduates were amalgamated with the graduate students, and even younger Faculty members, into groups who would eagerly listen to Keynes' lectures, then debate among ourselves what he had said, what would be our position on what he had said. Then we might send a spokesman to Keynes, whoever that might be, to present to Keynes what we had thought or put any questions to him that we couldn't cope with; and then Keynes would send a message back and we would discuss that message. There was one lecture a week in Mill Lane in the lecture rooms by the river, and that was a very focal point. And then of course Keynes wrote during those years the *General Theory*, so the progress of the *General Theory* was another focal point. The favoured man in that case was David Bensusan-Butt,[7] because Keynes used him as a sort of assistant, for writing the references, for literature search and so forth; and therefore David Bensusan-Butt was the best informed about the progress. And he would report to us, to this group, 'He is now writing the chapter on liquidity preference'; and we would all eagerly ask, 'What does he say about liquidity preference?' And then we would discuss this back and forth. That was the second outer circle. In the first inner circle, there, of course, the great and envied man, the closest to Keynes, was Richard Kahn. So we all would beleaguer Kahn, pump him on the progress on the book; and then, third, in addition to that, there was the weekly seminar in Keynes' room. Somebody would read a paper, the graduate students would be in the audience, and we had to draw lots. Richard Kahn would go around with matches. You had to draw matches. He would present a group of twelve or fifteen matches. We had to draw out a match, and if you had a broken match, that meant you had to speak! You couldn't choose, you had to speak and that was sometimes a dreaded moment, partly because you were mortally afraid of making a fool of yourself in front of Keynes; and also partly because it might be a subject that you desperately had to look for something to say, you really felt you had nothing much to say but you had to speak. And also it was an ordeal – a vivid memory for me – you had to stand in front of an open fire, close to the open fire, and it burned your behind all the time! It was dreadfully uncomfortable on the occasion when I drew the half match. But you had to speak.

Another important seminar was the Oxford–Cambridge–LSE seminar where the graduate students and young Faculty, had lively debates, very lively debates. Among the leading people there I remember Kalecki, who was a very lively debater. Frank Burchardt, in Oxford. We met in term-time, I think it was on Sundays, it was certainly on weekends. One week in Oxford, the next week in Cambridge, the next week in London, and these were very important

---

[7] David Bensusan-Butt (died 1994) entered the Civil Service in 1938 and worked after the war chiefly in the Treasury. In 1962 he became a Professorial Fellow at the Australian National University, retiring in 1976. See the obituary by M.W. Arndt and R.M. Sundrum in *Economic Journal*, vol. 105 (1995), pp. 669–75.

centres of discussion. I remember a famous occasion when Kalecki and Tjalling Koopmans came to blows physically over the definition of liquidity preference of all things – and had to be separated by the rest of us! So that is an illustration of how seriously we took this. There is nothing quite like this today. Today you discuss it in a much more detached way, but we felt very strongly involved in the issues. Difficult to convey this, but it was a different atmosphere, yes.

Keynes' weekly seminar was also a tremendously powerful job market, because in the background there would be sitting important visitors to Cambridge. Keynes was already beleaguered with visitors. Let's say, for example, there might be the Finance Minister of New Zealand sitting there listening to this, and then after the formal seminar was over you got a cup of tea, and over tea Keynes and the Finance Minister for New Zealand, let's say, would talk to each other and Keynes would beckon one of his younger, one of the graduate students or research assistants, introduce him to the Finance Minister; and the next thing we knew, but perhaps some months later, that person was appointed Economist in the Ministry of Finance of New Zealand. So there were lots of examples like that. I got my first job after I took my Ph.D. with the Pilgrim Trust Unemployment Enquiry. And the man in charge was Dr Temple, Archbishop of York then, later he became Archbishop of Canterbury. Among the chief advisers to him and to the Pilgrim Trust on setting up this enquiry were Beveridge and Keynes, and one or two other people. Keynes simply designated me as the economist and statistician for this enquiry. There were two other equally young men. One of them I think was designated by Beveridge, that was David Owen.[8] I think he was designated by Beveridge, because he had started work with Beveridge on the forerunner of the Beveridge Report. This was an example of this powerful influence of Keynes simply to shift people into jobs. I had no real qualifications for that particular job. I had not studied unemployment problems. My dissertation was on something quite different. But then in the event I became deeply interested in it; but I started without real qualifications. But Keynes had said to Dr Temple, I am the man for it. That was good enough for Dr Temple. So there I was.

TRIBE: So that was two years?

SINGER: That was two years. 1936 to 1938.

TRIBE: Where did you work? Were you still based in Cambridge or did you move?

SINGER: No, we lived in what were then called the depressed areas, among unemployed families, in mining communities in the Rhondda Valley, County

---

[8] (Arthur) David Owen (1904–70) had worked on the Sheffield Social Survey Committee 1929–33, was General Secretary of Political and Economic Planning 1940–41, Personal Assistant to Stafford Cripps in 1942 and at the Ministry of Aircraft Production 1942–43. In 1944 he joined the Reconstruction Department of the Foreign Office in charge of League of Nations affairs, in which capacity he attended the 1945 San Francisco conference and subsequently worked for the United Nations.

Durham, Blackburn in Lancashire, Liverpool, and by contrast also one or two more prosperous areas, Leicester and part of London, Deptford. In fact, one of the findings of our study was that the unemployed in the really depressed areas, where everyone was unemployed, were better off in many ways than the unemployed in otherwise prosperous areas. That was one of our findings. In fact the book that resulted from this was *Men Without Work*.[9]

TRIBE: It was based on a sample survey?

SINGER: Yes, that's right. Yes. We didn't have any computers then, so it was quite a tricky business for us.

TRIBE: It was just you three? You had no other assistants?

SINGER: Well, if you look at the 'Preface', we had one or two, but essentially it was the three of us. Eleanora Iredale was the Secretary of the Committee which supervised this enquiry, but her contribution was really limited to the chapter on women. She was responsible for the report, to some extent, but all the rest of the book, was written by Walter Oakeshott, David Owen and me. Later Dr Wagner. Well, Dr Wagner was a refugee from Austria, and she had worked in the earlier unemployment enquiry in Austria which in some ways was a model for us.

TRIBE: Did you bring in the work from Marienthal? I was thinking because of your ability to read German . . .

SINGER: Well, I could read it in the original German, therefore I acted as a sort of translator; but I was not involved in the Marienthal study. My part was to draw attention to it. And, by the way, I followed this up with another book that was entirely my own, not jointly with others, called *Unemployment and the Unemployed*, published in 1939. Shortly before the outbreak of war and therefore it became very rapidly obsolete, because unemployment disappeared quickly.

TRIBE: You went to Manchester in 1938. How did that come about? Your going to Manchester coincided with Hicks.

SINGER: No, no, I came there before Hicks. Hicks must have come half a year or a year after me. I don't think Hicks at that time had any plans to go to Manchester, not as far as I remember. Frankly, I don't quite remember how I was recruited. There were two professors then in the Economics Department. The senior Professor was G.W. Daniels, an old cotton man, but more an historian than an economist.[10] The real economist in the department was not the Professor but the Reader, but who also had a strong interest in economic history rather than economics, T.S. Ashton. But I was not recruited directly for the University, I was recruited for the Economic Research Section, which was a bit separate from the Faculty, and the man in charge of that was Jewkes, Professor John Jewkes.[11] Whatever happened, I must have been recruited

[9] Cambridge University Press, Cambridge, 1938.
[10] See the comments by Sir Henry Hardman on Daniels and Ashton, p. 14.
[11] See for details of Jewkes, Cairncross interview, footnote 26 on p. 49.

because John Jewkes agreed. How it happened I don't . . . I hadn't known John Jewkes before, so it was not from any direct knowledge, or he didn't know me from any direct contacts. I would not be a bit surprised if that again was just simply Keynes' doing. That Manchester people asked Keynes for advice, and Keynes, knowing that my activity in the Pilgrim Trust Enquiry had come to an end, recommended me. It is quite possible. And of course my work, the fact that I had done these unemployment studies was probably an important reason for Manchester to appoint me because, well, that was in 1938 the big problem in Manchester, of course.

TRIBE: So when did you start? In the autumn of 1938?

SINGER: It must have been the autumn, yes. September–October 1938, yes.

TRIBE: But did you know Daniels, because Daniels in fact died the previous December, so when did you know Daniels?

SINGER: Well, I knew Daniels. How did I know him? Well, very likely I went for an interview in Manchester just before Daniels died but I am guessing now. My recollection there is very dim. How did I get to Manchester from the Pilgrim Trust Enquiry and why Manchester? I had no previous links with Manchester that I remember. I knew some people in Manchester. Some friends in Manchester, but not at the University but at the Cotton Board, and of course my studies on unemployment conditions in Blackburn, where the unemployed there were very largely from the decaying textile industries, cotton weaving and spinning, so that must have brought me in touch with the Cotton Board people.

TRIBE: At the time that you went to Manchester a major change of regime, from the Daniels' era to that of Hicks, was about to take place. From the vivid way you describe the work in which you were involved in Cambridge, I was wondering what your impression of Manchester was when you first went there?

SINGER: I got to Manchester late in 1938. At that time Jewkes was the dominant figure in the Economics Research Section. I am not speaking of the University now. In the Faculty probably, when he arrived, Hicks was an important figure. Ursula Hicks (or Ursula Webb as she was before she married him), I had known her very well in Cambridge already.

TRIBE: Arthur Brown suggests that it was a good year or two before Keynes' *General Theory* was properly understood in Oxford.[12] It was read and widely discussed, but he thinks that few really understood the major principles. Now you describe the time in Cambridge before publication as one of constant and close discussion of Keynes' work. Did you notice a difference between you from Cambridge and the Oxford economists when you were discussing issues such as liquidity preference?

SINGER: Well, you see, in Oxford it took a year or two after the publication of it for Keynes to sink in. I can tell you exactly the reaction to that that we

---

[12] See interview with Arthur Brown, p. 161.

would have had in the Cambridge School. 'Yes, of course, that's Oxford!' We had a deep contempt for – not just for Oxford, but for anything non-Cambridge. I mean, for us Cambridge was the centre of the universe, and King's College was the centre of Cambridge, and Keynes was the centre of King's College: so we had the holy of holies and we didn't care tuppence! I mean, I am not defending it, I am not trying to . . . we didn't care what the rest of the world, including Oxford, thought.

TRIBE: The only one that was half-accepted was Roy Harrod in Cambridge.

SINGER: Yes. He was more or less treated as an honorary Cambridge man, yes, who only by accident was Oxford. He was accepted because he was a loyal follower of Keynes, so he was accepted.

TRIBE: What would you have thought of the LSE?

SINGER: Oh, the LSE! The senior levels of the LSE they were the demons, they were the great enemies! Hayek, Lionel Robbins at that time, were treated as despicable heretics. Of course, later Keynes collaborated very closely with Lionel Robbins in the preparation for Bretton Woods, and at Bretton Woods; but at that time Lionel Robbins was ranked with Hayek and Mises as untouchable, despicable, yes.

TRIBE: But what was Hicks' role in this in Cambridge because he came from the LSE to Cambridge? Where did he fit in?

SINGER: Who, Hicks? Where was Hicks in that connection? I mean, Hicks was not included in this contempt for Hayek, Mises, Lionel Robbins. I think he was considered as a young genius. My recollection is, that certainly I in Cambridge during the years of the unemployment enquiry, I was beginning to realise that Hicks was a very important figure, a brilliant economist, but he was not part of the Cambridge Circus, certainly not, and he was a little outside that debate. They treated him I think more or less as neutral, he was not part of the enemy camp, but he was not one of us! He was in-between, and I think probably, I don't know, we watched him, I mean we read him, we are hoping he would soon see the light and become a more convinced Keynesian! Yes. Yes. I think that sums it up, I don't know.

TRIBE: I understand the view from Oxford was the mirror image of that: that Oxford had this wider view of the world, but that Cambridge was very much closed in on itself . . .

SINGER: Yes, well, that is quite justified. As I said, we thought we were the universe. We didn't pay much attention to what was going on outside. Even in my reading; my reading was very strongly concentrated on what came out of Cambridge. Quite excessively. I mean with the benefit of hindsight I know this. I am not justifying it but that was the spirit. And in a way it was necessary to create the enthusiasm that was behind all this.

TRIBE: So your journey from the Rhineland, from Switzerland to Istanbul, and then to Cambridge: when you came to the unemployment survey that must have been quite a startling experience personally, because of the kinds of situations you would have found yourself in, the kind of living conditions in

Britain at that time. The areas you describe as poor regions were exceptionally poor, there was a lot of ill-health and a very great deal of deprivation. How did you experience that, having spent two years in Cambridge, which is obviously very much a world closed in on itself?

SINGER: Well, to me it was a new world. I was unfamiliar even with the language. I had great difficulty at first certainly in understanding people. I remember a dreadful occasion, Miss Iredale was very religious, she was the Secretary of the Student Christian Movement also, very religious person, a prim Victorian lady you could call her. And I remember after the first week, we used to more or less be separate but we would meet in the evenings to exchange our experiences. We had cards to fill in about what we observed, we gave a lot of thought to the devising of the cards, and we exchanged our experiences; and I remember a dreadful occasion when I said to Eleanora Iredale, in the presence of David Owen and Walker Oakeshott, 'One thing that puzzles me, the people that I met today and the family with whom I stayed, when they talk about the Unemployment Assistance Board' [that was the body which was responsible for the dole, for the means-tested payment for the long-term unemployed who had run out of their automatic right to unemployment insurance], and I said to Eleanora, 'What puzzles me is that they never call it Unemployment Assistance Board, they always speak about those *buggers*, and I don't know what it means!' And poor Eleanora got red in the face, and David Owen and Walker Oakeshott took me aside, and told me what this term meant! It was new to me! And at first I was rather doubtful how I would be received. I mean, I was visible and audible as a foreigner, or of foreign origin, and I probably still am today, I don't know. I don't think I have lost my accent. So I was marked as a foreigner, and I thought that might work against me, strongly against me. I was rather worried. But I found exactly the opposite. The very fact that I was a foreigner helped me, because nobody suspected me of being a spy for the Unemployment Assistance Board. They knew that they could tell me without fear. That was the great danger, that we were treated as spies that if we observed that somebody was quietly making a bit of income on the side, that we might denounce them to the officials. And we always had to be very careful to establish our completely non-official credentials, which was easier for me to do because I was audible as a for-eigner. Yes.

TRIBE: How did the others experience this? What were their backgrounds?

SINGER: David Owen was Welsh by background. He had been an econo-mist in PEP. Political and Economic Planning which was a think tank, slightly left of centre. That is why Beveridge was associated, he took a lot of assistance from PEP; it was financed by the Sieff family, from Marks & Spencer. David Owen had been working on this, and had become an expert on social insurance questions, social legislation, labour market problems, wage problems.

I should, of course, talk a bit about Manchester. You see, I had only been in Manchester for a few months when the war broke out. And Jewkes, immediately the war broke out, disappeared to London. Anyway he disappeared, and goodbye to all for the duration of the war. And gradually all the other Faculty members disappeared into Whitehall: Harry Campion, Jack Stafford, and several others disappeared. So Jewkes disappeared, and I was left with Hicks. I mean, Hicks then was the only Professor during the war. Daniels had died. Jewkes was in Whitehall. I had to switch from the Research Section to the University and therefore I worked under Hicks, and on the whole it was very harmonious. But there is one thing that I still have a slightly bitter memory of. Hicks lived quite far outside Manchester, deep into Cheshire, in Prestbury. I also lived a little bit out but not that far, I lived in Cheadle, not so far from the University; and my bitter memory is that Hicks had a terrible habit at the last minute on raw winter mornings to phone me and say, 'I can't take that lecture, will you take it over for me?' On the whole, it was very harmonious, but Hicks did have a tendency to exploit me in that sense. Well, I had to do it, and when I could I did. But on the whole my relationship was always closer with Ursula than with John, but I got on very well with Hicks.

TRIBE: How many students did you have then at the time?

SINGER: Quite a number. In spite of the war, the University went on quite normally. None of the courses was cancelled. There was a predominance of women, I remember. I remember the lecture rooms were bitterly cold because of the lack of heating. But nothing like as cold as my winter in Glasgow after the war. No, I remember the University life as being fairly normal. I mean there were the usual problems of the blackouts, of air raids. At one time during the heavy air raids on Manchester in 1940 when the cotton warehouses burned, and it was very tricky and dangerous – on individual days lectures had to be cancelled, but the University itself was never hit. Rather miraculously. All around the University there was a lot of damage. But neither the University, nor the Economic Research Section, which was a bit outside. I mean, on some days I remember lectures had to be cancelled because of air raids and disruption, and in any case I was also a fire fighter, so that was exhausting me.

TRIBE: Was that in Manchester or in Cheadle?

SINGER: Manchester.

TRIBE: So you taught the economists and the B.A.Com. and the B.A. (Admin.) people together, did you?

SINGER: The general division of labour with Hicks was that Hicks gave the main theoretical courses, and I did more the applied courses. There was a course on Industrial Organisation as it was called, I remember, and rather surprisingly, Hicks concentrated more on the international problems and I concentrated more on domestic problems. I remember I gave a course on wartime planning, for instance.

TRIBE: You gave a talk to the Manchester Statistical Society on that as well, didn't you?[13] If you taught the more applied courses – industrial organisation – what other things can you remember?

SINGER: Statistics – took that over from Harry Campion, because originally I was trained as much as a statistician as an economist; I always had a strong interest in statistics, which was another link with Colin Clark, of course. Industrial relations, statistics, wartime planning, I forget now. I am afraid I can't reconstruct the curriculum.

TRIBE: Coming back to the point when you got to Manchester and you were in the Research Section to start with; can you think of any general features which differentiated the kind of work or the kind of teaching that they did in Manchester from that which you had encountered in Cambridge? The nature of the students, for example, or the kinds of work they did, or the way they worked?

SINGER: Well, of course, in Manchester I was very predominantly concerned with undergraduates, very predominantly. I mean there were a few graduates around, but not many. In Cambridge my contacts with the undergraduates were limited to that very small elite of undergraduates who were more or less accepted as especially brilliant. And they were not all economists, necessarily. We were already interested of course in Wittgenstein, and debated Wittgenstein's views; and there was Piero Sraffa around, who was greatly admired by us, partly because he was so obscure. I mean none of us understood quite what he was after, but . . . so we adopted people from other disciplines also. One of my fellow students was a man whose name is very rarely mentioned now; but if you can say that any man won the war, it was him. It was a man called Alan Turing. Bletchley Park. The man who broke the code. He was a member of that group. He was a mathematician of course, and he was a very difficult person, but he was recognised as brilliant.

TRIBE: He was at King's College as well, wasn't he?

SINGER: Yes. Yes. Top brilliant, and for instance he was one of the few people who fully understood, *critically* understood Wittgenstein. So he was more or less our Wittgenstein interpreter. He was a genius, Alan Turing.

TRIBE: Did you have any contact with him after you left Cambridge at all?

SINGER: No. No. I cannot say that.

TRIBE: What was the age of the students you taught in Manchester?

SINGER: Ah, during the war, I forgot to mention this, I was very active during the war with the WEA. The Workers Education Association. It was very powerful and active in the Manchester area. The Secretary of the WEA was a great character, Ely Bibby, and he had his office in the Economic Research Section or next door to it. And a lot of my lecturing activity was in fact WEA lecturing; and I did a lot of travelling, sometimes in very difficult

---

[13] H.W. Singer, 'The German War Economy', *Transactions of the Manchester Statistical Society* (1942–43), pp. 1–26.

conditions during the war, to places around Manchester, Poynton and Stockport, extending also towards Leeds and Sheffield.

TRIBE: Were you the only economics lecturer on that circuit?

SINGER: Well, I was the only economics lecturer from the University. I don't think Hicks took any part. I don't think WEA lecturing was his cup of tea. I don't think he wanted this. He was probably above the heads of the students. In fact, one of my functions was often to explain Hicks' lectures to the students. Very often Hicks lectured above the heads of the students. And then they came to me, and it was my job to explain and interpret Hicks, and Ursula knew this. She often talked half-jokingly, she described my role as an intermediary between John and the students. Yes. That I remember.

TRIBE: What other subjects were covered? Did other people from the University teach on the WEA? You said you were the only economics lecturer?

SINGER: Well, of course anything to do with the cotton industry. There were lots of technical people from the cotton industry. History was a popular subject on the WEA circuit, especially of course recent history. There was a lot of interest in biology, health problems, I remember. But the WEA was a very powerful force in Manchester at that time; and the WEA was, you might say, an adult education of mature students, an extension of the University.

TRIBE: So you taught occasional lectures and courses of lectures. What was the make-up of the people who came along? How big were their groups?

SINGER: You mean to the WEA?

TRIBE: To the various meetings.

SINGER: Oh well, it partly depended on where you lectured. If you lectured in a middle-class area, in Cheshire let's say, it would be housewives. There was of course a gap. The younger males were usually in the army, they were not there. But housewives, but in the poorer areas you would find remarkable things. Women who worked during the day in the factories would come to the WEA lectures. There was a great thirst for knowledge. Older workers. Sixth formers would come. Lots of women. Lots of women always. But as I said, it depended on what your subject was and where you were. But what I vividly remember is usually crowded classes. Crowded audiences. There was a great interest in it. It was partly that there was not much else to do. I mean it was not like today. There was no TV. There was BBC, there was radio of course, but there was no TV and the cinemas, well very often the performances were interrupted by air raid warnings, so I suppose part of it was that it was an outlet from the drabness and difficulties of normal life; but there was a great thirst for knowledge then. Especially among women. I think many women who, before the war, were set up in their homes and when they emerged now into production they wanted to inform themselves on what they were doing, what it was all about. That is a strong impression I had then.

TRIBE: So, how did they compare then to your students, coming back to the students at Manchester, you said there was still quite a number of them. Were they the same age – well, between 18 and 22, say – or were they generally older? How come they were studying at university, and not on war service, for instance?

SINGER: Well, there were all sorts of reasons. I mean, some were not on war service because of illness. There were lots of women, of course, again, but because of illness. Later in the war, in the later stages of the war years, there were some returned servicemen, and of course when I lectured in Glasgow after the war, there practically all the students were ex-servicemen who got a grant to return to the University to complete their studies. And to some extent that was also true in the later war years in Manchester.

TRIBE: And so you stayed in Manchester through until 1946, then?

SINGER: Yes, although with some interruptions. On some occasions I usually was in London on some kind of assignment. Sometimes at the Ministry of Economic Warfare, and at one point I was drawn into the preparatory work for Bretton Woods that was going on in the Treasury. Mainly Ministry of Economic Warfare. During the war I published in each issue of the *Economic Journal*, an article on the German war economy. One of my unofficial functions, I had no official standing, but the Ministry of Economic Warfare gave me access, or sent me the material on Germany that was penetrating to England. Not confidential military information, but economic information that came through neutral countries like Spain or Portugal or Sweden or some other ways. And on other occasions they also asked me to interview businessmen from neutral countries who had visited Germany and had acquired some knowledge of German war production. And Keynes was very keen. I did this because Keynes wanted an article in the *Economic Journal* on the German war economy. That led me then also to do some work in the Ministry of Economic Warfare. I was a casual collaborator – I had no official standing until I joined the Ministry of Town and Country Planning. Essentially my job was in Manchester but on occasions, especially during the summers, I got leave to work in London.

5

BRIAN REDDAWAY

Brian Reddaway was one of the Cambridge undergraduates of the 1930s who switched their studies to economics because of a desire for an understanding of the causes of and cures for, the mass unemployment of the time. His father was a Fellow of King's College, and so he found himself among several of the most prominent economists of the time: Keynes, Pigou, Kahn, and Shove. He first worked in the Bank of England, but finding this undemanding, and being acquainted with Keynes, he was recommended for a Research Fellowship at the University of Melbourne. After two years in Australia he returned to a Fellowship at Clare College, Cambridge in 1938. He has lived in Cambridge ever since. During the war he worked in the Board of Trade, where he contributed greatly to the development of the clothes rationing scheme. In 1947 he resumed teaching in Cambridge, and during 1951–52 spent a year at the OEEC in Paris. In 1955 Reddaway became Director of the Department of Applied Economics in Cambridge, succeeding Richard Stone; and in 1969 he succeeded James Meade as Professor of Political Economy.[1] The following is an edited version of an interview conducted on 6 September 1994 in Cambridge.

REDDAWAY: I was an undergraduate in Cambridge from 1931 to 1934. In the first year I was doing Mathematics, with the intention of going on to do Chemistry; but it was purely an accident of the school that I went to that I graduated into natural science and in the course of coming up I was advised that it was sensible *not* to do Part I Natural Science, but to do Part I Maths. One could do that in one year, avoiding repeating a lot that you had done for a scholarship, and then have two years for whichever branch of more advanced Natural Science you wanted. So that was the plan. But in the course of the first year, i.e. 1931–32, there was, as you well know, a recession on; and I became very interested in the reason why we had poverty in the midst of potential plenty, and anyhow I realised that Natural Science was not in the Reddaway

[1] See Brian Reddaway's own account of his career in the *Banca Nazionale del Lavoro Quarterly*, vol. 48 (1995), pp. 3–16.

family at all. I had only got there *via* mathematics, so I changed after one year from Maths to Economics. This was a very fortunate choice, because I was an undergraduate at King's; and King's had Keynes, who wasn't doing the basic teaching, but he gave all King's undergraduates, once a fortnight, an extra supervision. You only got one supervision a week as an undergraduate then, but this was an extra with Keynes. And he taught not about the Tripos as such, but about subjects in which he was interested. Which was, of course, marvellous teaching. Apart from that there was Richard Kahn, who was extremely good; and there was Gerald Shove, who was also very good. So I had an absolute plethora of excellent supervisors in economics and also went to the Keynes Club, as it was called, the Monday Club. It was open to recommended undergraduate students who were Firsts or potential Firsts, plus research students, and also members of staff. Somebody read a paper, and then the order of batting was started with the undergraduates, and then the research students, and then the junior staff, and then the senior staff, and then Keynes; and so that was how that all worked from 1931 to 1934 for me.

TRIBE: You mentioned Keynes, Kahn and Shove as supervisors. Were they all formally your supervisors?

REDDAWAY: Well, that is a fair question. Shove[2] was in a sense the primary supervisor in King's. The idea at that time being that you had one supervisor for the whole subject. They might farm you out on something special if you were doing Principles of Politics or Statistics or something; but otherwise you went to one supervisor who looked after you. Who looked at your reading list, and considered what lectures you should go to, and so on. Well, I suppose Shove was my supervisor in that sense, but, certainly in my final year, Kahn took me in alternate weeks from Shove, so I had the two of them. I am not quite sure what happened in the second year, but I think probably I went to Shove only at that time.

TRIBE: What about the supervisions with Keynes then?

REDDAWAY: They were very much supervisions, but the subjects were not integrated into the Tripos, as such. They were jolly useful for the Tripos, but they were not built up as part of a programme to cover the field or anything of this kind. I mean, for example, the World Economic Conference was on in 1933. This was a matter which naturally interested Keynes, and he called on his supervisees to write an essay on what should be done at the World Economic Conference. You then talked about it with Keynes. And we had one about protection. The very first supervision was about protection. And I went in fear and trembling, because I thought free trade was the doctrine for economists, and I couldn't see that free imports without free trade was really the best policy for a single country. And I put this forward very tentatively, and Keynes welcomed this as a contribution, and made very nice remarks about

---

[2] Gerald Shove (1887–1947) studied Classics and Economics in Cambridge, gaining a First in Pt. II in 1911. He was a Fellow of King's College from 1926.

my essay being a very good effort; and he said he thought I should get a First, straight from the very first supervision! But it was a supervision just like any other, no distinctions except that the subject was one that *he* chose, largely because he was interested in the subject, but that made it a perfectly good subject; and of course there wasn't any method adopted to stop getting the same supervision from Kahn or whatnot.

TRIBE: You, in fact, got the only Upper First of that day?

REDDAWAY: I did, yes. I don't think one should take too much heed of that. I don't think Pigou thought I ought to have had it. Pigou was an examiner at that time. I don't think it was really a good idea to divide the Firsts. Very much an accident of what questions you happened to get and so on. But you are quite right that I was one of the few people in the history of the whole of Cambridge economics who got it and later on, quite soon later on, the whole thing was abolished.

TRIBE: When you were talking about King's earlier you didn't mention Pigou.

REDDAWAY: No. That is an absolutely pertinent question. Pigou, I don't think did any serious undergraduate supervision. I never heard of any.

TRIBE: Well, Professors weren't allowed to supervise at that time, I think.

REDDAWAY: That is true. That must be the answer.

TRIBE: But also within the College – although you were doing economics, would he not have had a prominent position?

REDDAWAY: Well, Pigou was a very shy man and he and Keynes were at daggers drawn in some degree, and he didn't push his views. He never invited me to lunch or anything of that kind. What was the nearest I got with him? I don't think I really had anything personal to do with him. I went to his lectures. He gave rather good first-year lectures. I didn't go to any of his advanced lectures – I don't know that he did any advanced lectures. He was rather an isolated figure, if you want to see it that way. He was an Examiner. He was an Examiner for the exam where I got a 1.1 and as I say, I rather think that he didn't welcome it with enthusiasm. I am not saying he was against it. That emerged from a very unexpected development, which was that my intention was not to do economic research as such but get on with a job. A Ph.D. was not an automatic thing by any manner, only a minority did it. So the first job I got was with the Bank of England; and through a rather odd chain of events – my father was a lecturer on Eastern Europe, and after I had finished my degree he took me and my mother and my sister to Russia for the first time, and the Bank of England had the idea I was to start in September. I was to have a long vacation first. Their expert on Russian money, a man called Hubbard, was anxious ·to go to Moscow to find out various things that he wanted to know. Little was known about Russian money except very garbled accounts in anecdotal form; so Hubbard said to the Bank he would like to have someone with him, and someone who was an economist. They said, 'Oh, that is easy, we will get Brian Reddaway to stay in Russia and you can join him.' Well, the only snag about that was that I had no address in Russia, so I arrived back from Russia to Cambridge somewhere about early July, and found a note saying would I turn around and go back to Moscow for a month or so with Hubbard. I was furious! I had arranged all sorts of walking tours, and so on. But of course it was a silly thing to be furious about, and in point of fact the bureaucracy of getting visas and so on ensured that I got some holiday first; and I went with Hubbard to Moscow before I had ever done a day's work in the Bank of England! We had quite an interesting time. I didn't speak any Russian, which was a great handicap, but Hubbard was quite good at telling me what the discussions had been. So I arrived back in the Bank of England and I thought, 'Well, I have got an awful lot of information, rather scrappy, organised by a banker rather than an economist. I ought to try and make sense of it all, even if what I am writing is what is supposed to happen rather than what does happen.' There was a Cambridge prize then, known as the Adam Smith Prize, which was open to all research students in Economics and anyone who had graduated as a B.A. in the last three years. So I thought that I would write up my knowledge for the competition. It had got to be in by December, and I wrote it up and I put in for this Prize. Well, having a subject that was far better than anybody else's, and making quite a good fist of it, I got the Prize. Keynes was not an examiner, but Pigou was. And Pigou wrote a note to my father saying that he was very glad that I had got the Prize, and that he thought in the exam I was a bit repetitive; but that this essay was all organised on one stalk, beautiful arrangement, and so on! He knew that Keynes was interested in Russian money, and so he passed the essay to Keynes. I got back to Cambridge, because I used to go home from London every weekend and found a note from Keynes saying, 'Dear Reddaway, I have read your essay on the Russian financial system for the Adam Smith Prize. I think it is very good and it ought to be published. If you like, I will send it to Macmillan's with a recommendation that they publish it.' Well, needless to say, I did like! And although it was rather short for a book, I said that in point of fact I would want to add an appendix because they had abolished the rationing of bread and this affected a whole lot of prices. So we included that. And having sworn that I was not going to rush into print, within a year of taking my B.A. I had a book published, not just an article![3] And that is why Pigou came into it. He was enthusiastic about it. He said he wasn't an expert on the subject but he told my father, and my father was a Fellow of King's, so it was all in the family.

TRIBE: So your family home was in Cambridge then?

REDDAWAY: Yes, indeed. I was born in Cambridge. I am 81 and I have never had a permanent address anywhere other than in Cambridge! I had two years in Australia, 1936 and 1937, when I was still a bachelor; and at that time of course I had an address in Melbourne. But if I had been asked what

---

[3] W.B. Reddaway, *The Russian Financial System*, Macmillan, London, 1935.

my permanent address was I would have said 2 Buckingham Road, Cambridge. And in the war I was working in London in the Board of Trade, and only came down to Cambridge for weekends, but even then I had an address in Cambridge, and, indeed, I was paying rates on it. So one could fairly say I am Cambridge, born and bred.

TRIBE: In your book on the Russian Financial System you start off with a comparison of the capitalist system and the communist system, saying that if we are looking at money, then there are common functions in both of them. This would have been rather unusual at that time?

REDDAWAY: Well, I don't know whether it was unusual or not, but I started firmly from that – that you did in fact go into a shop and you bought things, and you hired a taxi, and you couldn't escape having money in Russia doing a good number of the jobs. Of course, there were various compulsions and prohibitions unless you had the relevant qualifications, that was the important difference, but nevertheless money did have a fairly important set of functions which were at least intelligible in terms of the European or Western view of things; and which would have been, if I may say so, a lot more intelligible in the war, because during the war we had this mixture of compulsions and free markets. So I suppose one would have been able to write a more interesting account if it had included comparisons with the wartime economy.

TRIBE: That was the question I was going to follow up with: because you supervised Alan Prest, and his thesis title as given in the *Cambridge Reporter* is precisely that comparison, 'The Differences between Free and Regulated Economic Systems in Wartime as Exemplified by the Economic Structure of Different Countries'.[4]

REDDAWAY: Alan Prest was one of the first pupils I had when I became a Fellow of Clare in 1938. He was taking his Part I, in 1938, Prelim in 1939, and he did go on and do Part II and came out in 1940. You are perfectly right that I did help him with his Ph.D., and it certainly would have been a subject like that. I had forgotten the exact nature of it, and there was a lot of cross-fertilisation between the two of us on this.

TRIBE: So the idea does come from you? I hadn't realised that you had supervised his Ph.D. as well as being his College Supervisor as an undergraduate.

REDDAWAY: Yes. I came back from Australia in January 1938, so he had already done one term of his first year. He took Part I in June, and, on the whole, people were a bit surprised that he had got a First, because Firsts were very rare in those days. In Prelim, which he did just before the war, he got a First again, and I would say it was a more convincing one; and then in the war when he did his Part II he got a clear-cut First. Well, I suppose I supervised him right through, because the first year of the war started with the Phoney War, as you know, and then I got half-involved with the Ministry of

---

[4] Annual Report of the Board of Research Studies, *Cambridge University Reporter*, vol. LXXVI, no. 23, 26 February 1946, p. 533.

Information. It was only a half-time job, so I think I must have supervised Alan Prest and such other people as there were in the other half of the week. And then he got his First.

TRIBE: So in Clare from the period 1938 onwards you would have been the Fellow responsible for all the students studying Part I or Part II economics?

REDDAWAY: Yes I was. I don't know how far these stories amuse you, but at the time when I was in Melbourne on this economics job there, Clare decided that they wanted to expand their Fellowship. Do you know they had twelve Fellows! One of the subjects they wanted to cover was Economics. They had had their supervision done by Maurice Dobb. Anyway, the question was who would they get. And by pure coincidence a Fellow – Commoner – of Clare called Raymond Priestley, had gone out to the University of Melbourne as Vice-Chancellor of Melbourne, the first one they had, about a year before I went out. He had resigned because the government wouldn't give him enough money and came back to Clare. So when there was a discussion in Clare about getting extra Fellows and somebody said who should we ask, Raymond Priestley said, 'Well why don't you ask Brian Reddaway? He is coming to the end of his time in Melbourne.' Virtually nobody knew me, but they decided that a recommendation from Raymond Priestley was good enough! So at a time when I was just beginning to wonder what I was going to do at the end of my two years I got a letter from Henry Thirkhill, Senior Tutor, saying that Clare College would like to offer me an Official Fellowship, not a Research Fellowship, and I would get £350 a year for dividend, and £200 a year for doing supervisions, which would carry a commitment to do twelve hours a week of supervisions.

TRIBE: You have mentioned Melbourne several times: how did you end up moving from the Bank of England to Melbourne?

REDDAWAY: After the Russian episode in the Bank of England, which was quite exotic, I settled down in the Bank of England, and their system was one which doesn't bear examination now. They didn't recruit, as it were, a first grade and a clerical grade. They just recruited people. I went in slightly specially. They hadn't recruited anybody for some years, because they had got a promotion bottleneck. They had recruited people during the First World War and had to reinstate people who had returned from war service. After the Russian episode I spent rather over a year in the Bank of England, which wasn't a complete waste of time but was pretty nearly a waste of time. I learnt a bit about how things worked in a rather mechanical way.

TRIBE: So what you are saying is that the system they were operating then was like the pre-Northcote–Trevelyan reformed Civil Service where you started as a clerk . . .?

REDDAWAY: Yes, it was like that, but the main thing was that they had a frightfully narrow concept of what they were trying to do. What happened in the Directors' parlour I don't know, but no job that I did, or saw anybody do, was anything other than pure routine. Anyway I came to the conclusion that this was really no good, and that if I was going to get out I had better get out quick, because I wouldn't get to any worthwhile job for about six years, and by the time you have been there two or three years you get bedded down. So I went back to Keynes. Keynes had recommended me to the Bank of England, and I went back to Keynes and said to him that the job in the Bank of England was proving extremely slow-moving and could he suggest anything else? He said, 'Well, that is very remarkable. I have just had a letter from a man called L.F. Giblin', who was a contemporary of his at King's and was an applied economist and Professor of Economic Research in the University of Melbourne. Giblin had written that the Central Bank of Australia is appointing some non-executive Directors, 'And behold they have appointed me, Giblin, and I feel that I shouldn't reduce the amount of research that I am doing for the University of Melbourne. So I am telling the Central Bank to pay the money to the University of Melbourne to appoint a Research Fellow, and the Research Fellow will have the privilege of seeing Central Bank papers when I, Giblin, think it is worthwhile to discuss things with him.' And Keynes said, 'Well, what do you think about it?' As an undergraduate I had seen a certain amount of the Australian economists who had visited Cambridge. It was very apparent that at that time Australia was the country where they took heed of what economists said, and so I thought this was a good bet, so it was fixed up. I went to Australia as a Research Fellow in Economics at the University of Melbourne, under Giblin.

TRIBE: Did you have much to do with the teaching or with the department generally in Melbourne?

REDDAWAY: In Melbourne I gave one course, I think it was, and a little bit of supervision to the students of Queen's College, to which I was attached.

TRIBE: Were they doing Economics degrees then, or was it a B.Com.?

REDDAWAY: Well, both. But most of the people did B.Com.

TRIBE: Did you form any general impression of the kind of things they were being taught, compared with the experience you had had in Cambridge?

REDDAWAY: Well, it was fairly low-level.

TRIBE: The reason I ask is simply that I have been trying to figure out the way in which British teaching models transferred to South Africa, Canada and Australia. Such accounts as there are about Australia at that time deal chiefly with individuals, rather than the structures within which they worked.

REDDAWAY: Well, let me do my best. There was Giblin, who was Professor of Economic Research, and he had very little to do with teaching, a minute amount of rather specialised stuff for research students. He took research students, and there were two then. There was also a man called Copeland who was very much the business type, he liked being the boss. I don't think he was a great economist. A man called Wood, who was not bad, and there was a woman called Jean Polglaze. She wasn't bad either. That was more or less the staff, and they ran a course which wasn't that different from a Cambridge course, and you took exams. I think you did get your degree just in

Commerce. The lectures I gave were straightforward, what one might call Part I Economics here. Supply and Demand, and a certain amount of elementary Keynesian economics, which was just coming. You see, I was involved in a rather special way, in that I took with me to Australia a copy of Keynes' *General Theory*.

TRIBE: So when did you go out, then?

REDDAWAY: January 1936.

TRIBE: So it had not quite been published.

REDDAWAY: Yes. I think I had got an advance copy, I believe. And I read it, and I wrote a review of it in the *Economic Record*.[5]

TRIBE: What struck me was this section here, which is June 1936. This section here where you formulate these equations in what is obviously a forerunner of the ISLM model.

REDDAWAY: Absolutely. I didn't think of it that way at all.

TRIBE: Which didn't come until later in Oxford with Hicks at the meeting of the Econometric Society.[6]

REDDAWAY: I set it out this way. In my review there is no IS = LM as such. I never thought of it that way. I was simply counting the equations to see whether there was the right number for the number of unknowns, and emphasising above all the mutuality of things. That is what that was about as far as I was concerned; but my equations could be interpreted as giving similar results to IS = LM.

TRIBE: This is before the ISLM. Before Hicks . . .

REDDAWAY: What I can say, this I know positively, that my review owes absolutely *nothing* to Hicks or to anyone else. I had no contact with them. This review was sent to the *Economic Record* on the 17 May 1936. And, strange as it may seem by modern standards, it appeared in print in June. Hard to believe it now.

TRIBE: There seems a fairly clear link between the things you have just been talking about and the Russian work you did at the Bank of England; but the next book you wrote was on *Economics of a Declining Population*,[7] which is in a sense very prescient. The book reads very interestingly today, but how come you moved on to that?

REDDAWAY: Well, this is in a sense a personal thing – Hicks was in Cambridge in 1938–39, and he said to me that it would be a good thing to have a book about the economic consequences of a declining population. Well, that's one side of the story. The other side of the story is that Allen and Unwin intended to produce a whole series of books which were rather loosely linked together on macroeconomic problems, and they asked me, would I do a book, and had I any idea for a subject? I had just been talking to Hicks and

---

[5] *Economic Record*, vol. 12 (1936), pp. 28–36.

[6] See W. Young, *Interpreting Mr. Keynes: The IS-LM Enigma*, Polity Press, Oxford, 1987 for a detailed reconstruction of the emergence of the ISLM model.

[7] George Allen and Unwin, London, 1939.

I said, 'Well, Hicks suggested the economics of a declining population', and Allen and Unwin said, 'Oh yes, that will do fine', so I settled down to write the *Economics of a Declining Population*! Well, it has a lot in it which is very much in common with Keynesian ideas – saying that much more important is the question of managing the economy rather than changing the population in order to avoid unemployment. Indeed, Allen and Unwin said at one point, 'You seem to be writing a book on the theory of the trade cycle rather than a book on population.' Barbara Wootton was the commentator and she helped. I didn't realise it when I was writing the *Economics of a Declining Population*, but 1939 was a peak year for the proportion of active people in the country as against children and old people taken together.

TRIBE: Well, Beveridge drew attention to this problem during the 1930s, that there was going to be a decline in the number of younger people coming into universities. He argued that the post-First World War boom in the birth-rate would peak out in the adolescents of the 1930s, and then there would be a decline in each successive cohort of 18 year olds. But then, of course, entry into universities was disturbed by the war, and then afterwards there was both a secular rise in demand and an expansion of the cohort.

REDDAWAY: Well, I don't know whether we are getting off the subject, but I was persuaded by *Lloyds Bank Review* to return to the subject of the effects of a declining population in an article published in 1977,[8] and I found it very intriguing to look at a whole number of things to see how important or unimportant the population factor had been in a range of issues, like the shortage of teachers or the abundance of teachers, or the demand for cars, and so on. One key moral was that the population was by no means the over-whelming factor, housing being a good example. The reason why more houses were being occupied was partly demographic, but mainly lay in rising standards.

TRIBE: You came back in 1938 to Cambridge, to Clare College. According to your *Who's Who* entry you started as a statistician with the Board of Trade in 1940. You still lived in Cambridge, and worked in London?

REDDAWAY: Well, up to the war I was a Fellow at Clare College and doing a certain amount of lecturing, and so on. I was an academic, and I was busy writing the *Economics of a Declining Population*. In September 1939 war was declared, our first child was born and the *Economics of a Declining Population*, was published, so there were three appearances! So, essentially you could say I was a young academic founding a family, equipping a house, and so on. In 1939, when war was declared, as we had all filled in forms about what we were competent to do, I had expected, absolutely crazily, that the bureaucrats would have allocated me to something; but they hadn't. All they had done was to compile a database. Every economist in Cambridge was on deck at the

---

[8] W.B. Reddaway, 'The Economic Consequences of Zero Population Growth', *Lloyds Bank Review*, Part 124 (1977), pp. 14–30.

beginning of the October term, except Postan, who was an economic historian and an expert on Russia. He went into the Ministry of Economic Warfare.

The first effect on me was that somewhere towards the end of the Michaelmas Term I was approached – and it must have been from the Academic Register, because I don't see where else it could have been from – with the suggestion that the Ministry of Information wanted somebody to help with information, sorting and knowing what to do with it, and so on. I think I was rung up and I said, 'Is it a good job?' 'Oh yes, a wonderful job.' It wasn't! I went along there, and it was somewhere in the University of London, fairly near to King's Cross, and I found that they hadn't really got a clear-cut job. They wanted another pair of hands, and most of what they were wanting to do seemed to me to be a pure waste of time. So I said that as I was supervising and so on until the end of term I would come half-time, which I did. Then again, I think probably through the Register, Sir Andrew Duncan, who was the President of the Board of Trade, was said to be looking for somebody to help with writing his speeches. Was I prepared to be considered for this? I said yes. I couldn't have been less pleased than with the job in the Ministry of Information, and that was when I got transferred to the Board of Trade. I helped Duncan with writing one speech; but I was anchored in the Statistics Division, and the fact that I had been teaching statistics helped. That was how I came into the Board of Trade. Well, I never bothered to record the Ministry of Information post in my *Who's Who* entry. It was only a short while, mostly half-time. But I moved into the Board of Trade in 1940.

TRIBE: How much did you have to do with the development of the Central Statistical Office?

REDDAWAY: Well, that is a very fair question. I knew some of the people in the Central Statistical Office, and sometimes they would expect the Board of Trade to produce a lot of the statistics to go into their information, and sometimes we would discuss things; but it was rather a chancy thing, contact with the CSO.

TRIBE: So you didn't have much contact with people like Ely Devons?

REDDAWAY: Very little. One just saw them now and then, but in the main the answer is no. I got involved in statistical work that was coming out of the Board of Trade, they were concerned with concentration of industry, and so on. You would get people who wanted to know something about the Census of Production, and Limitation of Supplies Orders was another thing I was asked for advice about; and then the really big job I had, on which I suppose I started work around December 1940, was preparing to ration clothes. That was my big job. To be perfectly candid, I was rather good at it! It was a very tricky job, rationing clothes. Quite unlike rationing jam or anything of this kind. You invented a second currency in effect, for which everyone has the same number of units, and they had to give the same number of coupons, and there was a debate as to whether the whole ration should be in terms of value. My first instinct as a good economist was that it should be, but then one soon saw that administratively you couldn't work a control that way. But we then had to say that this currency would pass from the customer to the retailer, and from the retailer to the wholesaler. Now if we trace a shirt back to a shirtmaker or a dress to a dressmaker, up until then there are the same number of coupons, retail, wholesale, and so on; but when you come to a dressmaker buying cloth you had to fix the number of coupons for a dress to be equal to the coupon value of the cloth that would go into it. This involved guessing the average that you could impose on people. I used my mother-in-law's pattern book! It is not economics, it is common sense, if you like, but ingenuity also was needed, and I couldn't get anybody else interested in it at all, although fundamentally we were fixing the size of the clothes ration.[9]

TRIBE: How many people did you work with in the Board of Trade on this problem?

REDDAWAY: Well, on the problem of the launching of clothes rationing, about a dozen or something like this. It had to be kept frightfully secret.

TRIBE: What background did they have?

REDDAWAY: Civil servants essentially.

TRIBE: With no particular academic or economic training, or statistical training?

REDDAWAY: No. They kept saying, 'That's for you to do, that's your job!' And the statistics as to what was available by way of supply were *terrible*. Awful guesswork at what was available. You carried it right back to the making of the cloth, and, with hosiery, the making of the knitted garment. And with shoes to the shoemaker. And we refused to ration hats. People said, 'Why in the world didn't you ration hats?' We said we absolutely couldn't administratively ration hats. There were no means, since hats are made by anybody and everybody, and there was no material that they must use in a specified way. If we laid it down that any retailer selling a hat collected three coupons they could go and blue the coupons. So there was an awful lot of administration involved, along with the principle of the thing. And the charming start, you are probably too young to know, the initial coupons for buying clothes were the twenty-six margarine coupons in the food ration book.

TRIBE: When was that?

REDDAWAY: June 1941.

TRIBE: What did you move on to, after the rationing?

REDDAWAY: Well, I was the main odd-job man in the Statistics Division, and there were a number of things, some of them arising out of clothes rationing, that really I shouldn't have been doing. But it was the more interesting work, and so I did. I worked on the question of utility furniture. That had a nice economic side to it. It was recognised that there wasn't going to be much furniture, and that you couldn't have a general furniture ration which

---

[9] See W.B. Reddaway, 'Rationing', in D.N. Chester (ed.) *Lessons of the British War Economy*, Cambridge University Press, London, 1951 pp. 182–99.

would have amounted to one door knob or something per annum! But you couldn't escape having some system for people applying for furniture. There was the question of what categories of furniture people setting up house would need, you had to define these categories; and also the question of children outgrowing their cots and needing a bed. I got two utility beds under that formula! Separately, of course! I had a battle royal on one issue, and I am glad to say I won. People setting up house applied and said they needed this, that and the other, which of course came to far more than was available. And the civil servant wanted to say, here is your list, we pick out a bed, yes, you need a bed. Two chairs, you need two chairs. And a table, and so on; and we give you a permit for these specific items but not for the others. I said that will create a riot, because people will say, 'If you can't give me the whole lot, these are the ones I want, and who are you to say that I need this and not that?' It was nearly always *not* a case of 'Do you need a bed?' – you might not want a bed because mother-in-law can spare a bed out of their house, it was always a matter of people not getting all that they wanted, and being allowed a free hand. My view was that you attached points to the different items. More points for a wardrobe than for a chair, and so on. Pretty arbitrary points. It wasn't like clothing, where you had so many yards of cloth or anything of that kind; but you gave the person these points and they could use them for what they wanted if they could find it. There was no guarantee with utility furniture that you would find it, but you couldn't buy without.

TRIBE: Did you have any discussion with American colleagues? During the war the American economy was subjected to controls through price rather than rationing schemes; Galbraith built a large empire in Washington around price regulation.

REDDAWAY: Oh, he didn't control purchases through price. He fixed prices, and there was no guarantee that you would get supplies.

TRIBE: So your approach was more market-conforming than that of Galbraith, because fixing prices would simply mean that you might just get no supply, because the price was wrong.

REDDAWAY: Well, I wouldn't like to be so strong as this, but let me put it this way. If you have ultimate control through the raw materials, and these are generally allocated according to use, not in the sort of detail that there is with furniture or anything of that kind, you then didn't want the people who got the raw materials to make a killing by charging illegitimate prices. So you had a system of price control, the essential object of which was to stop the recipients of the raw materials making a killing; and the question then of who got these supplies became a very hugga-mugga question. In America they were never short in the way that we were short. By and large, you would get supplies, but you might have to wait, and you might not get the right size or pattern or whatnot; but the price control was there to ensure that a consumer did not get supplies by outbidding. So in that sense it was fair shares, but terribly weak fair shares. A person with time to hunt around lots of shops would get what he wanted. A busy housewife would just have to take anything that she could find. So it doesn't fit into these nice categories. You see, price is OK if price implies that you can deal at that price, and essentially in the war you were limiting the total quantity produced. If you had said, 'We are not going to do anything about prices', then you have the sky as the limit for prices. If you did as we did, have a completely nominal control of prices so people may not charge more than a fair price, it was a little better than nothing. But it became a lottery who got the things. If you had a ration you would ensure that they were allocated according to the ration. If you had utility furniture you had a partial ration. They didn't, strictly speaking, say that the seller couldn't sell anything to people who hadn't got these dockets. But he was to give priority to people with dockets. All very loose. They don't fit very neatly in with economists' normal concepts because economists' normal concepts imply that you can deal at the specified price, and at least buy even if not sell, and in the war of course selling was easy. Well, it meant in the furniture case that there was a rather limited quantity of furniture produced, because not much timber was made available. Care was taken to specify what types of articles were to be made. Rather loose definitions but no elaborate stuff, straightforward bed or straightforward table, no fancy carving and things of this sort. These could have been let loose on the market, but were sold to people who persuaded administrators that they had a need, and on the whole, in the war, people were fairly honest over these statements. Where they couldn't in a sense be honest was with respect to the alternative of scrounging off mother-in-law, and so on; and so there were rather global limits on how much you could get in the category of setting up house.

TRIBE: So these are the kinds of issues that you dealt with right through the war?

REDDAWAY: Yes. I have picked on some of the more interesting ones, but there were all sorts of things on exports, and so on. The Limitation of Supplies Orders that I mentioned were very largely to encourage exports; they limited the amount which could be sold on the home market, but if you could export output then you could sell as much as you could get materials for or means of production.

TRIBE: Did you work until 1947 in the Board of Trade, then, full-time?

REDDAWAY: No. In 1945 I went with one or two others to Washington and we produced, along with the Americans and the Canadians, a booklet called *The Impact of the War on Civilian Consumption.*[10] The object of producing it was to provide material for the people concerned with reconstruction after the war, so that they would appreciate that the UK had had a very much tougher time than the United States, and that therefore Lend Lease should be

---

[10] *The Impact of the War on Civilian Consumption in the United Kingdom, the United States and Canada*, HMSO, London, 1945.

cancelled, together with debts and all that sort of thing. So it had a real purpose, even though on the face of it, it is ostensibly an academic investigation. This is one of the things that took quite a bit of time and involved getting to the United States when there was no airplane that could fly across the North Atlantic. We had to go by seaplane, a requisitioned seaplane, which flew first of all to Lisbon, and then to the West African port of Bathurst and then across the narrowest part of the South Atlantic to Brazil and then to Trinidad and then to Bermuda, and then to North America!

TRIBE: When was this?

REDDAWAY: Oh, that would have been April 1945, I should think.

TRIBE: Why couldn't you have gone by boat?

REDDAWAY: Well, it only took five days and boats going across the Atlantic weren't all that easy. U-boats and convoys, and so on.

TRIBE: How long did you stay there?

REDDAWAY: About three or four weeks. There was a lot of work in this, as you can imagine. In the summer of 1945 when VJ day took place, the academics who were in government service were allocated for 1945–46 to university or to the government department according to a committee's decision as to which had the greater claim on you. I was simply allocated to the Board of Trade. Then in 1946–47 I saw that it didn't look as if I was going to get back to Cambridge; so I took the initiative, and said, 'What about half-time in London and half-time in Cambridge?' And that was agreed. So I was still half-time in the Board of Trade in 1946–47, and I was teaching, but not researching.

TRIBE: About that time the plan for setting up the Department of Applied Economics was revived, which had originally been planned for 1939.

REDDAWAY: That's right. Well it was pretty obvious that the person who was going to be Director of the DAE would be Dick Stone; he was the initial Director of the DAE. And he did a number of different things. I had a minor part in some of them. We wrote, jointly with Charles Carter, *The Measurement of Production Movements*,[11] we were much concerned with that, and with extending this from industrial production to GNP.

TRIBE: The Institute of Statistics in Oxford had, all through the war, conducted studies on the home economy. Was there any sense of rivalry with Oxford in the kind of work one should do, or carving out a kind of different area?

REDDAWAY: No, not really. Dick Stone was effectively the person who decided what the DAE did, within a budget. The budget wasn't very restrictive, it got money from Rockefeller and also the University; and, on the whole, the problem was manpower, skilled manpower, rather than anything else. They did quite a number of different things. Dick was very much involved in national income work.

---

[11] Cambridge University Press, London, 1948.

TRIBE: One post you had was Economic Advisor to the OEEC in 1951–52. Was that as immediate successor to Cairncross?

REDDAWAY: Yes. That was what one might call an interesting sabbatical. I enjoyed it and I think it was a fairly important job.

The thing I feel I haven't said is I became Director of the DAE in 1955, but there is nothing very much to say about what we were doing. We had a number of projects on which we were working, but Dick Stone, although he was Professor of Finance and Accounting, was in effect a supplementary director of the Growth Project, as it was called, arising out of the work with the National Institute. We had an arrangement that settled the finance of the department, which was that the University would make a contribution to the department which covered the staff salaries in post in 1955, and the department could beg, borrow or steal money from other bodies to do other work as well. Because of this there was a good deal of freedom of budgeting for the department, which didn't apply in a number of others, because it wasn't obvious whether it was more important to spend the money on hiring investigators or buying books or anything of this sort.

6

R.D.C. BLACK

Bob Black was born in Dublin, studied and taught economics at Trinity College, before moving to Queen's University of Belfast as part of a general reorganisation of the staff following the retirement of H.O. Meredith from the Chair in 1943. He remained on the staff at Queen's for the remainder of his career, until his retirement in 1985. He spent many years editing the Jevons' Papers and Correspondence, and he is a recognised authority on the history of Irish economics, although he had not initially intended to develop such a specialism as a historian of economics. The following is an edited version of an interview conducted on 16 October 1994 at his home in Belfast.

TRIBE: Perhaps you could tell me something of your early beginnings at Trinity College?
BLACK: I think I started from a position of great naïvety. When I was at school I was thinking of a career in industry or commerce, and so I was thinking about a business or commerce type of degree. But you see, I started from a rather different position from that of most of the people who have come into the subject, in that I went into Trinity in 1937, and I was then 15 years of age.
TRIBE: Was that the normal age of entry, like the Scottish system?
BLACK: No. At that stage very few people entered below the age of 17 – the normal age of entry would have been 17. I was fairly fed up with the school that I was going to. It didn't have a good Sixth Form. It was also very obvious by 1937 that the Second World War was going to happen, and happen quite soon, and I was rather anxious that before it happened I would have seen something at least beyond secondary school. There wasn't anything to stop anybody doing the Matriculation Examination in Trinity at any age, really. So I took the Matriculation Examination, which was pretty elementary in those days, got it, and went up in October 1937. Now in those days and for a long time before that in Trinity there had been a statute or regulation that you could not take any degree in the University until you had taken a B.A. It was first and foremost necessary to do the B.A. in some form. There were two ways in which you could get a B.A. Either by doing what was called the Ordinary Arts Pass Degree, or by doing Honours – what they in those days

86

called a Moderatorship. Now the Pass Course at that time was pretty basic. In fact until you got into the third year probably it wouldn't have been much beyond the normal A-level standard, if that. It laid a fairly strong emphasis on classics and mathematics, but pretty rudimentary in both cases and you would have been doing things like algebra, and a certain amount of physics or chemistry if you wanted. Interestingly enough, you had to do logic. But all these things were capable of being passed at a fairly low level, and medical students, for example, treated these subjects almost with contempt by comparison to their own courses, and got through them as best they could. And the pass-mark was 30 per cent: so it wasn't too difficult to get it if you wanted! Now that struck me at the time as pretty much a waste of effort really, trying to combine it with the Commerce course – but it seemed inevitable. There was one way in which you could get round it and that was to do Honours, do a Moderatorship. There was a Moderatorship in Economics and Political Science then, and I asked if I might enter for Honours in Economics and Political Science as well. I actually took both of those courses simultaneously. Now the Commerce degree was a three-year course. The Economics and Political Science Moderatorship was a four-year course, and you couldn't graduate until you had qualified for the B.A. So although I completed the commerce course in 1940 I didn't complete the economics course until 1941; and I got the two degrees in 1941, that was how it worked. Now actually that Moderatorship in Economics was a fairly recent development at that time. I am not sure when it began, but I think probably about 1932[1] – when George Duncan took over from Bastable. Bastable retired in 1932, and George Duncan became Whately Professor in 1934, and it was he, I think, and Johnston, who was the Professor of Applied Economics, who established that Moderatorship.[2] Prior to that there had only been a Moderatorship in History and Political Science, and another Moderatorship I think in what was called Legal Science, which included a certain amount of economics in its courses. So the Economics and Political Science Moderatorship was a fairly recent growth and although it was called Economics and Political Science, in effect it was a course in which the major emphasis was on economics, and politics was really an ancillary subject.

The School of Commerce really had a fairly loose relationship with economics. There were a lot of part-time teachers in subjects like bookkeeping or

---

[1] A Moderatorship in Economics and Political Science first appears in the Trinity College *Calendar* for 1932–33 at pp. 127–8; previously Economics had been included in the Law Moderatorship.

[2] C.F. Bastable (1855–1945) was Professor of Political Economy, Trinity College, Dublin from 1882 to 1932. His textbooks on *International Trade* and on *Public Finance* remained standard works from the late nineteenth century to the inter-war years. George Duncan (1902–) was appointed to a Fellowship at Trinity College in 1930 and succeeded Bastable in the Whately Chair in 1934, retiring from this appointment in 1967. Joseph Johnston (1890–1972) became a Fellow of Trinity College in 1913, studied for a time at Lincoln College, Oxford, held a Rockefeller Scholarship in 1928–29 and was appointed to a Lectureship at Trinity College in the 1930s. The Chair of Applied Economics was created for him in 1939, a post which he held until his death.

accountancy, and it was more bookkeeping than accountancy; and commercial law, subjects like that. What happened to me was that over the four years I got a lot less interested in commerce and a lot more interested in economics. And because of that shift in my interests and because of other things that were influencing the situation for me then, I decided to do graduate work in the subject, and enrolled for a Ph.D. in 1941 after I got the degree. They had this system, which I think is modelled on Oxford and Cambridge, that you got an M.A. by seniority when you had been there for upwards of two years. You could simply apply to get the degree of M.A. and you paid the fee and paraded up and got it; but there was no teaching at the Master's level at all. And the only way in which you could do post-graduate work was to submit a thesis either for a B.Litt. or a Ph.D. I did a Ph.D. which I finished in 1943, and then things turned out rather unexpectedly for me. I had not expected to have an academic career at all at that stage. In fact what I thought I would do was go into the administrative grade of the Irish Civil Service, and I was working towards that.

TRIBE: Can you estimate the number of students who would have been doing the Economics and Political Science Moderatorship compared with Commerce? How was the work of people like Duncan spread between the commerce side and the economics and political science side?

BLACK: To take an example, the year that I finished the course in economics, there were only two of us who actually took the Moderatorship examination that year. That had I think been a bit artificially reduced by the war, but in most years it wouldn't have been anything above five, or something like that. In commerce you would have probably have had twenty to twenty-five, that sort of number.

TRIBE: In each year?

BLACK: In each year, yes. You would have got something like about twenty graduating each year. Maybe not always as much as that, but fifteen, twenty, twenty-five, that sort of thing. But economics was much smaller. Some of the first-year courses in economics were common to both the economics students and the commerce students, so Duncan would have had a first-year class that might be twenty-five, thirtyish, and similarly Joe Johnston taught what was called Descriptive Economics – Duncan taught the theoretical side, Joe Johnston taught the applied side – and again, his numbers would have been about that size. But I remember in the last year, when Flann Campbell, the other chap who was in the final year with me, he and I were sitting in lonely state with the Professor, and the two of us listening to the lectures.

Now Duncan had actually been a Classics man originally, who had at some stage in his career switched over to an interest in economics. He had developed this interest in Swedish economics; and he never taught us Marshall at all. I think he was much more on the London wavelength in those days. His first-year course was closer to the LSE approach, I think; Hayek was at the LSE at that time, and Hayek was one of his great idols.

Duncan was a sort of Austro-Swedish economist. Instead of teaching partial equilibrium through Marshall, as most people did in those days, he used to teach general equilibrium through Cassel. It was an unusual approach; and then in things like macro or monetary economics, whatever you like to call it, it was Lindahl, Myrdal and Hayek that he concentrated on.

TRIBE: Had he been taught by Bastable?

BLACK: Oh yes, undoubtedly. Duncan had done the Moderatorship, I think, in Classics but he had also done legal studies, I think, and had an LL.B. You see this was a very common orientation at the time; and going further back I think that it probably would be true to say that almost every man who had been appointed to the Whately Chair, from the time that Whately founded it in 1832, had a legal qualification up to well, up to the time when Duncan retired, when Louden Ryan was appointed to succeed him. I think Louden Ryan was the first person to hold that chair who had gone through Trinity purely on the economics side. But right from Longfield through Bastable down to Duncan, I think you would find that almost, I believe, every one of these people had an LL.B. and were qualified to practise at the Bar. Whether they did or not, most of them probably didn't. But Longfield, for example, in his later years became a Judge. And this legal/political economy relationship, you know with people like Cliffe Leslie, Bastable, and so on, was always there.

TRIBE: With Edgeworth as well, of course. He went on and entered the London Bar, didn't he?

BLACK: He did, yes. It was a common way of looking for a certain amount of status. A position from which you could move in various directions. If you succeeded at the Bar, well and good; and if not, there were other openings which you might get in that way. So a lot of them used that approach, I think. Now I don't know exactly how Duncan got around to Economics. But I do know he had got a Rockefeller scholarship in 1928 or 1929, and went to the University of North Carolina, I think; and I think he did a certain amount of economics there, as well as a certain amount of sociology. He was interested in the race issue in the South, for example.

TRIBE: What was Johnston's background then compared with Duncan?

BLACK: Ancient History and Economics.

TRIBE: Classics again.

BLACK: Yes. But he got interested more in the Irish economy effectively and applied economics in a very institutional sense. Now you see actually, funnily enough, you have got there an extract from the *Calendar* for 1937–38. That was my first year. This was the course that I did as a junior freshman – 'Economics Introductory'. That was Duncan's introductory theory course. This one was Joe Johnston's. The syllabus there looks a lot better than the lectures! I read most of the stuff that was on the reading list. It wasn't even terribly onerous. But the lecturing . . . all you got there actually in Trinity at that time was lectures. There were no tutorials at all.

TRIBE: How many lectures would you have a week then?

BLACK: Two on each course. And the terms were only seven weeks, you see. So each lecturer would have fourteen lectures in a term. Forty-two lectures for the year. But there were no tutorials. There really was little opportunity if any to question the lecturer about anything, and you were on your own mostly to make up the reading list whatever way you could. But that is the course that I did, and the course in economics. But certainly the Diploma in Economics and Commercial Knowledge, I never knew anybody who did that at all. In the early days there may have been . . . I don't know when they introduced that, probably somewhere about 1910.[3] But it wasn't attracting any students to my knowledge in my day.

TRIBE: But coming back to this economics course in Junior Freshman, and the comments you made about Duncan and his LSE Swedish/Austrian leanings. The first item on the reading list here is Cannan's *Wealth*, which is Cannan's first-year lectures in the LSE. But the major textbook was Taussig, *Principles of Economics*. How far did the course correspond to this? When I first looked at this I thought, 'This is almost a standard, neo-classical, modernish course.' Because there is a lot about price, and what you said about equilibrium draws attention to that in that first section, the idea about general equilibrium.

BLACK: Well, I don't think it lived up to its name in all of these respects certainly. Actually the textbook that we concentrated on most was Briggs and Jordan, which you probably wouldn't even have seen.[4] And that is a funny thing because Briggs and Jordan is a textbook which was written in the 1930s almost more for commercial students than for economic students. It was written, I think, with an eye to the market of people who were doing things like the Institute of Bankers exams or Chartered Institute of Secretaries, and these kind of things, you see. But interestingly enough it was a kind of LSE-style book. I don't know whether Briggs or Jordan were LSE graduates, they may well have been.[5] But it did, for example, eschew the concept of marginal utility. It talked about marginal significance. It eschewed the idea of measurable utility, and it was going more into the idea of an ordinal rather than a cardinal approach to utility, and so it had that kind of emphasis to it. Taussig, as I remember, most of us found wasn't playing any great part in the course as Duncan taught it; and when we had had a bit of a look at that we found we weren't getting much out of it so I had played that one down. It was Briggs and Jordan that was the textbook for the most part. I actually lectured this

---

[3] The Diploma in Economics and Commercial Knowledge first appears in the Trinity College *Calendar* for 1906–07 at pp. 68*–72*.

[4] M. Briggs and P. Jordan, *Textbook of Economics*, 3rd edition, University Tutorial Press, London, 1935.

[5] Both authors held a London B.Sc. (Econ.), and Briggs, originally a graduate of Cambridge, was also a Gladstone Prizeman of London University. In the 'Preface' the authors describe their textbook as suitable 'for the Intermediate Examinations of the Universities, in Arts and Commerce'. They describe the book as having originally been based upon Marshall's *Principles*, but that the later, revised edition covered the 'leading ideas of Wicksteed, Wicksell, Davenport, Knight, Wieser, Hayek and Mises'. (Letter from R.D.C.B to editor, 4 February 1997.)

course later on. After I had finished my Ph.D., I was thinking of going into the Irish Civil Service, Duncan got a call to go and work for the wartime Civil Service in London. The College agreed that he could go provided that he employed deputies to do his work for him while he was away. I was one of the deputies, and that was really how I got my foot on the academic ladder, really through the accident of his wanting somebody to take on the job; because otherwise there was no regular vacancy on the staff there.

As for other textbooks, Bastable had actually written *Principles of Public Finance*, which was a kind of nineteenth-century classic, and it was still in use in those days, and actually still worth using, because it was a very well-written textbook on the structure of public finances up to 1914 or thereabouts. So Bastable was probably the key there, along of course with Dalton,[6] which again is an LSE product. But, in Distribution and Consumption Pigou's *Economics of Welfare* got a fair look in, but again Duncan was using things like Cassel's *Nature and Necessity of Interest*, the Swedish influence comes in again there; and Wicksell, and Böhm-Bawerk. But the earlier lectures didn't give a solid grounding in things that would have enabled you, for example, to tackle Wicksell and get a real grip on it, at that stage. I found that a problem. He was dealing with things like Austrian theories of capital, but you wondered what all this meant; and you went to the textbooks and tried to read it, and you did your best with it. Inevitably, at that stage there was a lot you didn't understand. Very little of the Money, Credit and Banking stayed with me, except for Withers, *Meaning of Money*. Well, the basic principles of central banking, commercial banking, credit creation; that got covered reasonably well out of that. This [the Trinity College syllabus] was, I think, fairly typical, if you've looked at other syllabuses, of the way that money and banking was taught in those days: on a very applied basis, not much emphasis on monetary theory.

TRIBE: So it was very institutional?

BLACK: Yes, very institutional. When I came up to Queen's in 1945 there was a Money and Banking course here, and I did half of that. And it was very much the same, very institutional approach: French banking, German banking, the Federal Reserve system. Then the last year in TC: 'Theory of Fluctuations', that was Duncan; 'International Trade', that was also Duncan; 'Recent Economic Changes', that was Joey Johnston. 'Political Theory' was one of the courses which was shared with the historians, and was taught by a good lady called Armstrong. She was a part-time lecturer who came in to give this course, she wasn't in either the History Department or the Economics Department – actually Trinity did not really have a departmental organisation in those days, people were just either full-time, as Fellows, or as Professors or Lecturers. Constantia Maxwell, for example, was Professor of Economic

---

[6] H. Dalton, *Principles of Public Finance*, George Routledge, London, 1922; LSE Studies in Economics and Political Science no. 66. The book went through twenty-one printings, was translated into six languages, and reached its fourth edition by 1954.

History, but Miss Armstrong who gave the Political Science was just a part-time person who came in. She set the Political Science paper for the historians, but Duncan set the Political Science paper for the economists! He had a stern approach to examination papers; he always set six questions on the paper, and he offered no choice whatever: that was it!

TRIBE: So you had to attempt all six?

BLACK: Either that, or take the risk of losing one-sixth of the marks.

TRIBE: That was a three-hour examination?

BLACK: Three hours, yes. And I remember one of the questions that came up on my final paper was something like, 'Comment critically on the political thought of von Gierke'. Miss Armstrong, bless her heart, had never even *mentioned* von Gierke, at any time, and nobody had suggested that we should read any of his works, if, indeed, they were available in translation, which I don't think they were! I remember looking in horror at that, and thinking, 'Well, there's no use writing anything about this, it is totally out of my ken'. And I just had to write that question off, and say OK, I'll try the other five and do the best I can. Just lose that number of marks. I managed to get a First, some-how or other!

TRIBE: You say that you had two hours' lectures on this course a week; but since for most of this four-year course there are only two lecturers, from their point of view there is a fairly large amount of work involved in teaching the courses for all four years.

BLACK: Duncan must have given about least eight lectures a week, and that I suppose was one reason why there were no tutorials, there simply wasn't the time available for them to take tutorials on their teaching load. Indeed, for some of the courses – Political Organisation in the first year and Statistical Methods in the second – no lectures at all were given, and students simply had to work up these subjects on their own, using the reading list which you see there in the *Calendar*. And presumably there wasn't the money available to employ anyone else to do part-time teaching.

TRIBE: But if this were on the Oxbridge model, then surely there should have been, along with the lectures, at least one hour's supervision a week?

BLACK: Should have been, yes. Well, you know, you can follow a model in some ways and not in others! The fact that Trinity was organised on the same lines as an Oxford or Cambridge college in having Provost, Fellows and Scholars didn't mean that it could do all the things that an Oxford college could. For although it was fairly well endowed, it was, I believe, in those days, in receipt of no government money whatever. The Irish Government provided no grants to either university – to the National University of Ireland, or to TCD. I think I'm right in saying that they had no money from the state at all, or only the most trivial amount. So everything had to come out of tuition fees or endowments. Now Trinity was fairly well endowed, but it was in effect not just a college, it was a university. And they had to run a Medical School, and they had to run a Law School, and they had to run an

Engineering School – and try to provide equipment for these, so I suppose their budget was tight enough as far as extra teaching was concerned. I could not put my hand on my heart and say that this was true of every subject, there may have been some subjects which provided supervisions. If there were, I didn't know of them.

TRIBE: So what happened when you went on to do a Ph.D.?

BLACK: I finished the Ph.D. before I became a deputy. I graduated in 1941, and I started the Ph.D. in October of 1941. In 1942–43 they did employ me for one course; they had introduced a new Diploma in Public Administration, which was being taken by people from the Civil Service, who came in on a part-time basis to evening lectures. And economics was included as a first-year course in that, it was a two-year Diploma. They employed me as a part-time tutor to give the elementary economics course for those first-year students. But that was just two lectures a week. So in the second year that I was a Ph.D. student I had that very small amount of teaching to do. For the most part I was doing the Ph.D. on a full-time basis with Duncan acting as supervisor. And then in the summer of 1943 he went – by that time I had finished the Ph.D. – and I started what was for me full-time academic teaching. I was then teaching six or eight hours a week, I started that in October 1943, and I was there until the summer of 1945, and Duncan came back when the war in Europe ended.

By that time, I had enough experience that I could try for at least an Assistant Lectureship somewhere. I did apply for several places; I remember I almost got an interview at LSE, Robbins had short-listed me for an assistant-ship, I think, but then I don't know what happened – this was at the time when LSE was still down in Peterhouse. But Meredith in Belfast gave me an Assistantship – a one-year appointment that could be renewed for up to three years, and there were three points on the scale, £275 a year, £300 a year, and £325; which to me was untold riches in those days! So I came here in October 1945, expecting to stay for a year, and I'm still here.

TRIBE: Before we move on to Queen's, have you any comments about the commerce degree which you did in parallel with the economics in Dublin?

BLACK: There was some overlap in the courses. The Economic Organisation course in the first year of Commerce was the same as that in the Economics stream. Economic History was a different introductory course which Miss Maxwell gave. Commercial Geography – I think that must have been the same as the Economic Geography course which I attended. That was given in the Geography Department by quite a good geographer called T.W. Freeman, who later became Professor at Manchester. He wasn't interested in Economic Geography at all, he was interested in Physical Geography. So it ended up that I knew more about the erosion cycle than the pattern of world trade! Languages – I did French and Spanish, you had to do two languages, I did French in the first year and Spanish in the second year. Those courses were given by the Professors of French and Spanish, both of whom were, I think, good scholars in their field. The Professor of Spanish particularly, Walter Starkey, was quite well known in those days; but they regarded the commerce students as rather less than the dust beneath their chariot wheels! But they taught us with amiable condescension.

TRIBE: Was it basic language learning, or literary? It wouldn't have been commercial correspondence, I imagine?

BLACK: Well, they did try to make it commercial correspondence to some extent. There was a bit of the commercial emphasis brought into the thing, you were supposed to be able to write a letter to your French wholesaler or retailer, and your Spanish one also. It wasn't terribly heavy going, for the most part, and obviously we had all done school French, though there was a problem with Spanish. We got the basic Spanish teaching and at that level it was relatively easy to adapt that to the commercial uses. Second Year Commerce: Economic Theory. Now I think that was Duncan's first-year course, so I think I got exempted; while Money and Credit, that was Joey Johnston again, there was an overlap of those two courses. So there was Business Organisation and Commercial Law and a second language in the second year. Now Business Organisation was a fairly harmless affair given by a local bank manager, who taught us about filing systems and commercial bills and a few things like that.

Commercial Law was an experience on its own, because it was given by a lady called Frances Moran, who was something of a figure in the Dublin of her day. She was one of the first women to be called to the Bar in Ireland, and she had been very successful, I think, and she was, to say the least, *formidable*! She came in and would sit at the front of the class, and begin to dictate notes from her file. And she dictated at approximately 55 words a minute, and as none of us knew shorthand that left us pretty breathless. But she expected you to get it down; and if you didn't, she would say, 'Why are you not writing this down?' We found this very tough going for the first couple of lectures, and so we thought of a good scheme. She had said that if anyone had any questions, not to hesitate to ask them; so we thought at the beginning of the third lecture that we would slow things down by asking her a question. And we did ask her a question. And her reply to this question was fascinating; and we got into a tutorial situation and she taught extremely lucidly and well, talking off the top of her head, she knew the subject inside-out, and we discussed it with her, and everything went swimmingly. We were delighted, until the next lecture when she came in and made up the difference by dictating at 70 words a minute! Because she actually had a line drawn in her lecture notes as to where she should reach at the end of every lecture, and if she didn't get there she speeded up until she did! So, it was heavy going, but it was impossible not to have a lot of respect for her, she really was a character, a very good lawyer I think, but those lectures were tough! The only thing you could do was take down as much as you could and read the rest in Stevens' *Mercantile Law*, which was the bible for the subject. Third Year: Public Finance, I think that was Duncan again. Accounting: well, accounting was given by a part-time lecturer who came in. He was either a partner in a local firm of accountants, or a Civil Service Accounting Officer, I am not sure which. He gave good basic training, starting with the basics of double-entry bookkeeping, but working up a bit beyond that. Statistical Method: now oddly enough there was teaching in statistical method in the B.Com. by a lady called Thekla Beere, who was a statistician in the Civil Service. She was a good statistician, but she didn't do much in the way of statistical theory. She took you through the basics of statistical method – correlation, index numbers – she didn't go much further than that, but she took people as far as she could reasonably be expected to take them in a one-year course. The trouble was that that course came in my third year and I had done the Economics' Statistical Method off my own bat in the second year.[7]

TRIBE: And so you said that there were twenty to twenty-five students doing this each year?

BLACK: Yes, about that.

TRIBE: Have you got any idea of destinations, or what these students might have intended to do? Was it similar to you – going into government administration?

BLACK: Probably private enterprise. I think what a lot of them probably intended to do was accountancy. In those days you could go into accountancy without a degree at all, but if you had a degree you could then go along and become an articled clerk, and you got certain exemptions because you had the degree. You would be able to qualify that little bit quicker. I think a fair few of them did that. There were some who had family businesses to go into, and they were trying to get some broader training before they did that. Civil Service – I don't think many of them would have gone in that direction, because, unless you went into the Administrative Grade, the openings weren't great, and the Administrative Grade was only open to people who had an Honours Degree; it was the same as the British system, really. I lost touch with most of them, because when I moved up here I moved into the economics network. I think a lot of them went on and probably were fairly well-to-do in the Dublin of the time.

TRIBE: You said earlier that you could see a war coming, and you talked as if this was the same perspective as if you were in Britain, in England or Scotland or Wales. But the Irish Republic wasn't actually involved in the war.

BLACK: That's right. You see, looking at it in advance, nobody before the Second World War would have anticipated that it would develop in the way it did. The idea that you could have neutrality, and that the neutrality of countries would be respected – most people didn't believe it in the 1930s, seeing the way that Hitler was going on. The impression was that when the war broke out certainly the whole of Europe would be involved in it willy-nilly. That it

---

[7] As noted earlier, there was no formal second-year teaching on Statistics in the Economics degree.

would start with mass bombing raids and so on in a matter of days after the declaration of war – if, indeed, there was any formal declaration – and that there would have been massive destruction in a very short space of time. That nobody would be immune from this kind of thing. Everyone was going to be involved. Now it didn't happen like that, you see, as far as the Republic of Ireland was concerned; and it was a very strange experience. It was like living in a trance, because Trinity went on working, and most of the institutions of the economy went on working, but of course they were affected in various ways. For example, my father was Company Secretary of a small group of companies which were in the grain trade. Well, the import of grain and many other essentials virtually disappeared after the first few months of the war, but there was a certain amount. And there was a fairly rigid allocation system for what imports came in, and there was substitution. Wheat wasn't much grown in Ireland in the early part of this century onwards; there was a free trade regime until 1932 and it was Canadian, American, Australian wheat which mostly was imported. Irish wheat came to be grown again on quite a large scale, but you got rationing of the basic foodstuffs. You had fuel shortages. Coal virtually disappeared. Petrol was extremely scarce. Bicycle tyres became a black market item. All this sort of thing. But with all these changes life still went on.

TRIBE: What was the degree being taught in Belfast when you arrived in 1945?

BLACK: The only degree was the Bachelor of Commercial Science. That was the only game in town. Even if you wanted to become an economist. But it was differently organised, because of course Queen's didn't have this constraint that Trinity had – that you had to do a B.A. before you could get anything else. So they had this arrangement, not uncommon at the time, I think it was perhaps more based on a Scottish model than anything else, that you could do a pass degree in three years. You could take the degree of Bachelor of Commercial Science at a pass level in three years. If you wanted to do Honours, and if the department allowed you, if they thought you were good enough to do Honours, you stayed on for a fourth year and in that year you concentrated really on economics in the fourth year and then you got an Honours degree. But it would still be a B.Com.Sc. There was also a substantial difference in that the B.Com.Sc. at Queen's could be done at the pass level either on a full-time or on a part-time basis. If you were a full-time student you got it in three years, and if you were a part-time student it took five years. I am not quite certain whether part-time students could do Honours on a part-time basis then. What happened subsequently was that part-time students were allowed to do Honours provided that, for the Honours year, they switched to full-time study. But as the thing stood when I came, there would have been again a goodish number of full-time B.Com. students, again may be around the thirty mark or something like that. And probably a similar number in the part-time course. And then in the Honours year you got smaller numbers again, but probably something like eight or ten.

Now two things I think worth saying there. First of all, there was an arrangement between Queen's University and what was then known as the Belfast College of Technology. The Belfast College of Technology provided some courses in what was called Applied Science and Technology, which was to a large extent engineering. But they also had a working arrangement with Queen's School of Commerce and a lot of the part-time students attended in the first year at any rate in the College of Technology, and then came to the University in their later years; and there were a certain number of what were called recognised teachers in the College of Technology who were allowed to teach University courses. There was a chap who taught economics there. There was somebody who taught economic geography. Somebody who taught commercial French, I think. Things like that. Now the other point which I think is worth mentioning at this stage is that amongst the part-time students, both then and subsequently, predominantly the largest number of those students were not what perhaps you would have expected. You would have expected, and what had been intended obviously by the people who started this movement for commerce degrees, was that you would have got people who were, say, working in a bank or an insurance company or linen warehouse through the day coming along to qualify for a degree by evening study. Now you got a few of those, but very, very few. The major proportion, and I would say it was 80 per cent to 90 per cent, or more, of the part-time B.Com. students then were teachers. Because in those days of course a lot of primary school teachers had no teaching qualifications, no degree qualifications either. But in order to get promotion, to get promotion to a principalship, for example, in the primary school or promotion into secondary school, a degree was often a prerequisite for that. The only degree they could get by part-time study was the B.Com.Sc., which wasn't the degree that most of them would have chosen. They would have preferred a B.A., but there was no evening teaching in arts. So they did this course instead. And I would say, you know, they were mostly very good students. Because they were totally self-motivated. They wouldn't have been there unless they wanted to be there. They paid their own fees. They sweated like hell to do the degree over five years because it meant being at the University or the College of Technology at least two evenings in the week, maybe three. A lot of them travelled quite substantial distances. They would come anything between twenty and fifty miles, perhaps, to come to their lectures and they had to read the stuff in their own time. In addition to whatever they were doing as teachers, all the homework and so on that they would have had to correct. So anyone who did that degree really wanted it and they were by and large some of the best students you could ever have asked for. They really were. So that is how it was come 1945.

Now as regards departmental organisation. There was a Department of Economics in Queen's, which officially there wasn't in Trinity. There you just had economics taught by people who had chairs or fellowships. Now, as I am sure you have already found in other smaller civic universities in England at that time, it was not uncommon for small departments to be run by a man and a boy. The man was the Professor and the boy was the assistant. And so it had been at Queen's. Meredith had been the Professor since 1911. He was a one-man band for quite a long time, I think. At some stage or other they decided to have an assistant, and in the years immediately before I came that job was held by Arthur Beacham, who subsequently became Vice-Chancellor of a University in New Zealand, then came back to a Chair in Liverpool towards the end of his career. Anyway, Beacham had departed before I arrived and so had Meredith, because Meredith was supposed to have retired in 1943 and he was quite glad to hand in his cards; although he went on to do other teaching elsewhere, at Magee College in Derry, for example. The University had decided on quite a dramatic expansion in the economics department at that stage; they had decided to double the staff. And they were going to have one Professor, two full lecturers, and an assistant. They had actually filled all these posts. The new Professor, who was to succeed Meredith, was Keith Isles, who stayed at Queen's until 1957 and then went to become Vice-Chancellor of the University of Tasmania – not surprisingly because he was a Tasmanian. He had been Professor at Adelaide before he came here, and prior to that I think, he had been Professor at Swansea.[8] The lectureships were filled in the first place by Duncan Black, who subsequently went to Glasgow and then to Bangor. He got the Chair at Bangor, North Wales and I think finished up on Hayek's Committee on Social Thought in Chicago. Then there was Tom Wilson, who had been in the Cabinet offices during the war. He subsequently moved to Oxford and became a fellow of Univ[ersity College], and then got the Chair at Glasgow, as Professor of Political Economy. And then there was me at the bottom of the pile; and come October 1945, Keith Isles was in Germany with the Australian army sorting something out and Tom Wilson hadn't got out of the Cabinet offices, so there was nobody there when the term began this time forty-nine years ago except Duncan Black and me. And he used to sign his name 'D. Black' and I used to sign mine 'R.D. Black' so there was a lot of confusion.

There was a lot of work to be done, because all these courses, first, second, third, fourth year had got to be taught. They were running, the students were enrolled and we had to keep the show on the road between the two of us, and, believe me, that was an experience. We taught everything. You name it, we did it. There was, for example, a Special Subject that the students in the third year did and they were supposed to write some minor thesis on some aspect of it; and the subject which Meredith had laid down for that year was transport. Neither of us knew anything special about the economics of transport, but Duncan Black had read something in Edgeworth about railway rates and the

[8] Keith Isles gained a First in Pt. II of the Cambridge Economics Tripos in 1929; after teaching in Edinburgh he was Professor of Economics at Swansea 1937–39 before returning to Adelaide as Professor 1939–45.

theory of discriminating monopoly, and I worked up a bit about air transport; so we had quite a sweat to cover all the bases. It was about half-way through the second term when Keith Isles arrived. Then Tom Wilson got there about Easter, and so we had the full complement before the year was out. But then Tom Wilson was offered the fellowship in Oxford and decided to go in 1946. I was by then busy applying for other jobs elsewhere: I went to Swansea for an interview, got shortlisted for a Fellowship at Balliol to my surprise, but didn't get it. And then Tom decided to go, and Queen's advertised the lectureship and I applied for it and was appointed. And, you know, that was the way my career at Queen's worked rather strangely; there was always a point at which I decided that I must not stay any longer. I was going to go somewhere else. And at that point something always happened that turned me in the direction of staying. So I finished up in the odd position which I think very few academics possibly had in their careers, that I had been on every rung of the academic ladder from Assistant Lecturer up to Professor. I had been Assistant Lecturer, Lecturer, Senior Lecturer, Reader and then Professor, but all in the one place.

TRIBE: The first major publication listed in your *Who's Who* entry is the *Centennial History of the Statistical Society of Ireland;* and, indeed, from your publications, especially your work on Jevons, one would get the impression that you were mainly historically inclined. But in your description of the way you learnt economics in the late 1930s and 1940s there is no suggestion of a particular historical bent. This is the training, actually a rather good training, for a standard economist at that time.

BLACK: Well, yes. There wasn't much historical emphasis in it. There were the courses in economic history and there was a small mixture of history of economic thought in the second year, but, as I say, there wasn't a lot of time given to that. No, it was really the Ph.D. which started me down that road and funnily enough it was not the undergraduate course in history of economic thought that gave me the idea for my thesis. In that fourth-year course at Trinity there was a course in international trade, as you have seen; and one of the textbooks which Duncan prescribed for that was Ohlin – Ohlin's *Inter-regional and International Trade*. And in Ohlin, which we read pretty thoroughly in relation to that course, there are a couple of references to Longfield as someone who had made original contributions to the theory of international or inter-regional trade, mostly through his analysis of the effect of Irish absenteeism on the price–income structures of the two countries. That caught my attention. When it came to the question of doing the Ph.D., George Duncan made a few suggestions, and I mentioned this thing about Longfield, and he agreed it would be a suitable subject. At that time you could get all the materials for that in Trinity; one of the difficulties about a subject in international trade is that a lot of the sources which you might normally either want to get from overseas or go overseas for would be inaccessible, because of the limitations of postage and censorship of the mails, apart from the difficulties of currency and whatnot. During the time that I was acting as Duncan's Deputy I didn't have much time for research, but what time I had I spent first of all compiling a bibliography, first of all, of all the Whately Professors, and then of all the other TCD graduates I could find – people like Edgeworth, and W.R. Scott, and so on – who had become what could be called professional economists. I had access to all these books in the Trinity Library and I read them; and found that actually Longfield had really established a kind of tradition, a subjective value tradition. Where everybody else was kind of hooked on Ricardo and Mill, in Trinity a lot of people had followed Longfield's lead in using a supply and demand type of analysis with a concentration on the consumer preference angles, and I wrote that up. I sent the thing off to *Economica*, because I knew that they had published quite a bit of history of economic thought under the influence of people like Robbins and Hayek – Hayek actually was the editor of *Economica* at that time – and Hayek accepted it much to my surprise, and it came out August 1945.[9]

But it is probably more important from your point of view to talk about what was happening about the organisation of the courses at Queen's. There were big changes there. Because when Keith Isles came, he was Cambridge-trained. He had been a pupil of Keynes and Pigou. And he was quite clear in his mind that economics was a science, but commerce wasn't. And he argued, let's wash away this pretence that we can teach commerce to people; and if we are going to teach economics it has got to be clearly named Economics. And so he originated the idea of changing the degree title from B.Com.Sc. to B.Sc. (Econ.); and we did that, if I remember rightly, in I think 1947–48; and, you know, that changed the focus of the thing. And from being a Faculty of Commerce, under Keith Isles' inspiration, it became a Faculty of Economics. But a variation I think from what was happening in most of the English and Scottish Universities at the time, was that the part-time course continued. It became a part-time course for the B.Sc. (Econ.). We continued to draw on the same sort of students. Again they were to a large extent teachers, but sometimes drawn from commerce and in the broad sense sometimes Local Government, that kind of thing. And we continued to get a very good bunch of students from that area, some of whom actually went on to academic careers as economists. The most outstanding example of that was Jack Johnson. Jack Johnson was Professor of Econometrics at Manchester. I think actually he was one of the people Charles Carter appointed there. He subsequently went on, I think finished up, at Stanford in California. Now Jack Johnson, when I knew him first, was a part-time student with us, and his day job was as a clerk in the Gas Department. Belfast Corporation in those days ran the gas works, and Belfast Corporation Gas Department took in the money and sent out the bills, and so on; and Jack was a clerk in there and he

[9] R.D. Black, 'Trinity College, Dublin, and the Theory of Value, 1832–1863', *Economica*, n.s., vol. 12 (1945), pp. 140–8.

came and did the course, and did very well in it. And Keith Isles said to him, 'Now what about coming and doing full-time for Honours?' Which he did, and from there on he went into academic life, and he wasn't the only case. Quite a few people like that moved in that way. And I always felt that that course was very well worth having. Nobody else at the University wanted to teach in the evenings! One of the problems we always had was that we needed to get the supplementary courses in economic history, in languages, all the other things that were necessary adjuncts to the degree, because we expected the part-time students to cover all the courses that the day-time students would have done, but in five years instead of three. And there were not a few people in the more academic departments like History and so on who very much resented the idea that they would be asked to teach after five in the afternoon; or, indeed, sometimes after 3 p.m.! But we managed to persuade them to keep giving the courses, and the thing actually lasted until 1986. The last student got the last degree in 1986. So it was B.Sc. (Econ.) from about 1947; as far as I can remember, when I started here, the B.Com. course that Meredith had wasn't greatly different from the sort of thing that Trinity had. The thing that distinguished the Queen's degree from most English universities, not so much the Scottish, I think, was that you had this four-year course; it was in the 1960s I think that we got two fairly substantial changes taking place and I think this is putting them in the right order. By the early 1960s, indeed, by the late 1950s, the expansion of universities meant that a lot of other subjects which had been part of the economics degree had become independent degrees. When I came in 1945 economic history and political science were both taught, but they were taught by one man. There was one man who did all the economic history and all the political science.

TRIBE: Who was that?

BLACK: That was a man called Joe Lemberger, who was a strange character. A very good teacher who never published anything all his life, but read everything and was known by the students as a very good teacher; but he had that very heavy teaching load. Then quite early, round about 1948 to 1949, we got a lecturer in Economic History separately, and Lemberger was left with just the Political Science. Things gradually developed from that: from being one economic historian there came to be two. Ken Connell came in 1952. And then he got an assistant, and it came to be two or three. Political Science got a Chair towards the end of the 1950s; and Social Studies, that had started off really as a kind of Social Work Diploma, but gradually social studies was moving towards Sociology. So we got a fairly substantial reorganisation of the Faculty after Keith Isles left and Stanley Dennison took his place in 1958. I think at the end of the 1950s or early 1960s, the name of the Faculty of Economics was changed to Faculty of Economics and Social Sciences, and you got Honours degrees in Political Science, Economic History, and so on. By that time we felt that the Queen's B.Sc. (Econ.) had become pretty well known and fairly well established. It was rather different from the LSE B.Sc. (Econ.),

101

as you say, because I believe in the earlier years that used to be taught on a fairly general level. You know, you got B.Sc. (Econ.) even if you hadn't done very much economics, if you had done a lot of economic geography or something like that. Now the B.Sc. (Econ.) in Queen's had always been an economics degree. It was a Bachelor of Science *in* Economics as such really, and we wanted to keep it that way! So we had battles with our colleagues about that, but eventually we compromised on the idea that the Bachelor of Science in Economics would remain for people who did what by then I think were beginning to call a major in economics and a minor in some other subject. And people who did, say, a major in economic history or political science would do what was called a Bachelor of Social Science degree. So we did that. Then by this time I had been appointed to the Chair, and Jack Parkinson had come as Professor of Applied Economics.

And in or about, I think it was 1966, the University made the decision to go into UCCA, which meant that for the first time entrance into Queen's was on a par with entrance into any other university in the UK – not as an individual application to Queen's itself. But you see, what it meant was that if they did Economics, say, at Bristol, at the end of three years they would come out with their Honours degree, and at the end of a fourth year they could have their Masters. After four years at Queen's they had just got their B.Sc. (Econ.). Now we thought that the B.Sc. (Econ.) was a damned good degree, as a four-year degree! Students used to come back to us after having started, say, the Masters degree at LSE, and we would get them coming back to us during the Christmas break of their first year and saying, 'Oh, honestly, we haven't heard a single thing yet that we haven't heard already from you people!' And we used to think to ourselves, 'That shows how good we are!' Then we got to thinking about it, and realising that that wasn't right, that we were short-changing these kids. At this time the New University of Ulster, as it was then called, was just starting up in Coleraine, and they decided on starting on the English model, on a three-year course, whereas Queen's had always been on the Scottish model. Jack Parkinson and I thought hard about this, and we thought that if you took two kids down there at Methodist College, or Campbell, and they each want to do Economics, and they each put in for that; but one of them decides to go to Queen's, and the other decides to go to Manchester or whatever: this is the result. It makes us non-competitive, we are going to lose the best students this way. So we switched over to a three-year Honours' system at that stage, from about 1967 or 1968. Now we had expected that our colleagues in other Faculties would follow that lead very quickly; actually they didn't. And right up almost to the time that I retired, certainly in the early 1980s, most courses at Queen's were four-year courses, but not ours. And, of course, all that got shaken up in the University reforms of the 1980s, when they *had* to go on to the three-year system, like it or not. But we were out of step for fifteen years, I suppose; we thought that we were a step ahead, anyway!

102

TRIBE: Stanley Dennison only stayed for a short period, 1957–60?[10] Some people have suggested that he was not an entirely happy appointment in Cambridge.

BLACK: Well, first of all, looking at it from the ideological point of view if you like, he was definitely right-wing, no doubt about that. He was a member of the Mont Pèlerin Society,[11] for example, he used to go to their conferences; he was a friend of Hayek's and all the Mont Pèlerin people. He was very much an industrial economist; and he did revise Dennis Robertson's *The Control of Industry* when he was at Cambridge. He was quite close to Dennis Robertson, and eventually became the custodian of Robertson's papers. Robertson was, I think, his master, if you like. And that must have made him very unpopular in the Cambridge of the Keynes–Kahn–Robinson days. He frankly didn't get on at all with Kahn or Joan Robinson. Or, so far as I know, with Keynes. He agreed very much with Robertson, and Robertson's way of teaching and thinking. He was, I think, a good economist, and there were no difficulties, so far as I know, with colleagues here. Some people maybe might have thought him a bit stand-offish, even a bit snobbish; he was very much the perfect old-style don. He was a bachelor, of course, all his life, and he was something of a *bon viveur* – he liked good food and good wine, he knew how to entertain very well, he liked good music, and could play the piano extremely well, he was an excellent pianist. But he wasn't going to play you any boogie, there was no doubt about that! It was going to be strictly Bach or Brahms! And some people got on with that, and some people didn't. It made it very difficult, I think, for him to relate to students, particularly in a provincial university. The type of student that he would have met and entertained at Cambridge was a fairly rare bird here! But the Department was quite happy with him; he didn't make favourites, he didn't quarrel with anybody that I'm aware of. I regarded him as a very decent individual. No, I liked Stanley Dennison, I think he was a good man. A lot of people underestimated him, I think; and he didn't do as much as he could have done in economics, there's no doubt about that. He got interested more in administration as he got older, that was why he decided to become Vice-Chancellor at Hull. But I don't think he really liked that very much, in the end . . .

TRIBE: Well, it was a difficult time, wasn't it, 1972–79? He would have come into contact with Jack Straw, wouldn't he?[12]

BLACK: He certainly wasn't the sort of man to have great sympathy with student activists and all that!

---

[10] Stanley Dennison (1912–92) was an Assistant Lecturer in Manchester 1937–39, Professor of Economics at Swansea 1939–45, and Lecturer in Economics in Cambridge 1945–57.

[11] See for an outline of the membership and programme of the Mont Pèlerin Society, R. Cockett, *Thinking the Unthinkable*, rev. edn, Collins, London, 1995, Ch. 3.

[12] Jack Straw established his reputation as a student militant at Hull University, was later Secretary of the National Union of Students and in early 1997 was Shadow Minister of Education on the Labour Party front bench.

TRIBE: You implied earlier that there has been for some time something systematically different about the students at Queen's – that they were mainly local.

BLACK: Well, that went through certain phases. I think Queen's was always very much a regional university, and, for example, it used to be quite common for students from Northern Ireland to go down to Trinity. A lot of the students who elsewhere might have gone to Oxford or Cambridge here would go to Trinity. So the students who came to Queen's were often much more local. From 1945 to the early 1950s anyway, they were predominantly local. And they probably would have come from what would have been a more middle-class, lower-middle class, even working-class background sometimes – the more well-to-do types, the landed gentry here, probably sent most of their children across to public schools in England and they would have gone on from there to Oxford or Cambridge. Those who weren't quite as well-heeled as that might have sent them to some of the boarding schools here, like Campbell, for example or others which rated as public schools, and on down to Trinity. The ones who came to Queen's were more likely to have been at one of the local grammar schools, and probably had an ordinary enough family background. The majority of them probably lived with their parents, or their relations. When I came here first, for example, I lived in what was then the Men's Hall of Residence; it was the only Men's Hall of Residence that was attached to the University, and it contained forty students and four members of staff. That more or less met the demand, although there were a lot of student digs at that time as well. But the proportion of students who were living away from home was relatively small. In the late 1950s and early 1960s, when the pressure on University places was heavy, there was a fair sprinkling of English and Scottish students coming here. But by and large I doubt if the proportion of students from literally overseas, across some sea however narrow, was much above 10 per cent of the total. And of course it virtually dried up once the Troubles started. When it got to 1969–70 there was no parent of any rational character, who, if they didn't have any connection with Northern Ireland, was going to allow their son or daughter to come to Northern Ireland if they could help it. And that was understandable. And of course recruitment to staff positions didn't become any easier at that time. But that's rather come back now. Interestingly enough, under EU Regulations there is a much higher proportion of students from the Republic of Ireland now than there used to be.

TRIBE: You went to Princeton in 1950 for a year; what impression did you form of the place then?

BLACK: I wanted to work with Jacob Viner, and I lived in the graduate college where the bulk of the graduate students from outside New Jersey lived. And so I got to know a fair number of the graduate students, and I attended some graduate courses. I attended Viner's graduate course in International Economics. I attended Friedrich Lutz's course in Micro. I did some lectures with Bill Baumol for a time, and one or two other people, but I couldn't go to all the courses that I would have wanted to go to without cutting too much into the time that I wanted to use to get on with my own research. There was a very good set of people in the graduate courses at that time. Martin Shubik was there, Harvey Liebenstein, Otto Eckstein. They were a good group and people like Viner and Lutz set pretty high standards.

TRIBE: Boulding made the comment that Viner's teaching method was extremely aggressive, rather forceful. Did you find that?

BLACK: Yes – he was forceful, there is no doubt about that! In the old saying, he didn't suffer fools gladly. He did sometimes push students fairly hard. He wouldn't have criticised any student for admitting that he didn't know a thing, but he would cut hell out of any student who pretended to know a thing and didn't. From that point of view he was a forceful kind of teacher and a lot of people stood in fear of him, there is no doubt about that. He had the reputation of being a peppery kind of person with a very short temper. I never found that, actually. I was in a rather different position because I was one of the students he was supervising and I wasn't doing any courses, except as an auditor. When I took stuff to him I used to find that he would say, 'Come and talk to me on such and such a day about what you are doing, tell me what you have done', he'd have a supervision every couple of weeks; and I used to find that when you went in there you felt a little bit as if you had put your finger into the electric mains, because he was so sharp. He took everything up instantly and he would start to generate ideas about it; but if something that he thought you were doing was interesting, he would say, 'Well look, leave that with me and I will see what I can find for you, and I will bring it in to the next class.' And he would come in the next day or two with a fistful of cards out of his card index. He had this phenomenal card index in his study at home which filled something like fifteen filing cabinets. It was incredible! He never went anywhere without a bunch of cards in his pocket and he was always going through the library at Princeton or wherever he was; he was never out of the library reading something, and he would make these notes on these cards. From that point of view his own standards were so crackingly high it was hard to keep up with him; and that I think was what most people feared. They just wouldn't be able to keep up with him! I stood in some awe, but he was very straightforward.

TRIBE: How did the work on the Jevons material come about?

BLACK: When I was finishing up *Economic Thought and the Irish Question* I spent an awful lot of time in the National Library in Dublin, and the chap who was in charge of the Manuscripts Department at the time said, 'Oh look, we have just got Cairnes's papers in. Maybe you would like to have a look at them?' And I went through this, and there was a lot of correspondence between Cairnes and Mill and so on, and I knew a lot of that had already found its way into Mill scholarship, but in the middle of it somewhere there was this half dozen letters from Jevons. And I was very surprised, because I had always thought of Cairnes and Jevons as being at opposite poles. Classical and Neo-classical as it were. But obviously Jevons thought very highly of Cairnes, and Cairnes equally seemed to think a good deal of Jevons. And I thought, 'I could have an article out of this, if I could find the letters that Cairnes sent back to Jevons! Well, that has got to be easy. After all Jevons was at Manchester, and he was at UCL. His papers have got to be at one or other place. Bound to be. No problem.' So I wrote off to the librarian at Manchester and the librarian at UCL. Neither of them could produce anything. No Jevons papers here, they said, much to my astonishment. Then I got a letter a few weeks or more later from a chap called Wolfe Mays who was in the Philosophy Department in Manchester and had been working on Jevons as a logician. He had got to know H.S. Jevons, Jevons' son, who had died in 1955; and he suggested I get in touch with Jevons' daughter, H.S. Jevons' sister. So I thanked him very much and wrote to Miss Jevons, who was alive. She was just over 80 at the time I think, but she was an extremely sharp mind still, very definitely *compos mentis* and she wrote back a very polite letter and said she hadn't got the papers any longer. She had passed them on to her niece, her brother's daughter who was a Mrs Rosamond Könekamp, and she enclosed her address, which was in Pembrokeshire. And so I contacted her, and she wrote back and said, 'Yes, I have got these letters and I have looked them all out and I will copy them all for you.' Which she did in her own hand, and she sent me back the letters from Cairnes to Jevons, and that made my article. Mostly it was material relating to the gold question, and so on. But I pieced the thing together and published the result in *Economica*, after sending a draft to Mrs Könekamp for her comments.[13] I think I said to her at the time, 'How much stuff do you have?' And she wrote back and said, 'Actually, I have got a couple of suitcases full of it; and this may be of no interest to you at all but here is a letter from Alfred Marshall which I copied out.' I thought, 'Crumbs, what are we on to here!' Well I talked to Charles Carter, who was just going to Manchester, and I said to him, 'Look, you're the Stanley Jevons Professor at Manchester now, Charles, what are you going to do about this? We ought to get this stuff properly looked after. It can't be left in a suitcase in Pembrokeshire. You ought to get it taken up to Manchester. Let's do something about it.' So he and I eventually went to see Lionel Robbins who agreed that this material should be preserved. By that time I think what had happened was that Mrs Könekamp had brought the suitcases up to her Aunt's house in Harlesden, somewhere near Heathrow, and she had shown it to me, and it was amazing stuff! And the striking thing about it was that there was a whole lot of stuff there which the family had never shown to anybody; if you read Keynes' memoir of Jevons written in 1936, he says that he had been unable to gain access to Jevons' personal journal, and this is because Miss Jevons wouldn't allow him. And when I was in her house on that occasion she

---

[13] R.D. Collison Black, 'Jevons and Cairnes', *Economica*, vol. 27 (1960), pp. 214–32.

sat me down in her dining room, I think, and she and Mrs Könekamp went off to the drawing room; she had all the papers piled up on the dining table, and I was looking through the letters and hadn't got as far as the Journal. After about half an hour Miss Jevons came back in, took the Journal up and said, 'I suppose you have finished with this now'; and took it out of the room. She knew quite well I hadn't looked at it! But she wouldn't allow anyone to see it. It was only after her death . . . Mrs Könekamp hadn't the same problem and she allowed me to see it; and the reason for it was that the journal was very personal. It contained Jevons' innermost thoughts about the fact that his elder brother had gone out of his mind, had been committed to a mental home and never recovered; and that had been a tremendous tragedy to Stanley Jevons. But that secret had been kept from the day in, I think it was 1852 or earlier, that Roscoe Jevons went out of his mind, and it was kept from then until 1961. It never went outside the family. But anyhow, I had seen the stuff and I knew there was a lot in it. And I said to Charles Carter and Lionel Robbins, that I thought a proper edition should be put together; Robbins agreed but said that I ought to do it! And so I came to take on the Jevons job, and I never really got away from that for twenty years. One of the reasons why I hadn't gone on with the economic thought and policy project was that I had realised that the period of production for anything you did in this area was so extremely long, and anyway I didn't really want to get typecast as an Irish economic historian. I wanted to get more into the mainstream of economic thought, and so the Jevons edition was appropriate enough from that point of view. But what I didn't realise at the time was of course that the period of production for a thing like that is a great deal longer; I started on that job in 1961 and we didn't get the first volume out until 1972.

7

RONALD TRESS

Ronald Tress studied economics as an external London candidate at University College, Southampton. After a year studying at Hawarden he became a Research Fellow in Manchester, where among others he encountered Harry Campion, John Jewkes, and Hans Singer. After a brief spell teaching at the University College of the South West (now Exeter University) he joined the War Cabinet Office as an economist in 1941. He left government service in 1947 and taught first at the LSE before being appointed Professor of Political Economy at the University of Bristol in 1951. From 1968 to 1977 he was Master of Birkbeck College, University of London. The following is an edited version of an interview conducted at the home of Dr Tress in East Molesey, Surrey, on 6 June 1995.

TRIBE: How many B.Sc. (Econ.) students were there at the time you were in Southampton, which was 1933–36?

TRESS: There were about a dozen, I suppose.

TRIBE: In that one year, or all together?

TRESS: In the one year. At most a dozen. I was the only one doing Special Economics as distinct from the other Special Options which were available, notably Geography and Economic History. I had done Higher School Certificate with Intermediate exemption, so that I went straight into the Finals course. The degree pattern was one year Intermediate, two years Final. I spent three years as an undergraduate, so I spent all three years on the Final stage, but the majority were doing the Intermediate and then the Final. That was likewise true of Exeter, where my wife, in fact, was a student of mine. She had gone into Exeter with Higher School Certificate to do a B.A. in History, but then she switched to the B.Sc. (Econ.), not because of me I hasten to add, with Economic History as her specialism.

TRIBE: What was your educational background?

TRESS: My family background was that of the two villages of Upchurch and Lower Halstow, east of the Medway towns, with an employment mix of largely fruit-farming and market-gardening, along with brickmaking (cherries before, but not after, the clay had been taken for bricks). I was one of the earliest to get what were then described as 'scholarships' to a secondary school: to Gillingham County School by bicycle and tram or bus. It was a new school, with building going on throughout my seven years and after. H.C. Barnard arrived as Headmaster in my first year, 1926. He made the school. When he left in 1937 it was to become Professor of Education at Reading. As regards the Higher School Certificate, there were three choices. You could do the (London) Higher School Certificate in Arts, or in Science, or in Economics. For the Higher School Certificate itself you had to do the equivalent of three 'A' levels. For the Intermediate exemption you had to do four in the cases of Arts and Science. In the case of Economics, it was five, three plus two. For the majority of schools, teaching was in Arts and in Science. It was exceptional that one could do Economics at all. I happened to be at a school where one could, though there weren't more than one or two of us at a time, because it happened that the deputy headmaster, besides being the senior history master, also taught economics. The fact that he was a Douglasite,[1] a heretic, didn't affect his teaching! He was conscious of what the syllabus required, as distinct from what he read in his magazines – if one could get hold of them, you could find out what the old boy was teaching himself! He was an exceptionally good teacher, not just in the subject matter he taught, but I learned how to take notes from his blackboard technique, and the notes that I used for my own teaching, up to 1968 when I ceased to teach, were very much designed in the way he had taught me. I knew how to put things in order rather than just scripting them, and I learned how to take things down likewise in that form. I wasn't the first to do Economics; in fact there were two of us at the same time and others would follow, and there were one or two before me. It was exceptional, but you could do it. I opted for it because I was no good at languages which was necessary to Arts, and I didn't want to do Science, because I didn't like Chemistry and Physics.

TRIBE: What were the five subjects you did then?

TRESS: Economics, Geography and Mathematics. The first two were compulsory; for the third, you could either do Mathematics or a language, so I opted for the Mathematics. They were the three for the Higher School Certificate, but I spent three years in the Sixth Form, so I didn't just do the other two for the Intermediate exemption, I did the whole lot again. So I got distinctions in Economics, Geography and Maths, and passed British Constitution and Economic History. Those were the five which got me exemption from the Intermediate B.Sc. (Econ.). I also got a scholarship in

[1] I.e., a follower of Major Douglas and the idea of Social Credit. Clifford Douglas (1879–1952) had been Chief Engineer for British Westinghouse in India before the Great War. During that war as a Major in the Royal Flying Corps he was directed to reorganise production and cost accounting at the Royal Aircraft Establishment at Farnborough. From this experience he developed ideas about the relation of sales receipts to production and distribution costs which he began to expound in 1919 in Orage's journal *New Age*.

Economics at what was then University College, Southampton, offering London external degrees.

TRIBE: So you did three years in what was the two-year course for the B.Sc. (Econ.); how was the syllabus organised? How many teachers were there at Southampton at that time?

TRESS: Well, I went straight into what was the College's second year for Economics. For the Final B.Sc. (Econ.) there were ten papers: compulsory papers in Economics, in Banking and Currency, and in Economic History, and in Statistics and Scientific Method, two half papers. Three papers on the Special Subject, a language translation paper in French and German, and finally papers in each of two optional subjects. The examination week for the Finals started on Monday morning and, for me, finished on Friday afternoon. The only break I had was that I had been allowed to do the language paper a year earlier, it being a Pass requirement only. It was also true that, for the optional papers, two were on the Friday, the other two were on the following Monday. It happened that the two I chose were both on the Friday. At dawn on the Saturday, which was 21 June, I was on Salisbury Plain, watching the sunrise at Stonehenge! But that was the pattern.

TRIBE: How was the teaching organised then?

TRESS: Well, as far as Special Economics was concerned, for the specialised three papers, I was the only one doing it. So it was personal teaching, or more especially reading, with Percy Ford, who was not Professor by then.[2] The Department didn't warrant a Professor for the number of students. Percy Ford taught the Economics and the History of Economic Thought; the course in Banking and Currency was taught by R.A. Hodgson, who is still alive, he is blind, I am sad to say, but he is still living in Southampton with his wife; we exchange Christmas messages. They were the substance of the Economics Department itself. There was Donald Tyerman, who taught the Economic History, but he was in the History Department; as was David Quinn, who taught Political History. David Quinn went eventually to a Chair at Belfast. Donald Tyerman went to *The Economist* and became Deputy Editor under Geoffrey Crowther, eventually Editor and then subsequently Deputy Editor of *The Times*, I think. He was at Southampton long enough to marry the girl who had been the Woman President of the Students' Union.

TRIBE: You have described in a letter to Fred Lee[3] how you started off at the beginning with Cannan's *Wealth*, which was Cannan's introductory lectures from, I suppose, before the First World War; and of course also Robbins,

---

[2] Percy Ford (1894–1983) studied economics at LSE and after a period at King's College, Durham he moved to University College, Southampton in 1926, was promoted to Professor of Economics in 1938, and retired from this position in 1959. From 1951 to 1962 he and his wife Grace devoted a great deal of effort to editorial work on the British Parliamentary Papers series.

[3] Letter to Lee concerning P.W.S. Andrews, with whom Tress overlapped as an undergraduate at Southampton: F. Lee, *Oxford Economics and Oxford Economists 1922–1971: Recollections of Students and Economists*, typescript, 1993, pp. 221–4.

Knight and Wicksell; but what caught my attention was the fact that you wrote a final special essay on Chamberlin. If you take the Cambridge-centred view of all this, it seems that firstly, Robinson and Chamberlin are equated; but there seems to be very little early reception of Chamberlin in Britain. His book came out in 1933, and there was very little reaction even in the journals until the mid-1930s. Was it Percy Ford who brought Chamberlin's book to your attention?

TRESS: Remember that the B.Sc. (Econ.) was a London external degree with the papers set by London (primarily the LSE) and external examiners: not Ford or Hodgson. A powerful guide therefore was the published *LSE Calendar* with a complete list, not only of the subject of the lectures, but the course content of the lectures and the recommended reading for the lectures; and Joan Robinson and Chamberlin were features of those. I in fact took more to Chamberlin than I did to Joan Robinson!

TRIBE: There is a big difference between Robinson and Chamberlin. Robinson has very little about oligopoly theory, there are lots of graphs, but it is very Marshallian in style. Chamberlin is in retrospect much more modern. He links to modern developments because he relates his exposition of oligopoly to ideas of product differentiation and advertising. This is very different to Robinson.

TRESS: Note first that the basic text for Lionel Robbins' prime Principles course at LSE was Frank Knight's *Risk, Uncertainty and Profit*. So I was started from Knight, not from Marshall. I think that Joan Robinson was much more in the Marshall tradition. Her notions about profit were more Marshallian, I think. Whereas Chamberlin was more mathematical in concept, and I had done mathematics, and kept up with mathematics. I found Chamberlin more attractive. The big problem for London External students was the differentiation between LSE and Cambridge in respect of macroeconomics. Because, of course, you had got Fritz Hayek at LSE, with *Prices and Production* as the prime textbook; Keynes' *Treatise on Money* was featured, but I graduated in 1936, the year that *General Theory* was published, so that book didn't get into the list. One was much more dominated by the Austrians, and after all, not just the Hayek Austrian concept, but the Robbins' influence is Austrian too, in terms of Menger, for example. I am talking about being Austrian, but this includes Pareto, Menger and Wicksell. Cambridge, on the other hand, was very self-sufficient: Marshall and Pigou, and then the Robinsons, and Richard Kahn come in at that point. Whereas the LSE influence draws from much wider sources: not only the Austrians but also the Swedes – Lindahl and Wicksell – I read those as well.

TRIBE: Bob Black in his interview has referred to the same phenomenon: orientation to the LSE in the 1930s meant to the Swedes and to the Austrians, not Marshall.

TRESS: John Jewkes always referred to the *Economic Journal* as the *Cambridge Economic Journal*!

111

TRIBE: Yes, there is a lot of truth in that! But to come back to your student days. After you graduated in Southampton you spent a year as a scholar at Hawarden. How did that come about, and what did that involve?

TRESS: Well, first, I was very much involved in religion; I had contemplated going into the Church. And the second thing was the Gladstone Library. The Gladstone seat was at Hawarden Castle, because he had married a Miss Glynne. The principal pub at Hawarden was, and still is, I believe, the Glynne Arms; and it was Glynne money, and the Glynnes were Liverpool shipping people. The story as I recall it (ahead of reading Roy Jenkins' biography)[4] was that Gladstone had established this library for his own books to give to the nation; and in fact he would wheel them down in a wheelbarrow to begin with and stack them. That was then subsequently endowed, initially through Morley's biography of Gladstone. The family commissioned this work, took all the royalties, put the royalties into the building of the library and, eventually besides an extended library, established a residential wing, and three studentships. One from Oxford, one from Cambridge, one from modern universities. It is not what you know, it is who you know! Albert Cock was the Professor of Education, and therefore the most powerful person in the University College of Southampton since the majority of students were education students. He was a bachelor, he was involved in religious things. He later became a Church of England priest. He was one of the Hawarden trustees. So that he advised me to apply for a Gladstone studentship, and surprise, surprise, I got the one for the modern universities! It was conditional, I think, on my getting a First, but as that happened too (he didn't have any influence on that), I spent a year there. Apart from the three Gladstone students, there were a number of residents coming and going, mostly for short periods. There were a number of scholars who came. Michael Ramsay, subsequently Archbishop of Canterbury, would come there to work; but also there were notably Rhodes scholars because during vacations they would come to work and it was pretty cheap living. So I got that studentship there, by the end of which time I had decided that I wanted to do more economics, and not go into the Church.

TRIBE: What did you do while you were there?

TRESS: I did work on Christian social thought either side of 1900, from the late nineteenth century into the twentieth. I have still got the collection of papers, I have never written it up. The latter part of the nineteenth century was very much dominated by perfectionism, liberalism, the expectation of continuous growth, with co-operation and social betterment as features of a Christian social gospel preached first by Frederick Denison Maurice (Joan Robinson's grandfather) and followed by the Christian Social Union led by Scott Holland and Charles Gore, as well as by the more radical Christian Socialists. Westcott, a distinguished biblical scholar and Bishop of Durham,

---

[4] Roy Jenkins, *Gladstone*, Macmillan, London, 1995.

would address the Miners' Gala. Then, with the new century, the background to the argument changed. A kind of romantic medievalism replaced the progressive optimism, with such as G.D.H. Cole arguing for guild socialism and Roman Catholics like Hilaire Belloc and G.K. Chesterton taking up the cause. There was also some espousal of unorthodox economics, like Douglas' Social Credit and A.R. Orage's *New Age*.

TRIBE: You should write it up, because that is all coming back again, isn't it?

TRESS: Yes! Even the Social Credit people. New Age.

TRIBE: Do you think that was stimulated by your deputy headmaster in the school, this insight that in fact there are different ideas of economics and ethics, and their relationship to Christian socialist thought?

TRESS: Oh, I don't know about that. My father was a Methodist, but I got roped into the Church of England initially because Lower Halstow needed an organist. I got £10 a year, I think! But my great good fortune then was to be befriended by the vicar who came to the Parish, who gave me ready access to his library. So from schooldays onwards I was reading quite extensively in both economics and theology. And when you don't see much except the services – the armed services, the Civil Service, school teaching or the Church – that is a limit to your horizons anyway. On all scores the last was an attractive proposition. But at Hawarden I changed my mind, and headed back to economics.

TRIBE: So how did the link with Manchester Research Section come about?

TRESS: There was an advertisement for studentships. I began to look out for them. Manchester was advertised. I was conscious of course of the existence of Manchester, and since I was living seven miles west of Chester I submitted an application, about the application of monopolistic competition to the cotton industry! I knew about monopolistic competition, and I assumed that they knew about the cotton industry; so I said to myself, 'I will put in an application for some kind of research project on monopolistic competition in the cotton industry.' Anyway, I got summoned for an interview, and cycled from Hawarden between breakfast and lunch to Manchester, and cycled back from Manchester to Hawarden for the evening meal with the interview in between. I had a very agreeable interview, presided over by the Vice-Chancellor, John Sebastian Bach Stopford, an anatomist. George Daniels, who was the old type of economist, he took the line that 'We know something about the cotton industry up here you know!', or Lancashire words to that effect. But he left it to John Jewkes and Harry Campion to take me off, and they said, 'Well, now, look, forget all that about monopolistic competition. There is a study we want to do about unemployment and depressed areas, and if you are willing to take that on it is yours.' So I did.

TRIBE: What you have just described is what Stanley Dennison went on to publish in 1939.[5]

[5] S.R. Dennison, *The Location of Industry and the Depressed Areas*, Oxford University Press, London, 1939.

TRESS: Well, Stanley Dennison was there of course at that time, with a major study in hand on the location of industry, but the research I was set was separate and distinct.

TRIBE: So did you work with him on that or . . .?

TRESS: Not really: I reported directly to Jewkes. But we were all very much together in a pair of houses in Oxford Road.

TRIBE: Was that quite separate from the Department at that time?

TRESS: Only in an accommodation sense. The Department was in the main building. But the Economic Research Section, as it was called, was housed in Oxford Road. Jewkes, Campion, Chester, Dennison, Hans Singer, Philip Chantler and H.C. Hillman were all there in that one building, we had tea together and all the rest of it.

TRIBE: Hans Singer was working on the Pilgrim Trust Study at that time, wasn't he?

TRESS: *Men Without Work.*[6] That is right. I have a copy of it. I did the index. I didn't get any credit for it! I submitted an article on my own research to the *Economic Journal* which Keynes turned down, and it was published in the *Manchester School* in 1938.[7]

TRIBE: You read it at Cambridge, in fact, at the British Association meeting in Cambridge in 1938 as well, according to the first footnote.

TRESS: Yes, well, that was because Percy Ford was the Secretary of Section F. Who you know!

TRIBE: I was just going to say that these diagrams in the back here, they look interesting . . .

TRESS: The Lorenz curve, as a way of representing the concentration/diversity of industry in an area.

TRIBE: Did this relate to the kind of work that was done in Manchester?

TRESS: Well, there was an interest in unemployment all round, with *Men Without Work*, and the work Stanley Dennison was doing on location. And the practical point, of course, was that one was particularly interested in this in Lancashire; and one of the outstanding cases I took was Barrow. The North-West division of the Ministry of Labour was housed in Manchester. With John Jewkes' contacts I was given access to all the data at the Manchester Ministry of Labour offices, and I painstakingly extracted these data, writing them up. There were no screens where you just pressed a button and it came up, I went through the files and wrote them all up, with Barrow being one of the outstanding places because of the degree of concentration; and it is still there.

TRIBE: There must have been about five or six people in the section then when you were there. How was it all financed? There were certain people like Jack Stafford who was a Lecturer in the Department. And Jewkes by that time was also a Senior Lecturer as well, wasn't he?

---

[6] *Men Without Work: A Report made to the Pilgrim Trust*, Cambridge University Press, Cambridge, 1938.
[7] 'Unemployment and the Diversification of Industry', *Manchester School*, vol. 9 (1938), pp. 140–52.

TRESS: Jewkes was Professor. He, Campion, Chester, Dennison and Chantler all had teaching posts, as did Stafford (*not* a member of the Section). I'm not sure about Hillman. Singer's work was funded by the Pilgrim Trust. George Daniels died in the year I was there. In fact I was spending an evening with John and Sylvia Jewkes when they got a telephone message saying he had died suddenly. And of course they appointed John Hicks as his successor. John Hicks came the year after I was at Manchester.

TRIBE: How did that come about? There was a big lurch between Daniels and Hicks. Do you know anything about why it was that Hicks was appointed?

TRESS: Well, Daniels was a traditional type. I think that people like Jewkes were conscious of the need for a modern theorist, and Hicks wasn't a Cambridge man in the same way – he had been at Oxford and the LSE before Cambridge. He was acceptable.

TRIBE: You spent one year only at Manchester. Was that simply because there was no more money available, or did you decide you wanted a different sort of job?

TRESS: It was a One-Year Fellowship.

TRIBE: You were succeeded by Christopher Dow.

TRESS: I was succeeded by Christopher Dow, and I had succeeded Bryan Hopkin.[8] And Jack Stafford, I think, the year before that.

TRIBE: You went to Exeter. You must have been fairly familiar with the routine because of Southampton. Were there any particular striking differences between Exeter and Southampton as institutions?

TRESS: I was personally in a different situation, but of course the teaching programme was still the London External. In the structure of the institutions, Southampton in my time was very much dominated by the Professor of Education, because it was he who got the students in, and what's more that included, up until the last year that I was there, two-year students as well as four-year. Two years was enough to qualify as an elementary school teacher. So there were two-year people and there were four-year people; would-be teachers could complete their training in two years or they could do a degree plus a year's postgraduate training.

TRIBE: From the *Calendars* of Exeter you can see the range of students who were relevant here. There were Civil Service students, and then there was a link with the National Association of Local Government Officers (NALGO) as well. Have you any idea how that came about?

---

8 Christopher Dow (1916–) was Economic Adviser to the Treasury from 1945 to 1954 and was then at the National Institute for Economic and Social Research until 1962. From 1963 to 1973 he was Assistant General Secretary of the OECD. Bryan Hopkin (1914–) worked in the Prime Minister's Statistical Branch during the war, was a member of the Economic Section of the Cabinet Office from 1948 to 1950 before moving to the Central Statistical Office. He was Director of the National Institute from 1952 to 1957 and then rejoined the Economic Section at the Treasury in 1958 as Deputy Director. From 1972 to 1982 he was Professor of Economics at the University of Cardiff, during which time he was also Head of the Government Economic Service and Chief Economic Adviser.

TRESS: I have forgotten all about it, to tell you the truth! Well, Sykes[9] was there when I joined and he had an interest in Local Government, and this was a period when training for Local Government Officers was a bit like that for teachers. Employees could train up from clerks by gaining Local Government Examination Board qualifications. Sykes was, again like Ford, not a Professor, but at Senior Lecturer level. Sykes and myself were the Department. But whereas Southampton in 1933 was all on its future edge-of-town site, the bulk of Exeter in 1937 was still in the city centre. Exeter did have its future edge-of-town site, with two men's halls of residence, one (Rede) a converted big house, the other (Mardon) purpose-built. But the only teaching building thereon was one for Physics, the Washington Singer labs (originating from sewing machine funds). It also served social purposes, its big lecture hall was a gym and a dance floor. The bulk of the teaching was in Gandy Street in the city centre, alongside the Royal Albert Museum (RAM) – that is why a ram was the emblem of the Students' Union. The Principal and administration, the library and some teaching departments, were housed in the one major building. The rest, as in Southampton, were largely in First World War army huts.

So the Economics Department was in an army hut in Gandy Street. Sykes was very much a money and banking specialist, so he taught those Final subjects as well as the Intermediate Economics. I taught Principles of Economics, second and third year, I taught Statistics, and I taught British Constitution to the Intermediate students. Quite a lot of work, when you haven't done any teaching before! Sykes did all the rest. Well, there were two postgraduate students, Lewis and Firth, who did some tutoring in economics and economic history. History teaching, of course, was done by the History Department, as it had been in Southampton; likewise Geography. Very much the same pattern as Southampton, and the same sort of size of 200–300 students.

TRIBE: Altogether 200–300?

TRESS: I don't think it was more than that.

TRIBE: Well, these days it seems curious, because no school would be that small!

TRESS: Well, certainly Southampton, there was the men's hall that I was in, and they had just built a second, then called New Hall and subsequently called Connaught Hall. There was one Women's Hall. The rest were home students. I don't know of any people in digs. You were either in a Hall of Residence, or you lived at home. The same was true at Exeter. For men, there were on the University's eventual site the two men's halls I have already referred to, plus a couple of converted houses on Pennsylvania Road called Kilmorie. Further up the hill were two Women's Halls, again a mixture of converted and purpose-built.

---

[9] Joseph Sykes (1899–1967) studied Commerce in Leeds and Manchester and established the teaching of economics at Exeter.

TRIBE: Where did the students come from? You say you met your wife there. But why did people go to Exeter? Because they lived locally?

TRESS: Well, my wife was born in Plymouth and brought up in Torquay, came up from Torquay Grammar School; and that was true of a number of others, but not exclusively so. I mean why did I go to Southampton originally? One of the reasons certainly was that I was able to take the scholarship exam at school. I didn't have to travel to another place.

TRIBE: Was that the only entrance exam that was done at your school?

TRESS: Southampton and, I think, Hull were doing it that way. I don't know if there were any others. My headmaster knew Cock, which was another linkage; Southampton wasn't a cypher, but . . .

TRIBE: And also Hull was much newer then, wasn't it?

TRESS: Hull had not got full University College status at the time when I was an undergraduate. It was in the same category as Leicester, I think, whereas Nottingham, Southampton and Exeter had recognised U.C. status. Nottingham first, and then Southampton and Exeter were given their Charters one after the other. Leicester and Hull a bit later.

TRIBE: So you spent three years at Exeter?

TRESS: Well, I went to Exeter in October 1938. As far as being on the staff was concerned, formally I didn't leave until July 1945 when, for people like me, HMG joined the universities' superannuation scheme. But I was put in a 'reserved occupation' because I could do statistics. I spent the summer of 1940 working for the National Assistance Board going up and down the Teign Valley, interviewing householders, seeing if old-age pensioners deserved their supplementation, meeting the unhappy daughters, whom I had to question on the income of the household. She didn't know what her husband's income was, and what's more she wouldn't want him to think that he was having to pay for her father! One learnt a bit of social economics at that stage; but that was that, and then the old Manchester connection – come early 1941, the Economic Section of the War Cabinet Secretariat was expanding. Further, Harold Wilson, who had joined it in early 1940, had been reclaimed by Sir William Beveridge to work with him at the Ministry of Labour. I got offered one of the vacancies.

TRIBE: It is very striking in the recruitment to the Economic Section that Jewkes called upon all those people who had passed through Manchester. Dennison by that time was in Swansea, you were at Exeter, but you were all brought back into the Economic Section; the common thread among you was Jewkes and Manchester, which, as you mention, Cairncross' book[10] doesn't really pick up on at all.

TRESS: It wasn't exclusively Manchester. The prime link of course is Henry Clay, who had been Professor at Manchester before he went to the Bank of England. I think that when he joined Stamp, he then initially recruited Harry

---

[10] *The Economic Section 1939–1961*, Routledge, London, 1989.

Campion to sit in for him at the Bank of England. Then Hubert Henderson brings in Austin Robinson. Lionel Robbins from LSE had a direct connection with Stamp. Alec Cairncross was Cambridge after Glasgow. James Meade was primarily Oxford though in Geneva when the war broke out.[11]

TRIBE: But if you look at that, it brackets Cambridge–Oxford: Hubert Henderson brings in Robinson from Cambridge, and Hubert Henderson also has connections with Oxford. Robbins has connections obviously with the LSE. But in fact a Manchester connection is the most significant common factor among many of the members of the Section, or who then dispersed to other Ministries. Indeed, a key pair are Devons and Campion, if only because of the work that they did on what eventually became the *Monthly Digest of Statistics*.

TRESS: Besides the Manchester names I mentioned in the Economic Section, you had Harry Campion, Jack Stafford, Ely Devons and Joan Marley – who had been a research student at Manchester – all in the Central Statistical Office, though the CSO also included Richard Stone from Cambridge, Walter Taplin from Oxford and two from LSE, Ronald Coase and Ronald Fowler.

TRIBE: Is there anything other than the simple fact that they were in Manchester, and known to Jewkes or to Clay, or to Devons? Is there anything beyond that relating to the character of the work that was done in Manchester? If you look at someone like Austin Robinson, Robinson was in some respects quite unusual in the Cambridge context of having a relatively empirical and practical grasp of industrial organisation. But common to the Manchester people would be statistical ability, knowledge of industrial or labour conditions, general ideas about applied economics. This would clearly distinguish them from people like Meade and Robbins. Apart from the work being done in Oxford before the war, none of which fed directly into wartime administration, Manchester had the only serious research section in Britain at that time.

TRESS: It was again, who you know. You start with Stamp, Clay and Henderson. Obviously Henderson has a link with Austin Robinson, and with Robbins, because Robbins had been at Oxford for a period. Remember that Stanley Dennison was a Cambridge man who had moved very much towards the empirical side.

TRIBE: Could you talk about the work you did? You are quite unusual, because most of the economists who were taken on during the war period left again almost as soon as the war had finished; but you stayed on for two years, until 1947. You worked with Meade for some time, for instance. You worked on the balance of payments, and public finance.

TRESS: I think you have got to start with the fact that almost all the senior ones had jobs to go back to. I technically was still a member of Exeter, I kept

---

[11] See notes on these names pp. 14, 16, 48.

up my superannuation payments at Exeter, for example; but I wasn't particularly keen to go back to Exeter. Edward Bridges, who was Secretary of the Cabinet, was very keen for some of the younger people to stay on. He had recruited, of course, James Meade to take over the Directorship of the Section after Lionel Robbins. So Philip Chantler, one of the Manchester people, and myself, accepted invitations to stay on, as did Nita Watts along with two others who had been later recruited, Marcus Fleming and John Wood; likewise Christopher Dow. There were also substantial new recruits. Richard Sayers came in from the Ministry of Supply as Deputy Director. A.J. Brown joined from the Foreign Office, Tom Wilson, George Shackle and David Bensusan-Butt from what, through the war, had been Winston Churchill's 'Statistical Branch' under Lord Cherwell. So for me, it was a better job than any of the alternatives. I was by then married with one child, and another on the way, and I had a comfortable flat near Crystal Palace. Very attractive conditions to carry on with until the Readership in Public Finance became available at LSE, which I was encouraged to apply for. Chairs and Readerships were University of London appointments and there was this considerable external element always in their selection committees. But I got it.

TRIBE: You went into the Section in 1941. Had the work of the Section settled down by that time, after the early days when its role had not been quite so well defined?

TRESS: In April 1941, when I began, manpower was a major consideration, together with the concentration of civil industry, the concentration on to engineering, and so on, at the same time as recruiting into the armed forces. Stanley Dennison had prime responsibility for that, and had been assisted by Harold Wilson, I think. But certainly my first early job was to support him, and to work with him on that kind of manpower planning.

TRIBE: With Harold Wilson or Stanley Dennison?

TRESS: With Stanley Dennison. Harold Wilson had left to work with Beveridge. I never overlapped with him, and took his place effectively, in a sense both of the vacancy, and also of the work. My Manchester research had familiarised me with the Ministry of Labour's manpower data. That is where I got first of all involved, and that continued to be a major part of my activities all through the war period. So I was also able to get on to the data which the Ministry of Economic Warfare was circulating but that no one was looking at, including manpower figures for Germany and countries under German control. And I spotted that you could compare, in manpower terms, the British war effort with that of the Germans. The Germans, because of the greater significance of peasant agricultural production, were getting very close to their maximum of engineering manpower, which was 4 million I think; while we were 3 million and could move up to four. One could then add what was coming out of those countries which Germany had occupied: the extent to which forced labour was being used for German purposes. It pretty well balanced what the Commonwealth was providing in resources for us in that field. In short, the Germans were using a lot of their manpower on food production, whereas we were importing ours. And therefore there would pretty well be a balance, or a stalemate, apart from the prospect of the Americans coming in. The best thing that happened was that the Japanese bombed Pearl Harbor! One was getting Lend Lease, of course, and that continued all through the war. So my first and continuing concern was with manpower and the scale of the war effort. Then I got drawn into national income calculations. James Meade had started with Dick Stone. Dick Stone, earlier in the Ministry of Economic Warfare, had been hauled out to work with James Meade on national income estimation because of the disputes within Whitehall about what the right calculations were. But James, having along with Dick settled the methodological issues, needed to return to the Section's questions of budgetary policy and such. So I took over his share of the statistical input, using in particular my manpower know-how in estimating wage and salary incomes. I would spend every afternoon at the CSO working with Dick on the first White Papers on National Income Accounting; and that is how I got drawn into that. In the meantime, of course, one had people like Lionel Robbins getting deeply involved in other aspects of the war economy: first of all in food rationing and agriculture, for example. Lionel's father was very much an agricultural man, and Lionel had written things on agriculture himself, and so he became involved with the Ministry of Agriculture, and then moved on to Points Rationing and with the Ministry of Food. It developed from one thing to the next, I think, in that sort of way; and so that towards the end of the war all the Section was much involved in prospective post-war problems and policies, as Cairncross and Watts so fully record. In that context, I moved into forecasting national income for 1948, which was taken as the freedom year, so to speak, with demobilisation complete and the economy back to something like normalcy. More importantly, the Section, and James Meade in particular, was working on post-war employment policy, with Keynes, Henderson and, in particular, top Treasury officials all involved. Now, the official Report on Social Insurance and Allied Services, forever identified with Beveridge (though owing much to Norman Chester) had been published at the end of 1942. Beveridge, aided by Nicholas Kaldor, was now turning his free and independent attention to post-war 'full employment in a free society'. In government, there was a great deal of pressure to beat Beveridge to it. The result was the *Employment Policy* White Paper, including an appendix on varying National Insurance contributions to counter fluctuations in consumer demand. I think I pretty well drafted that appendix. The White Paper itself, of course, was an agreed government document even if most of the basic drafting had been by Meade.

TRIBE: So how did the interest in public finance come about? All of the things you have talked about so far, right back to Manchester, relate to labour supply and unemployment, industrial concentration, and statistics; but not taxation, or public finance . . .?

TRESS: Well, no, but the notion of income and expenditure accounting starts with Keynes' *How to Pay for the War*. So it was very much linked up with public finance and taxation at that stage, and the levels of funding required. So the public finance aspects that I was interested in were initially novelty things, like purchase tax, and what sort of basis would one operate that on, whether wholesale or retail. And at that stage wholesale won, just on the basis of the sheer administration costs. At LSE, the big course of lectures that I took early on was my National Income course to the mass of students, which was very much my field. The more specific public finance things were for the specialist groups. I also got involved very quickly in the London and Cambridge Economic Service; Frank Paish had managed it from before the war, and I effectively took it over and managed it, combining with Charles Carter and Brian Reddaway, both at Cambridge, as joint editors. I think that it was effectively superseded by all the output of the statistics, post-war. It was quite a dramatic change. Pre-war, there was a *Board of Trade Journal*, and the *Ministry of Labour Gazette*. National statistics were restricted to a single volume about that size published annually by the Board of Trade.

TRIBE: When you were in Manchester you said you got the material easily because of contact with the Ministry of Labour; so the data which they were publishing were far too aggregated to be of any use to the economists. Why then did they publish them? What were they for?

TRESS: How do you mean?

TRIBE: Well, for research purposes, or even for preliminary survey purposes, it seems you had to yourself go through the Ministry files and pick out the relevant data; the material they did publish was at such a level of aggregation that it wasn't suitable. Cairncross also emphasises in respect of the Economic Section that a lot of the early work involved trying to generate the information that was needed to get an idea about manpower and production from the relevant Ministries, because this didn't exist anywhere. Campion and Devons were particularly involved in this. So it seems to me that the statistical data published before the war were of little use to academics, and no use to public administration. So the question is, what were they for? Who were they for?

TRESS: Well, they were all that there was. The *Board of Trade Journal* was publishing trade statistics regularly, I can't recall if monthly or quarterly, imports CIF, exports FOB. The *Ministry of Labour Gazette* carried the unemployment data. There were occasional special surveys. Population statistics followed the Census, once every ten years. But that is all there was. Now one has data available and the technology such that they can be used. Compare my labour-intensive extracting of raw data to arrive at just half-a-dozen Lorenz curves depicting industrial diversity in 1937 with Michael Chisholm's study of regional specialisation, *The Changing Pattern of Employment*, published in 1973 which has maps of the whole of Britain depicting what he calls 'subregional Tress scores'.[12]

But the computer revolution is very recent. Let me illustrate from experience. It was some years after my going to Bristol, when we moved into a new building, I got the architect to design the interior very much how I wanted; and I got a Statistics Room which had desks with wires to them, so that the students could operate statistical machines, calculators.

TRIBE: Were these electronic calculators?

TRESS: Oh no! All the national income stuff that I did during the war, and Dick Stone similarly, was done turning a handle.

TRIBE: So how long did it take you to do this?

TRESS: Dick used to take work home overnight carrying his portable machine, and would come back with more work done the next morning. It was a revolution that I could have a dozen students in that room doing statistics, actually working with figures which they could cope with mechanically. And that must have been, well, late 1950s.

TRIBE: Do you know of anywhere else that had that kind of facility? You could set these students all working on a particular problem, I assume.

TRESS: This was just for statistical teaching, you know. Previously, illustrations of how to calculate averages and dispersions had to be within the capacity of mental arithmetic. My second illustration is that when I went to Birkbeck in 1968 one of the first things I had to do was to get the existing equipment dismantled and the two technicians made redundant or redeployed, for the first electronic computer in the University of London.

TRIBE: In 1968? They didn't have anything before then at all?

TRESS: Well, they were getting around to it, but Birkbeck's had been the first one ever. It was Desmond Bernal, Professor of Crystallography, who got it installed. The University had established a number of institutes in subjects which weren't represented in the colleges. One such was the Institute of Computer Science. And it was well into the middle of my ten years at Birkbeck when that Institute was broken up and its members dispersed to the various colleges. Birkbeck was teaching Computer Science to both B.Sc. and M.Sc. students, both with the same programme. If you weren't a graduate then you did it for a general B.Sc. along with mathematics and statistics. If you were a graduate it would have been in something else. There were no computer science graduates; it is all as recent as that.

TRIBE: Going back to the immediate post-war period, one figure that remains rather hazy is John Jewkes. After the war he became very critical of planning in general. Was he always of that opinion, or did his experience of administration in the war make him particularly disillusioned?

---

[12] M. Chisholm and J. Oeppen, *The Changing Pattern of Employment: Regional Specialization and Industrial Localization in Britain*, Croom Helm, London, 1973.

TRESS: I don't know what he did pre-war, before I met him. I think he was certainly very much of a liberal–free trade outlook, and became rather possessed by that; but if I had to look for a reason within the background that I know I would quote, for example, the cotton industry, which was having problems. The rise of the Indian cotton industry, doing the simpler forms of cotton manufacture, was creating problems for the Lancashire cotton industry. The government set up a Cotton Industry Working Party to try and ration out the work of the cotton industry, with a Control Board. Jewkes was very much against that because the more advanced parts of the cotton industry, like Tootals and several firms of that sort, were moving into the higher technology field, and doing well. This in a sense bears out the proposition that one shouldn't try to hold back technological change. I don't know if my Fellowship had technically run out or not, but during the summer vacation between my going from Manchester to Exeter I got taken into servicing the Opposition Committee to the Cotton Industry Bill. I started with one bare room in an office down in the centre of Manchester, from where the resistance was to be organised. Jewkes was very much backing that, since it was the bright innovative firms that were on the up and didn't want to be constrained by any rationing process. Now it could be said that that was part of Jewkes' education, but it fitted in very well with his outlook. I think he became absorbed by it. It was Thatcherism before its time, so to speak! Although Alan Peacock, of course, was in the same mould.

TRIBE: *Ordeal by Planning*[13] is very generalised in its argument. It doesn't have a very strong critique of the instruments of government, or even of their objectives. It is not clear from reading it what the nature of a preferred order would be. It is much the same with Hayek, it is not at all clear what specific institutions and arrangements they would support, what kind of economic organisation they envisaged for the post-war world.

TRESS: It is all anti . . .

TRIBE: Jewkes was obviously quite important at the time, because he then went on to Oxford as Professor of Applied Economics. Do you know how that move from Manchester to Oxford took place? Did you have any contact with him at that time, in 1948, when he went to Oxford?

TRESS: I always had the impression that it was a big mistake. I didn't see an awful lot of him after that. He did in fact become a somewhat isolated figure; a bit isolated in the general Oxford context, I fancy, although Henry Clay and Norman Chester were both at Nuffield; but also one didn't see him around. I suppose if I had been involved in the IEA I might have seen more of him: he figured there. But I think he was never very happy in Oxford.

TRIBE: You went to Bristol in 1951 . . .

TRESS: As far as economics was concerned, that had been pretty old-fashioned, a man called Hamilton Whyte had been Professor, and then he

---

[13] J. Jewkes, *Ordeal by Planning*, Macmillan, London, 1948.

had recruited H.D. Dickinson. I say H.D. Dickinson, because he was known as Dick by everybody. Reading recently the tribute by Dorothy Hodgkin to Desmond Bernal, she suggests that Dick was one of the prime influences on Bernal in moving him from Catholicism to Marxism.

TRIBE: What was the contact between them?

TRESS: They were students at Cambridge. Bernal was an undergraduate, 1919–23. Dickinson, along with Maurice Dobb, was very much in the same left-wing context. Dickinson was an incredibly knowledgeable person. It was quite incredible, the range of his knowledge, he was a polymath, but he didn't do a lot of writing. He wrote one book, *Institutional Revenue*.[14] He was a marvellous teacher, although I think students didn't realise how good he was, except the ablest ones in their third year. They never quite knew what his lecture was going to be about; it would be interesting, but what had it got to do with the syllabus? And therefore a very agreeable person. It was just the beginning of the expansion period, and they advertised two Chairs. There was the Chair of Economics and a second Chair, and the outcome of the interviews was that next morning Philip Morris, the V-C, said to me, 'We want to appoint Dickinson to one of the Chairs, and you would have the other if you can establish a *modus vivendi*.' Sad story. We chatted about this, Dickinson and I, and we went back to Philip Morris and said, 'We think we get on very well, the only thing we can't settle is titles.' I said, 'I am quite willing for Dickinson to have the Professor of Economics title (which was the established chair) but coming to Bristol I do not want to be a Professor of Industrial Economics or Applied Economics. That is not my field.' Philip Morris said, 'Well, what about Political Economy?' I said. 'That suits me fine!' and Dickinson's face dropped! He said, 'Yes, that was Marshall's title.'[15]

But we got on very well. Harking back to my Civil Service experience, I played the Civil Servant and he played the Minister. That is to say, I did all the donkey work of getting what we wanted to do worked out, but when it came to making the speeches in the Faculty and so on I let Dickinson do that. He was much more effective at persuading people, and I think they trusted him more than they trusted me. It worked very well. We were appointed joint Heads of Department. Formally we told Philip Morris that Dickinson would be responsible for these things, and I would be responsible for those. In practice, whenever Philip Morris wrote a memo to Dickinson he sent me a copy. On the research side, the Department had this Reconstruction Unit. They had rustled up local funds from various sources with a group of people whom Dickinson had recruited, or Hamilton Whyte had recruited, I suppose, to work on the post-war problems of the area. And they recruited a range of people: Hugh Mackenzie who was a straightforward statistician; Kate

[14] H.D. Dickinson, *Institutional Revenue: A Study of the Influence of Social Institutions on the Distribution of Wealth*, Williams and Norgate, London, 1932.

[15] Alfred Marshall was Professor of Political Economy, University College Bristol from 1877 to 1883, and first Principal of the College from 1877 to 1881.

Liepmann, who had done work on women and labour; Howard Bracey, who was a specialist in rural sociology; and Derek Brooman, who was very much the junior. Besides them in the teaching department there was Miles Fleming who was very much an economic theorist, who had been originally a Belfast graduate, and Bryn Giles who came from Oxford. The Department was effectively *the* social sciences as far as the University was concerned. It included a Lecturer in Government, R.S. Milne, and one in Social Work, Lulie Shaw. We had Accountancy in a Pass degree with Economics, taught by the local professionals part-time. Very soon, the Unit was wound up.

The subsequent period was one in which there was much talk about setting up Management Schools, and there was some motivation in Bristol particularly with the Bristol Aeroplane Company, and the Imperial Tobacco Company. One of the attractions of Bristol was that the top people were there. They lived in the neighbourhood, and were keen to encourage the development of management education. But it didn't happen, because the Franks Report led to the establishment of the London Business School and the Manchester Business School, which concentrated resources there and any efforts we had rather atrophied. One outstanding feature was, however, in Accounting. The first thing we did was to establish an Honours degree in Economics and Accounting with a Professor of Accounting. I managed to get local funds for that, from the Imperial Tobacco Company, Bristol Aeroplane Company and the British Institute of Management, covering the salaries for five to seven years. I then recruited David Solomons to the Chair – he died quite recently. He was there only four years before he went to Pennsylvania, and became a major figure in American accounting. Initially, there was strong opposition from the national profession. They hadn't realised that with the opening up of university opportunities the profession could no longer recruit school-leavers as clerks. So they were very anti; but the irony was that, some fifteen years later, it was David Solomons that the Chartered Institute brought back to advise on education in accountancy! We got that Chair established and one or two other appointments, prior to the post-Robbins expansion. Then, very rapidly in the early 1960s, we separated out into independent departments both Politics and Social Administration (Social Work), with a wholly new Chair and a Department of Sociology quickly following in 1965 and thence to our own separate Faculty of Social Sciences in 1966.

8

TERENCE HUTCHISON

Terence Hutchison was born in Bournemouth in 1912 but lived in London until he went to Cambridge in 1931. He graduated with a First in Part II of the Economics Tripos in 1934; in that year there were six Firsts apart from Hutchison, including Brian Reddaway,[1] V.K.R.V. Rao,[2] and the Canadians Robert Bryce and Lorie Tarshis. Without any immediate prospects of employment, Hutchison attended lectures at the LSE until the spring of 1935, when he went as a *Lektor* to the University of Bonn, remaining there until 1938. While in Bonn he wrote *The Significance and Basic Postulates of Economic Theory*, an essay whose approach to economics is strongly influenced by logical positivism, and which earned him an uncomprehending critique from the pen of Frank Knight. After leaving Germany he found work as a teacher in Baghdad, and then in 1941 joined the Indian Army. Consequently, when he returned to England at the age of 33 he had few academic contacts, and began his university career at University College, Hull in 1946, taking up a vacancy created by the decision of the former Professor, Eric Roll, to remain in the Civil Service after his period with the British Food Mission in Washington. In 1947 he moved to the London School of Economics, and then in 1956 he became Professor of Economics at the University of Birmingham, a post which he held until his retirement in 1978. While at the LSE he published *A Review of Economic Doctrines* (1953), and he has continued to publish in the areas of the history and methodology of economics up to the mid-1990s.

The following is edited from two interviews conducted in Birmingham on 1 February 1994 and 17 August 1995, plus additions and corrections in the course of correspondence.

HUTCHISON: I began to get much more seriously interested in economics and politics in the summer of 1931, especially when I was between school and university in August and September, which coincided with the major

---

[1] See the interview with Reddaway pp. 71–85.
[2] See the comments of Cairncross (p. 38) and Singer (p. 59).

economic–political crisis in Britain. The Labour Government, unable to agree on cuts in public expenditure, was replaced by a National Government, which was followed by Britain leaving the Gold Standard. A General Election in October resulted in an overwhelming victory for the (mainly Conservative) National Government. I went up to Peterhouse in October 1931 to read Classics, but soon decided I would switch to economics and politics.

TRIBE: You went to Peterhouse presumably because of the Classics connection?

HUTCHISON: Not particularly. Peterhouse later became a rather Conservative History college. Butterfield wrote his *Whig Interpretation of History* while I was there. They had no economists and they looked with some disdain upon economics – my classics tutor was rather shocked at my turning away from Latin and Greek to economics and politics. Part I in Classics normally took two years, but I did it in one year and only got a Third, but I was keen to get on to economics and politics. Since Peterhouse didn't have a tutor for economics I was sent to Joan Robinson, who lived just up the street from Peterhouse with Austin; and I had two years tutoring from Joan Robinson. On the analysis, which I wasn't very good at, she was very helpful. The last term – in 1934 – she was having her first baby, so I was sent out to Kahn in King's College.

TRIBE: I've got the lecture list here from that time.

HUTCHISON: Oh, I remember this document. Well I started with Pigou: I think he must have been giving that course for twenty to thirty years or so. I liked him. He was a dry, witty lecturer. He was very lucid. Pigou, Arts School. Yes that's it – twice a week – Wednesdays and Fridays at 12.00. That's right. But then the next item you see is Politics. I wish there had been more politics, and probably I would have done better in politics and history than economics. There was Ernest Barker who was highly distinguished. He was at Peterhouse actually, and I knew him slightly. Then there was John Hilton. He was a character. He had come from the International Labour Office. He'd started in, I think, the Ministry of Labour, and he was a sort of folksy, Lancastrian type. There was a special Chair, the Montague Burton Chair of Industrial Relations.[3] I remember he later became a very popular media person, through radio. He gave regular weekly chats, although by that time I wasn't in the country. He talked about everyday things – practical things. But he was not at home with the Cambridge Economics Faculty. He thought they were much too abstract in their approach, and I sympathised with him to a large extent, and I still do. He ran a little evening discussion group. In the second year we had one course in economic history from C.R. Fay: he was a bit comic, yes. I think his economic history included the history of economic thought. 'Mr Clark' – that conceals Colin Clark, who became an ardent

---

[3] A benefaction of 18,858 £1 7 per cent shares in Montague Burton Limited was accepted by the Senate in October 1930 (see *Cambridge University Reporter*, vol. LXI, no. 6, 21 October 1930, p. 183). John Hilton, Assistant Secretary to the Ministry of Labour, was appointed to the Montague Burton Chair of Industrial Relations as from 9 May 1931.

Catholic and a rather conservative member of the Institute of Economic Affairs, but was then a Labour candidate. I can remember the first political debate in the Union I ever attended. It was at the time of this very acrimonious election, when Labour had been thrown out, and the National Government had come in and Labour was almost wiped out. They were reduced to 50 seats from getting on for 300, and Colin Clark was a Labour candidate in that election. But he did Statistics. He was a pretty poor lecturer, I remember. There were the 'Mays' exams at the end of the second year, which would be my first year in Economics, which I didn't do particularly well in. I put in all my serious work in the last year.

Of course, I heard Keynes for two years. He gave just eight lectures a year; and I see it is called here the 'Monetary Theory of Production'.[4] That was really the *General Theory* coming up. I remember the parts of the *General Theory*. Well, it was a tragedy – I lost my lecture notes. A lot of people have got interested in Keynes' lecture notes you know, and they study his changes through the early 1930s between the *Treatise* and the *General Theory*. I kept some lecture notes – but somehow or other, those got lost, probably during the war in Iraq or India. I would not have deliberately thrown them away – I can't think what happened. But I heard those eight lectures. That would have been in the autumn of 1932 and again in the following year when he included, which was to interest me later a lot, that last but one chapter in the *General Theory*, on his predecessors in the history of thought. The next man on the list: Gerald Shove, 'Production, Value and Distribution'. He was the best lecturer of the lot really, I think. He was a very good lecturer. I remember him mainly on wages. If you had asked me what the course had been I would have said it was on wages and the theory of wages; but it was evidently a bit wider than that. I think I am right in saying there were four, or perhaps five compulsory papers. There was 'Principles', which we called 'Theory', I suppose; and then there was 'Industry', 'Money' and 'Labour'. I also did papers on Public Finance and Politics. Then there was a compulsory essay paper.

TRIBE: How was the subject determined for that essay?

HUTCHISON: Well there was really no preparation for it. You simply had three hours. They had a list of perhaps four topics and you just had to write an essay on one of these. They were fairly broad subjects. There is a famous saying from Burke about the age of sophisters and economists being now upon us – I think that is what I wrote my essay on. Yes, if you count the essay there were five compulsory papers plus two optionals. You could do International Relations, or International Law was the subject then. Or you could do Statistics, and that would have been a useful thing to do, but I didn't do it because I was more interested in politics I suppose; so as I said, I did Public Finance and Politics.

---

[4] *Cambridge University Reporter*, vol. LXIV (1 October 1933), p. 55. See T.K. Rymes, *Keynes's Lectures, 1932–35*, Macmillan, Basingstoke, 1989, pp. 35–128, based mainly on the notes taken by Lorie Tarshis.

TRIBE: Your supervisions with Joan Robinson – what form did they take? Did you just have a weekly supervision on an essay?

HUTCHISON: You had to write an essay each week. She'd give you an essay. I think she had a number of prepared subjects. I learnt a lot about the geometry of the theory of the firm, value analysis, and so on. She could be quite caustic.

TRIBE: In *The Economics of Imperfect Competition* she thanks B.L. Hallwood of Peterhouse for the term 'monopsony'.[5]

HUTCHISON: That's right – yes. He did Classics; he was my Tutor in my first year. He is still alive and in his nineties. I think, his last job was Vice-Chancellor of Nottingham where Bob Coats took me along to see him again.

TRIBE: When you got a First the other names were Reddaway, Bryce, Cuthbertson, Rao, Lorie Tarshis and Thomas. How much contact did you have with these people?

HUTCHISON: Oh, I made friends. I suppose the one I got to know best was Rao, who was considerably older. He must have been in his late twenties by then. Tarshis and Bryce – I knew them a bit, and I knew them by sight. A.R. Thomas – I knew him a bit. He went into the Colonial Service, and I knew Reddaway slightly. But Rao I knew best. I eventually saw him in India later when I was in the army. He was a big man in Delhi.

TRIBE: What about the Political Economy Club in Cambridge?

HUTCHISON: Well, as an undergraduate who hadn't got anywhere and even done well in the Mays – the second year exam – I was no candidate for that. Of course, I was very keen to get some work as a tutor after I graduated, but there was very little of that in those days. I remember getting an invitation to the Cambridge Political Economy Club when I wasn't able to go back to Cambridge.

TRIBE: Cambridge was notorious in the 1930s, unlike the LSE, for its intellectual isolation from the Continent and from the United States. How did you form an interest in Austrian theory and methodology?

HUTCHISON: It was really Robbins' work which inspired this idea. I got interested in philosophy and methodology because I had two friends in Cambridge who were note-takers for Wittgenstein. One, Goodstein, had been at a prep school with me, and the other, Francis Skinner, had been at St Paul's, where he had got to know Goodstein.

TRIBE: It was in your last year, 1933–34, that Wittgenstein dictated the Blue Book to his class.

HUTCHISON: I remember that, they were his *amanuenses*. I would very much have liked to have gone, but it was quite difficult to get in, and I was sweating away to get a degree.[6]

TRIBE: The classes were in Trinity?

---

[5] J. Robinson, *The Economics of Imperfect Competition*, Macmillan, London, 1933, p. 215.

[6] The Blue Book was a duplicated set of lecture notes dictated to a select group of five students, including Goodstein and Skinner, for circulation to other students – see R. Monk, *Ludwig Wittgenstein: The Duty of Genius*, Vintage Books, London, 1991, p. 336. See also p. 359 for Goodstein's views on Skinner's decision to discontinue academic life.

HUTCHISON: Yes, they would have been in his rooms in Trinity, Whewell Court, ten or a dozen people. Goodstein was still an undergraduate, he was about the same age as me, or even younger. I got interested in that kind of philosophy and I picked up one or two phrases, and quoted Wittgenstein. I suppose that was the beginnings of some sort of philosophical interest. I showed Goodstein Joan Robinson's book;[7] he and Francis Skinner were always rather sceptical, and now I think Goodstein was quite right in saying that, methodologically, it didn't make sense! But I didn't realise that at the time!

TRIBE: When you went to the LSE you said that you sat in on lectures.

HUTCHISON: That was in the winter of 1934–35: I was 22 at that time. I was an Occasional Student, I didn't have tuition. I could use the library, and I went to courses by Hicks and Hayek. Hicks did a course on the theory of value; he began it with a bit of history. He was a pretty difficult lecturer to follow, he has the reputation of *not* being a good lecturer! Hayek lectured on the Theory of Capital and on the Business Cycle, and they were both pretty difficult to follow. I was mildly interested in them, but I was more interested in doing my own work and using the library.

TRIBE: Did you go to Robbins' lectures at all?

HUTCHISON: No, I didn't go to his lectures then, I went after the war. But it was Robbins who aroused my interest in the Austrians, in Pareto and people like that; he made me want to read German by the way he had drawn on people like Max Weber and Carl Menger. His *Essay on the Nature and Significance of Economic Science*[8] came out in 1932, just at the time to capture me. English economics was very, very insular at that time and Robbins did broaden people's interests, and he had that effect on me at a distance; he made me want to learn German. I reacted in a very big way, both negatively and positively, to Robbins. I reacted rather negatively to his methodology, but his opening-up of windows on Austrian and German economics very much interested me. I thought he went for the wrong people, on the whole! I was beginning to learn a bit of German, although I hadn't done any in school. And I was not particularly good at languages.

I went to the National Union of Students with a view to fixing up an *au pair* arrangement, and was offered a job as a *Lektor* in Bonn, which I started in April 1935, the same month that my mother died and our home began to break up. My first idea was to go there for perhaps six months, at the most one year. It was comparatively well paid, as pay went in those days, I suppose I got the equivalent of £250–£300 a year, which was more or less an Assistant Lecturer's salary in those days. There was very little work, and not a great deal in the way of preparation, so I got on with my own work. There was of course this general atmosphere which gradually intensified and got worse and worse,

---

[7] *The Economics of Imperfect Competition*; in a letter of 12 November 1996 Terence Hutchison explained that it was Ch. 17, Section 1, 'A Digression on the Buyer' where Joan Robinson discusses what she described as 'The fundamental assumptions of economic analysis'.

[8] Macmillan, London, 1932; 2nd edn, Macmillan, London, 1935.

and I cleared out. It was high time to clear out, in the summer of 1938, just before the Munich crisis.

TRIBE: You must have done a great deal of reading in Bonn in method and philosophy. Did that come from the original ideas that you had started to pick up in Cambridge? Robbins' book created quite a stir, but there was not a great deal of related publication in English on methodological issues at that time.

HUTCHISON: No, I started with Wittgenstein's *Tractatus*! I can't remember the exact chain of events, but through Wittgenstein I got interested in the Vienna Circle. Carnap came to London and gave three lectures at Bedford College which I heard.[9] There was a Professor at Bedford College whose work I found pretty good, Susan Stebbing. Through those I got on to the Vienna Circle. I could use the LSE library, and when I learned German I was able to read more.

At the moment I am writing something on the spread of international ideas and the steps in that process. One such step occurred at the LSE in the early 1930s, when Hayek had recently arrived, and Robbins' interest in German material was reflected in the Reprint series, not always of course in translation. Later in the 1930s the climate was not so favourable, and Robbins distanced himself from the Austrian influence. I was against the Austrian influences he was keen on, especially Mises. But he played a major role in opening up economics to international influences. I can say that I already thought then, although goodness knows I was juvenile, that the only stuff that mattered for Cambridge was what was written in Cambridge! There might be one or two books that might be worth reading that were not written in Cambridge, but precious few! And I thought that was somehow rather narrow-minded and provincial. I was rather keen on seeing what other people had written. I thought that these people had something to say relevant to the criticism of economic theory; some of them did and some of them didn't.

TRIBE: When you were in Bonn you carried on this work, but you also visited Vienna?

HUTCHISON: Yes, but that was as a tourist, I didn't really see anybody. I went there in the summer of 1934 after I had finished at Cambridge, when of course I didn't know anybody and some of the economists were already beginning to leave.

TRIBE: Morgenstern didn't leave until 1938, did he?

HUTCHISON: Yes, but those contacts were only in writing; I did submit my work to them. The Vienna *Zeitschrift für Nationalökonomie* was a very great international journal in the 1930s until the Nazi takeover in 1938: they published Myrdal, American and English work, Hicks. It interested me. I didn't meet Morgenstern until after the war, but I corresponded, and he published two of my first four publications.

---

[9] R. Carnap, *Philosophy and Logical Syntax*, Routledge, London, 1935; lectures given at Bedford College, October 1934.

TRIBE: One of them, 'Expectation and Rational Conduct',[10] was a section from the book, but the other one does not seem to have such a clear relationship.

HUTCHISON: 'Theoretische Ökonomie als Sprachsystem'[11] was also more or less in the book, but a bit revised. There was a third piece for the *Zeitschrift*, a review of Lindley Fraser's *Economic Thought and Language*.[12] He must have been a bright chap – he was Professor at Aberdeen at a very early age, but then went into the German Service of the BBC during the war and stayed in it after the war; he never went back to economics. But he wrote that book, and Morgenstern gave it to me to review, it was about the first book review I ever wrote.

TRIBE: I hadn't realised until I looked at the *Zeitschrift* recently that Stonier was working on similar lines at this time; he published, in German, a piece on methodology, he reviewed Robbins in the *Zeitschrift* in 1934 . . .[13]

HUTCHISON: Did he? I must have read that but don't remember it. Of course, I didn't agree with Alf Stonier at all! I only got to know him later, and I knew him really quite closely for a few years as examiner in London. It was a mountainous job, and we would work for a week or two very closely together. We never argued about methodology; we knew we disagreed fundamentally, and this was after we'd both been interested in methodology. Yes, Robbins refers to Alf Stonier in the 'Foreword' to his *Essay*, in perhaps the second edition.

TRIBE: Yes, it is the second edition. Stonier was at University College at that time, together with Gaitskell and Rosenstein-Rodan. Gaitskell spent the academic year 1934–35 in Vienna as a Rockefeller Fellow,[14] and also published a two-part essay on Austrian capital theory.[15] It is usually assumed that the Austrian influence on British economics came through the LSE, with Robbins and Hayek, but in fact it is much broader than that. Reading through your 'Theoretische Ökonomie als Sprachsystem' it struck me, more forcibly than I remember in the book, the extent to which it is indebted to the basic distinction between analytic and synthetic statements which is fundamental to the Logical Positivist enterprise.

HUTCHISON: I think that's a useful distinction for this confused business of economic 'theory'; I've always thought that, and still think that. I would not be dogmatic as to whether this distinction should be regarded as a comprehensive or exclusive dichotomy. But I am not aware of any testable statements,

---

[10] 'Expectation and Rational Conduct', *Zeitschrift für Nationalökonomie*, Bd 8 (1938), pp. 636–53.

[11] 'Theoretische Ökonomie als Sprachsystem', *Zeitschrift für Nationalökonomie*, Bd 8 (1937), pp. 78–90.

[12] 'Review of L.M. Fraser, *Economic Thought and Language: A Critique of Some Fundamental Economic Concepts* (1937)', *Zeitschrift für Nationalökonomie*, Bd 9 (1938), pp. 109–11.

[13] A.W. Stonier, 'Review of L. Robbins, *An Essay on the Nature and Significance of Economic Science* (1932)', *Zeitschrift für Nationalökonomie*, Bd 5 (1934), pp. 417–24.

[14] P.M. Williams, *Hugh Gaitskell: A Political Biography*, Jonathan Cape, London, 1979, pp. 52–8.

[15] 'Notes on the Period of Production', 2 parts, *Zeitschrift für Nationalökonomie*, Bd 7 (1936), pp. 577–95; Bd 9 (1938), pp. 215–44.

significant in economics, which cannot be adequately interpreted as *either* analytic, *or* synthetic. I am reasonably clear as to how one can try to test analytic and synthetic statements (i.e. purely logically or mathematically, on the one hand, or empirically or historically, on the other). Those who think otherwise should first, list clearly a number of statements *in economics* (not simply in academic philosophy) which cannot adequately be treated as analytic or synthetic, and are not seriously ambiguous; and second, explain *how these statements are conceivably testable.* I object, in a serious and highly controversial subject, to being confronted with statements which are not conceivably testable and are not to be interpreted as ethical. Incidentally, I was never a thoroughgoing Logical Positivist.

TRIBE: Another part of that essay which becomes a major section of the book is the treatment of rationality and expectations. Shortly before that in the *Zeitschrift* Morgenstern had published an article on foresight. Was that influential for your work?[16]

HUTCHISON: 'Vollkommene Voraussicht' . . . Yes, I think that article would have been 1934; I remember struggling to read that when I didn't know German. I couldn't read it properly until about a year later.

TRIBE: You said that you had differences with Stonier; were these theoretical, or methodological?

HUTCHISON: Methodological, or philosophical – Stonier produced what must have been his doctoral thesis, in German, in Heidelberg; and I would have read that at some stage.[17] But it was on very different lines – he would have followed Max Weber, developing an argument about *Verstehen*, which is alright as far as it goes, but one can make too much of it. But I went off in the opposite direction.

TRIBE: At LSE the Continental tradition in the 1930s has come to be associated with Hayek, and so 'Continental' has become equivalent to 'Austrian'. But there were others, for example, Moritz Bonn came over as an exile, together with a few others. But this importance ascribed to Hayek is a later construction; what strikes me is that Hayek's direct influence, even upon his immediate colleagues, was during the 1930s relatively slight.

HUTCHISON: I would say that there was great initial interest, but that it fairly soon faded.

TRIBE: People who were at the LSE as students or as staff in the late 1930s and 1940s never seem to mention him as a major figure.

HUTCHISON: No, I don't think he was, until later. I'm just reading Ronald Coase's book of essays, he's got one on the LSE in the 1930s.[18] He says that

---

[16] O. Morgenstern, 'Vollkommene Voraussicht und wirtschaftliches Gleichgewicht', *Zeitschrift für Nationalökonomie*, Bd 6 (1935), pp. 337–57.

[17] A.W. Stonier, *Der logische Charakter der Wirtschaftswissenschaft*, Carl Winter Universitätsbuchhandlung, Heidelberg, 1935.

[18] R.H. Coase, 'Economics at LSE in the 1930s: A Personal View', in his *Essays on Economics and Economists*, University of Chicago Press, Chicago, 1994, pp. 208–14.

Hayek's initial lectures, before he was appointed, on prices and production, created terrific interest. They may have done, it was something very strange, but I don't think it lasted. It rather fizzled out. A man I came to know later was Ludwig Lachmann. He was at the LSE, had emigrated in 1933 as soon as Hitler came to power. Lachmann was from Berlin, he was a pupil of Sombart. One could quite understand that he wouldn't call himself a German on arriving in London in 1933! He linked up with Hayek and always called himself an 'Austrian economist'. But the idea that had come through in that brand of Austrian economics was thoroughly German. Lachmann remained influenced by German philosophy right to the end; for example he championed Gadamer and hermeneuticism, which I am afraid is not my line at all! You could say that many influences on Carl Menger were more German than Austrian. If you can say that there is Austrian philosophy, then it is people like – I can claim to have quoted them in my book – Ernst Mach, Wittgenstein, Popper, Schlick. Schlick was born in Berlin, but he was the pillar, or even the leader, of the Vienna Circle. And, if you like, that could be Austrian philosophy. But it is pretty fundamentally opposed, on most points relevant to methodology and economics, to German ideas. When you think of the *Methodenstreit*, many people seem to think that it is an argument between Germans and 'Austrians'. Well, it was more often a battle between two sorts of Germans!

TRIBE: The names that you list with respect to Vienna, or Austria, do bring out a clear German–Austrian difference – Popper and Schlick and Carnap and Neurath . . .

HUTCHISON: I would say that the oldest of those was Ernst Mach. I have read *Erkenntnis und Irrtum*, although I can't claim to have read a terrific amount of Mach; I like some of his phrases, though, and I think he influenced Popper. I was puzzled to read that Hayek said he been influenced by Ernst Mach. Now I don't know enough about Ernst Mach. It could be to do with his writings on psychology, and the one book of Hayek's that I haven't read is *The Sensory Order*.[19]

TRIBE: Did you try to get a post in Britain before leaving for the Middle East in 1938?

HUTCHISON: I remember trying for one in Bristol and not getting it. But I was very keen to see the Middle East; so I went out there, I was at Baghdad for two and a half years. Academic positions were very few and far between in the 1930s. By that time the war had started so I left there and joined the army. So you see I didn't really get a job in economics, or see anything of economics departments in England, or any other country. In Baghdad I was supposed to be teaching the social sciences, but really they knew so little English I was teaching them English. Trying to explain to them what these very elementary little textbooks meant, rather than anything else; and I didn't know any Arabic, of course. So I had written this book which appeared in 1938, but

---

[19] F.A. Hayek, *The Sensory Order*, Routledge and Kegan Paul, London, 1952.

then the war came; so I didn't really take up with economics departments until I came back after the war in 1946.

TRIBE: But the book got reviewed and noticed – you had the exchange in the *Journal of Political Economy* with Frank Knight.[20]

HUTCHISON: It was marvellous publicity! He wrote an absolutely blistering review which they had to give me space to reply to. I was in Baghdad then. I must have had a copy of my own book, I think – I don't quite know – but that was about it. I mean, there may have been a few books around. I had read the odd books, and Hicks' *Value and Capital.* Apart from the Knight review, there was one by Stonier, who reviewed it rather unfavourably and rather curtly in the *Economic Journal.*[21] It wasn't reviewed in *Economica,* I've never had much of a press in *Economica.* The best review article came from a chap who was a very nice man, though of course I regard him as totally misguided: Maurice Dobb in *Science and Society* in 1938.[22] It was mainly kind and favourable. I think that review lost me a job after the war! When I got back from the army in India after the war I was applying for jobs and I went up to Leeds, where there was a chap called Richardson. I don't say that I was all that strong a candidate, but I had a reference from Dobb. I hardly knew Maurice Dobb – once I went to his house in Cambridge, must have been about 1934 – and I had pretty few referees, and as he'd written a favourable review I asked him to be a referee.

TRIBE: You got a job, however, at Hull.

HUTCHISON: Yes, the man who took me on there was the Acting Head. Eric Roll had gone into the government, and they were hoping that he would come back. They kept his post open, but then he carried on in the Civil Service. In 1945–46 Lachmann was Acting Head, but he didn't get the Chair: they gave it to Ian Bowen in 1947, I think, when I left. Soon after that Ludwig got an offer from Leicester, but then went out to Johannesburg.

TRIBE: How did you get that job?

HUTCHISON: Adverts in the paper. We came back in April 1946. I had three children by then – I had a sort of gratuity, but I had to get a job at that stage, and I applied to one or two places. I didn't get a job at Manchester, I remember. Or Exeter. And then I thought I might try for the Civil Service; but then I got one at Hull, and was, and remain, very glad I did.

TRIBE: When I talked to Eric Roll about his teaching in Hull during the 1930s it seemed that the bulk of his teaching was taken up with extra-mural work. Had that changed by the late 1940s?

HUTCHISON: It must have changed quite a bit; I taught one extra-mural course over in Grimsby, I remember it was quite an expedition across the

---

[20] F. Knight, '"What is Truth" in Economics?', *Journal of Political Economy,* vol. 48 (1940), pp. 1–32; T.W. Hutchison, '*The Significance and Basic Postulates of Economic Theory.* A Reply to Professor Knight', *Journal of Political Economy,* vol. 49 (1941), pp. 732–50; F. Knight, 'A Rejoinder', *Journal of Political Economy* vol. 49 (1941), pp. 750–3.

[21] Review by A.W. Stonier, *Economic Journal,* vol. 49 (1939), pp. 114–15.

[22] *Science and Society,* vol. 3, no. 3 (Summer 1939), pp. 389ff.

estuary. No, I did all my teaching in Hull, this was an extra, to make a little extra money.

TRIBE: Roll was heavily engaged in this work . . .

HUTCHISON: He probably had very few students, but by my time I presume there were quite a few more. They weren't big classes, and the History of Economic Thought was a comparatively small one, it may have been around eight or nine people. This was of course the external London degree.

TRIBE: Was that both B.Com. and B.Sc. (Econ.)?

HUTCHISON: Well, I didn't do much B.Com. teaching. I did an elementary statistics course for the first year, that might have been for the B.Com. Goodness knows what I knew about that! There was Ludwig Lachmann; Dennis Rotheray from Cambridge, very bright but I don't think he published anything; he spent his career there, retired recently. And then coming up from London to teach economic history was a man who became subsequently famous – MacGregor, who ended up in the Press Commission. He was a social historian, a pupil of Beales, he came up for about one day a week. Otherwise it was me, Rotheray and Lachmann. They probably had someone in to teach accounting.

When I came back in 1946 I needed a terrific re-education in economics, I'd been out of the subject for ten years, I hadn't done any serious work since 1937 when I finished my book. Included among the bits and pieces was a course on the History of Economic Thought, which was the first I'd ever taught. I was reading the stuff up each week before giving the lecture. Then I applied for a job at the LSE, and got it. Robbins gave me two very congenial courses. I gave a course on the History of Economic Controversies. It wasn't my idea. Robbins suggested it. My other course was on the History of Economic Thought after 1870, which eventually I wrote up. I wish I had written up the course on methodological controversies.

TRIBE: So, when you started with that course in Hull did you use Alexander Gray's book?[23] Bob Coats says that you used that in Hull.[24]

HUTCHISON: Yes, I used that on the course up at Hull. Well, that was the little textbook – that was what I began from, and I was sort of reading the stuff about a week ahead of the students, I suppose. Oh, it was a nice bright little book in its day, and we could do with another book like that.

TRIBE: It is very striking that book, because it stops with the Austrians, doesn't include Marshall and devotes a lot of space to . . .

HUTCHISON: Isn't Marshall somehow mentioned?

TRIBE: He was mentioned at the end.

HUTCHISON: Oh, that's about it, a mention – yes.

TRIBE: There is also a chapter on Bastiat and Carey, and also on Müller and List; and so the balance of the nineteenth century, given it starts with the

---

[23] A. Gray, *The Development of Economic Doctrine*, Longmans, Green and Co., London, 1931.

[24] A.W. Coats, 'T.W. Hutchison as a Historian of Economics', *Research in the History of Economic Thought and Methodology*, vol. 1 (1983), p. 191.

Greeks, is quite interesting, and relates to the sort of work and the sort of writing that you later did. Did you choose that deliberately, or was it simply because there was . . .?

HUTCHISON: Oh no. It was the obvious book. I mean, I don't know if there was any competitor around then. A purely elementary book, which is really all we could do. I am trying to think of what other stuff I had tried to get them to read, but I can't think of it now. Well, there were various articles like Keynes' *Essays on Biography* and his piece on Marshall, and so on. Certainly Gray's book was rather peculiar. It certainly looks that now, as he treated the later part of the nineteenth century.

TRIBE: You also later wrote a book on economic policy, where you deliberately use newspapers as your principal source.[25]

HUTCHISON: I wrote a new introduction to the new edition, about two or three pages. When I began, the idea was to do a rather waspish pamphlet about how wrong leading British economists had been when they wrote about economic policies; the wrong predictions they made. Particularly people like Harrod and Balogh, who were my two *bêtes noires* – one on the Conservative side and one on the Left. But then there seemed to be so much of it. I don't think academic economists these days are sticking their necks out to the extent that they did after the war, when economics was riding very high.

TRIBE: These days we are used to reading economic journalists in the press, not academic economists. But up to the late 1960s much of the comment was written by academics, and you used this material in your book.

HUTCHISON: On the whole, the decent economic journalist hadn't really appeared. Samuel Brittan is *the* type. Peter Jay wrote an appalling, a very severe review, well, I mean he was a great Kaldor fan, and I answered him in *The Times*.[26]

TRIBE: So in fact these journalists – Brittan, Lawson, Hutton, Jay, and so on – are a product of the expansion of economics in the 1950s. Sam Brittan graduated in 1955, I think.

HUTCHISON: That's right. He began being noticed as a writer not until the 1960s, I think.

TRIBE: But you use a lot of newspaper material in this. Had you been collecting it for some time, or how did you find the material?

HUTCHISON: I waste too much time reading newspapers, and always have, including the weeklies! There are certain sources, you don't find them in *The Times* correspondence column these days. But, I mean, Harrod and Balogh were writing to *The Times* about every month airing their views.

TRIBE: You kept all those?

---

[25] T.W. Hutchison, *Economics and Economic Policy in Britain, 1946–1966*, George Allen and Unwin, London, 1968; reprinted 1992 by Gregg Revivals, Aldershot.
[26] Peter Jay, *The Times*, 15 August 1968, p. 18; reply appeared 10 September 1968, p. 23.

HUTCHISON: Oh, I kept those, yes. I collected them for a few years and then it seemed to grow. I have never had a research assistant except on this occasion for a few months when I was at Yale during 1963 to 1964. I had a research assistant there, I got him to look up all the things in *The Times* index for me; that was for a few months in 1964 and I've never had any other research assistant for any of my jobs.

TRIBE: But your reputation in the 1950s was established mainly as a historian of economics?

HUTCHISON: Oh, yes.

TRIBE: How, then, did that fit with the move to Birmingham? I understand that in Birmingham around the mid-1950s Gilbert Walker had been Professor of Economics, but when Sargant Florence retired, he shifted over to Commerce . . .

HUTCHISON: That's right.

TRIBE: . . . and then the Mitsui chair became free . . .

HUTCHISON: That's right.

TRIBE: But Frank Hahn says of Birmingham in the early part of the 1950s that Gilbert Walker encouraged them in mathematical economics.[27] By the late 1950s there was an equal number of commerce, economics and econometrics and statistics appointments. Weren't you really a bit of a surprise appointment?

HUTCHISON: I should think I was for some of them! Well, there were the most awful tensions, I think. I certainly didn't get on with Gilbert Walker at all well.

TRIBE: He was primarily a transport economist, wasn't he?

HUTCHISON: That's right. He had done PPE at Oxford. He made a good many enemies around the University and these young mathematics types were regarded as highly bumptious. Don't ask me whether that was justified or not. And the Vice-Chancellor was a rather grim Scottish New Zealand type. He was a really efficient man and one must pay him that tribute, and I think the Faculty was split between Walker, who was popular with the younger lecturers like Hahn and Walters, and the other more senior people in chairs and the Vice-Chancellor. And I was brought in, I suppose, as the candidate of the forces of 'reaction', if you like! It was a very split Faculty. But these Young Turk types: well, they varied a lot. Some were awful and some were not so bad. They went on to higher things more or less in due course. Alan Walters at least had some interest in the real world. I suppose Hahn and Gorman *thought* they had an interest in the real world, but they didn't realise it *wasn't* the real world up on the blackboard which they were manipulating so magnificently.

TRIBE: Walters was there from the early 1950s, wasn't he, until 1968 or 1969 when he went to the LSE?

---

[27] F. Hahn, 'Autobiographical Notes with Reflections', in M. Szenberg, *Eminent Economists: Their Life Philosophies*, Cambridge University Press, Cambridge, 1992, p. 162.

HUTCHISON: That's right.

TRIBE: Birmingham is relatively unusual in the British scene, for it had right from the early 1950s a number of strong representatives of the new, for-malised mathematical economics . . .

HUTCHISON: That was Hahn and Gorman. That's right.

TRIBE: Whereas, for example, in Cambridge, where they also have a lot of appointments in the late 1940s and early 1950s it doesn't go that way at all. Why should places like Birmingham, and also Nottingham, become the focus for the development of mathematical economics?

HUTCHISON: Well, that certainly wasn't the intention of Sargant Florence, who would have been the senior man responsible. Or the intention of Gilbert Walker. Gilbert Walker and Sargant Florence were quite non-mathematical, but they chose these bright young men. In a way, you see, they had the new ideas. Gilbert Walker, except for transport economics, wasn't doing much and there wasn't anybody else. And they rather dominated the economics.

TRIBE: During your period as Professor in Birmingham, staff exchanges with American universities became more common.

HUTCHISON: Well, the great thing about Birmingham was they were very liberal about giving leave. You could almost get leave whenever you wanted it, provided you didn't want your salary. If you are getting paid twice as much in America that was quite alright.

TRIBE: What did you teach in Birmingham?

HUTCHISON: I taught a big first-year course – that was the main thing I taught.

TRIBE: What textbooks did you use?

HUTCHISON: The pretty obvious ones: I have always quite liked Samuelson. I quite like Lipsey.

TRIBE: But Lipsey's *Positive Economics* wasn't published until 1963?

HUTCHISON: No, I would have used Samuelson. Well, Cairncross was still available. And I taught a History of Economic Thought course, and I taught on a subject which I still think is a good one – and, indeed, a very necessary one – called 'The Principles of Economic Policy'. Robbins had given a course called 'Principles of Economic Policy' which I only heard bits of. I went to hear him give it at the School.

TRIBE: When did you retire?

HUTCHISON: 1978. I could have gone on one more year. I wish I had retired earlier now, really. I have seen so many complaints from the people who have become economists in business or government that what they learned at the University wasn't much use. You might well ask who am I to castigate aca-demic economics, having devoted much of my life to the History of Economic Thought, which is a highly academic subject. I think it provides an under-standing of the relation between institutional change and the development of analytical argument.

9

ARTHUR BROWN

A.J. Brown was born in 1914 and attended Bradford Grammar School before going up to Oxford to read Physics in 1933, switching to the PPE in which he gained a First in 1936. He stayed on in Oxford, completed graduate work, and was in 1937 a Fellow of All Souls and a temporary Lecturer in Economics at Hertford College, Oxford. During the war he worked for the Foreign Office, moving to the Economic Section in 1945. In 1947 he was appointed Professor of Economics at Leeds, a position he retained until his retirement in 1979. The following is an edited version of an interview conducted in Professor Brown's home in Headingley, Leeds, on 25 May 1994.

TRIBE: In your memories of Oxford,[1] you state that when you went to Oxford you intended to do natural science?

BROWN: Well, it would have been physics, I think.

TRIBE: What made you choose to change to PPE, and choose to focus upon economics within the PPE curriculum?

BROWN: Well, I had always been interested in that sort of thing. I had been brought up very conscious of political and quasi-economic discussion. My parents were manager and manageress of the Liberal Club in Bradford, so it was that sort of atmosphere. So I got very interested in current affairs when I was in the sixth form. I knew that there were one or two precedents of people going up from Bradford Grammar School on science scholarships and changing to PPE. So when I got my scholarship I asked if I could change and they said, 'Well, come up and do an examination.' So I went up and did an examination and they let me change.

TRIBE: So you changed before you started in Oxford, rather than after your first year?

BROWN: I didn't actually do any sciences at Oxford.

TRIBE: Have you got any idea of how many there were similar to you within the PPE doing the economics stream?

---

[1] A.J. Brown, 'A Worm's Eye View of the Keynesian Revolution', in J. Hillard (ed.) *J.M. Keynes in Retrospect*, Edward Elgar, Aldershot, 1988, pp. 18–44.

BROWN: No, I figure . . . Would it make sense to say that the number taking PPE altogether in the year was about 150? Well, how many were taking the two special subjects in economics, that is the mark of an economist, I suppose. I should have thought that it was a fairly good proportion – more than a third.

TRIBE: But, for example, when you took Macgregor's seminar?[2] How many people would have been at the meetings?

BROWN: At Macgregor's seminars there would be about six or ten.

TRIBE: What determined who would go to the more advanced economics seminars like Macgregor's?

BROWN: It was inclination plus the advice of their tutors so far as I can remember. Macgregor would offer this seminar and a few people would be advised to go to it. Macgregor was a bit of a lone wolf. For one thing he wasn't the man he had been. He was blown up badly in 1918 and he was never quite himself after that, I think. He remembered things before better than he remembered things since. I always thought he was very good value because his approach was just a bit different from everybody else's, and he was knowledgeable, and he was extremely conscientious. He was my examiner for the D.Phil. and he informed me that one of my correlations would sink from 0.9 to 0.6 if I missed two dates out, you know. He was all there. But people regarded him as somehow speaking from a different world. He was not fashionable.

TRIBE: He came before the newer developments, or the recruitment in the 1930s.

BROWN: I remember being told that he was very much wanted by Oxford. He was Professor at Manchester at that time, and he was perfectly happy there. He didn't want to move again, I think. And eventually he received a personal letter from the Chancellor begging him to accept the appointment in Oxford. They were very short of people who they thought were good enough.

TRIBE: Who was your tutor at Queens?

BROWN: Lindley Fraser[3] first, and then Charlie Hitch.[4]

TRIBE: Hitch was the one who suggested your D.Phil. topic, wasn't it? So would you say Hitch was one of the major influences on you while you were . . .?

BROWN: Oh, very much, yes. Very much.

TRIBE: Was there anybody else who you can think of particularly?

BROWN: Well, I suppose, Fraser influenced me a lot. After all, he taught me for two and a bit out of the three years.

---

[2] D.H. Macgregor was Drummond Professor of Political Economy from 1921 to 1945.

[3] Lindley Fraser (1904–63) was Fellow and Praelector in Economics, Queen's College, Oxford from 1928–35 and then Professor of Economics at Aberdeen from 1935 to 1946. He subsequently became head of the German and Austrian section of the BBC World Service.

[4] Charles Hitch (1910–95) was Fellow, Lecturer and Tutor in Economics, Queen's College, Oxford from 1935 until 1948 when he left to join the Rand Corporation. He was leter U.S. Assistant Secretary of Defense 1961–65.

TRIBE: Was that because you started off with him and then you went over to Hitch?

BROWN: That's right, yes. Fraser went to the Chair at Aberdeen at the end of my second year, and he came back to Oxford once a fortnight to take those who were doing a special subject with him. Whichever it was I was doing with him. Money, I think it was. I did take that with him actually, not with Charlie. Charlie Hitch tutored me in my second term of my final year. And in the final term I think he ran a seminar which I went to. He was a different sort of animal from Fraser. Fraser was a philosopher turned economist. Charlie was just an economist *ab initio*.

TRIBE: In retrospect, looking back at your time as a PPE student, how far do you think there was a difference between you as a representative of Oxford PPE, and those who had gone through the economics course at the LSE or out of the Cambridge Tripos? Have you any idea, comparing the approach you were taught, or the strengths or weaknesses that you had, compared with people trained in Cambridge and London at the same time?

BROWN: Well, my impression is that it was different from Cambridge because in Cambridge you had the older generation who thought it was all in Marshall, and you had bright young things like Joan Robinson, who were breaking the mould. Oxford wasn't like that. There wasn't anything corresponding to the founding fathers who thought it was all in Marshall. They were all bright relatively young things and they were all a bit different from each other. The influence of Cambridge wasn't as great as you might have expected considering how important Cambridge had been and was then being in economics, apart from the influence of Keynes, which came through Harrod and Meade, and a bit more indirectly through some of the others. I think the main difference is that we didn't have a bible called the *Principles of Economics*.

TRIBE: You say in your reminiscences that after you had done your first year they used Taussig in Oxford. Taussig's *Principles of Economics*.

BROWN: Taussig, yes. Not an inspiring work. Well, the question is, what sort of alternative was there? Taussig was a bit like Marshall, but not quite. The books that were really new were not written. I always thought the first book that was really new and different that might have been regarded as a general textbook, some people might think it was a general textbook, was Meade's *Introduction to Economic Analysis and Policy*. That was produced in the year I took Finals. And, then, of course the book that really got into circulation as the new kind of textbook was Hick's *Social Framework*. Before that there was Taussig and there was Benham.

TRIBE: The other thing that relates to Oxford is that it appears to have a much more empirical, statistical kind of bias than Cambridge. In Manchester, for example, there are a number of people, Devons and others, who ended up in the Ministry of Aircraft Production. Were you conscious when you were doing your graduate work that there was this difference between, say, Oxford and Cambridge, and also to a large extent the LSE as well?

BROWN: Oh, yes. Oh, yes. The empirical influence in Oxford was the Institute of Statistics, and Marschak,[5] ably supported by Phelps Brown.[6] I went to the Institute for my graduate work, a year after it was founded. It was founded in 1935. There was a bunch of people there who had come from various places. All were doing empirical work of one sort or another, with Marschak very much in the middle.

TRIBE: How did you finance your graduate work then, when you decided to do the D.Phil?

BROWN: The Webb-Medley Senior Scholarship. There is a sort of university prize or scholarship called the Webb-Medley, which has a junior version for which you compete at the end of your second year, and senior versions for which you compete at the end of your third year. The third year, the senior, is given on the results of Finals. The Junior Scholarship was small, it didn't revolutionise my life! But the Senior Scholarship was such that I didn't have to bother about being financed.

TRIBE: The existence of the Institute must have been a focus for a number of graduates. Do you know roughly how many graduates there were in total working there at the time? At that time in Cambridge, as opposed to the LSE, there were no more than about a dozen people doing graduate work.

BROWN: Yes. I don't think there would be anybody doing graduate work of anything like an empirical nature in Oxford that I wouldn't have come across in the Institute. There would be about a dozen I suppose. There was Teddy Jackson, who became the Director of the Institute later on. There was George Shackle. George Shackle had a composite nature. He was partly himself and partly a research assistant to Henry Phelps Brown. He combined these two. There were people who were on various tickets. There was Betty Ackroyd who finished up as being Dame Elizabeth Ackroyd – Chairman of the Consumers Council. Which ticket was she on? I rather think she was doing . . . there was an Oxford Social Survey going on. I think she was connected with that. The two bits of it that I ever caught up with were the bit that was about employment at Morris' and the bit that was about mobility of labour – labour migration. I think Elizabeth Ackroyd was attached to that. And then there was another character who was attached to that, and who worked for the Institute. The Institute was a sort of lost dogs' home, you see. If you wanted to do empirical work you came and sat there. Goronwy Daniel, who finished up as Principal of Aberystwyth. He was Permanent Secretary to the Welsh Office in Harold Wilson's Government. He went to Aberystwyth. And then there was Helen Makower. Yes, Helen Makower who was working with Marschak on labour and mobility.

[5] Jacob Marschak (1898–1977) was Director of the Oxford Institute for Statistics 1935–39 and then Director of the Cowles Commission, Chicago 1943–48.
[6] Henry Phelps Brown (1906–94) gained a First in PPE in 1929 and then spent a year in the United States, at Columbia and Chicago Universities. In 1930 he was appointed Fellow of New College, Oxford; in 1947 he moved to LSE where he was Professor of the Economics of Labour until 1968.

TRIBE: Harold Wilson was working with Beveridge as well, wasn't he?

BROWN: Harold Wilson, yes. He came a year after that. He overlapped with me. He was really working for Beveridge at that stage, and Walt Rostow worked there as well. I should say we didn't do too badly because we had among us a future knight, a Dame, a millionaire and a Prime Minister. Yes, the millionaire was a man called Robinson. Little Yorkshireman from Hull, who was working with Marschak on the econometrics of building activity, house-building activity specifically . . .

TRIBE: You got your D.Phil. in 1939 and stayed on in Oxford.

BROWN: I was a Fellow of All Souls and I was also involved with Chatham House. I got into All Souls in 1937 as an Examination Fellow. Chatham House had mostly decamped to Oxford in the war. Part of it was enlarged and situated in Balliol, as the foreign press service for the Foreign Office. The bits that weren't so occupied, mostly bits that produced the *Bulletins of International News*, were partly moved to Oxford. First of all I got drawn into writing for the *Bulletin of International News*, and then in some time in early 1940 I got drawn into the other thing and became a member of their economic section under A.G.B. Fisher. When they moved to London in 1943 and became the Foreign Office Research Department, Fisher left and went back to peacetime Chatham House, and I became head of their Economic Section.

TRIBE: How many people were in that, then?

BROWN: By the time I left there I had three assistants.

TRIBE: Was the Foreign Office post wound up in 1945, or did you work there until 1946?

BROWN: I worked there until 1945 and then I went into the Economic Section of the Cabinet Office. I was recruited by James Meade.

10

SIR CHARLES CARTER

Charles Carter was born in 1919 and attended Rugby School before going up to St John's College, Cambridge in 1938 to read mathematics. During the war he worked with the Friends' Relief Service, and then he became Lecturer in Statistics in Cambridge. In 1952 he was appointed Professor of Applied Economics at Queen's Belfast, moving in 1959 to Manchester as Stanley Jevons Professor of Political Economy. During the 1950s he was Joint Director, with Bruce Williams at Keele, of research into technology and the innovation process; based on this work they published *Industry and Technical Progress* (1957), *Investment and Innovation* (1958) and *Science in Industry* (1959). He became the founding Vice-Chancellor of the University of Lancaster in 1963, retiring from the post in 1979. The following is an edited version of an interview conducted at Professor Carter's home in Seascale, Cumbria, on 28 November 1994.

CARTER: I went up to Cambridge in 1938 and took the Maths Tripos; in those days, if you had done enough at school you went straight to Part II of the Maths Tripos, so after two years I took Part II, completing the examination requirements for the degree. But Cambridge wouldn't give you a degree unless you had spent the appropriate number of nights, so it was necessary to go back. Well, it didn't seem very sensible to go back in 1940; and the Friends' Relief Service was working with various problems of old people who were evacuated and that kind of thing, setting up hostels in the countryside. I worked with them for some time, and then I went back to Cambridge in 1943 to 1944 and took the second part of the Economics Tripos. So my total training in economics took eight months! Then I worked for another year or so with the Friends' Relief Service, and then I was looking for a job. I nearly got myself appointed as editor of a journal in the building trade, God help us, and then I got a telephone call from Dennis Robertson concerning a lectureship in Cambridge that they would like me to apply for. So I applied for it and got it. It was in statistics, to succeed Colin Clark, who had gone to Australia. There was always a Lecturer in Statistics in the Economics Faculty, so that is what I did for the following six years. I didn't really know any statistics, but there is nothing which teaches you things so quickly as having to teach them to somebody else!

TRIBE: Who was your tutor when you were an economics student?

CARTER: My supervisor was Guillebaud, who was, of course, a great enthusiast for Marshall. In fact his first act when he knew I was going to do economics was to send me away to read Marshall's *Principles*, which I obediently did! The Faculty at Cambridge was thin. Keynes was away, of course. A number of other people were away. People from the LSE one saw bits of. I went to some lectures by Hayek and by Grebenik, who lectured in statistics. I think they were the only ones who I actually took any notice of. And, no, you were very much left to your own devices, reading. When I came back to Cambridge as a lecturer of course they were all coming back, but Keynes never came back. I think he died before he really re-established himself at Cambridge, and I never met him.

TRIBE: You came back then as Lecturer in Economic Statistics at a time when they were resuming their immediate pre-war plans for the creation of the DAE?

CARTER: Yes.

TRIBE: That was actually quite a late development; originally it was meant to be established in 1939, but it came into existence about 1947.

CARTER: It had no real impact on teaching, but it gave one the renewed focus for research. My first major work was a book called *The Measurement of Production Movements* with Richard Stone, who was running the Department of Applied Economics, and Brian Reddaway – setting up a new index of production.[1] There was various work in the national income area and so on with which I used to spend quite a lot of time in the Department of Applied Economics, and they certainly were a very considerable help in research, because they were pioneering a whole lot of things in the statistical field which were of interest to me.

TRIBE: In your later career, you moved away from statistical work.

CARTER: Well, I think I always believed what Marshall said about economics, as being the study of mankind in the ordinary business of life; and it seemed to me therefore – I was probably too much influenced by Guillebaud? – that one had to keep the statistics and the econometrics very much as servants and not as the primary subject of study. It seemed to me at that time, in fact it still does, that a great many economists manage to make their reputation on rather bogus and not very interesting little bits of mathematics which actually have very little to do with the ordinary business of life. So you know, I was quite glad to get away from being typecast as a statistician to a position in which I was typecast as an applied economist using statistics, I hope intelligently, for the purposes of my trade, but not as the be all and end all.

---

[1] See the interview with Reddaway p. 84.

146

TRIBE: You then went to Belfast. How did the appointment in Belfast come about?

CARTER: I was recruited. I never found out what they had done before they got hold of my name, but I was the only one being interviewed, and as you will gather I was not averse to being regarded as an economist, and not just a statistician. It was a Chair of Applied Economics. There was another Chair of Economics held by Keith Isles, an Australian. A large department, lecturers and students, together with a considerable amount of evening work in those days, which actually was very interesting. It is a pity that it has died out so much.

TRIBE: What was your impression then of Belfast compared to Cambridge with respect to say, the courses?

CARTER: Well, Cambridge had large numbers of brilliant people around, but whatever the Faculty may have thought, they had practically no control over what was taught. I mean, the idea of having any sort of syllabus and systematically covering it was absent from their minds. There was supposed to be an annual meeting of all members of the Faculty to discuss the syllabus, and for years and years, I think probably more than twenty years, this was never called and you had to guess, or deduce from your supervisees, what was being taught. So it was a change to go a place where you actually sat down and thought what an economist should learn, in the round. The other thing about Cambridge was, it was then beginning to fall apart in internal dissension; there were various people who didn't speak to each other, and in particular there were what you might call the diehard Keynesians and others who didn't agree. This didn't really make for sensible co-operation. On the other hand, of course, Belfast was a very much less eminent place, but it was also a place where it was easy to work, and easy to use it as a springboard, I think. It seemed to me that Belfast was a place where one could really do things. You know, the Faculty worked together well. They listened to each other's ideas. We had a great deal of discussion with each other. That was one drawback about Cambridge. You had to manufacture occasions for discussion with other members of the Faculty. And the idea that Dons at high table talked about serious matters is quite untrue. They talked about the *Times* crossword! It was enjoyable to be at a place that really was a community of economists. We had our problems occasionally, but it was a very interesting place, and I think from my point of view it led on to further developments which were very valuable.

TRIBE: When did you start the move towards your interest in innovation and science policy?

CARTER: Well, that was 1953 or 1954. The British Association met in Belfast and, following that, a body called the Science and Industry Committee was set up, with support from the Nuffield Foundation and various other bodies, to look into the factors affecting the use of science in industry. The Committee was partly economists and partly scientists, but the economists rather arrogantly decided they had better take the lead because scientists couldn't be trusted to talk sense on these issues. So we very much controlled the research programme. I think it was an extremely interesting period. What we said now looks all too familiar. It is also true that very few people have since gone anywhere beyond what we said. I think if people had listened to the implications a bit earlier, the situation with this country would be better.

TRIBE: The publications coming out of the project date from the late 1950s, but in my mind the line of argument they supported is most closely associated with the Labour Party in the 1960s, starting with Wilson's 'white heat of technology' speech in 1963.[2] There were great hopes for economic modernisation here, but the result was not as great as one might have hoped. How were your ideas received when they were first published?

CARTER: When the work first came out, there was a very generous reception. We got a lot of publicity and a lot of people of significance in the industrial world thought it was splendid. But, of course, you then say, what should be done? There were certain things the government needed to do, and moving government is a very slow business, because they tend to have ideas which are set in stone. There were some things which industrialists had to do, and there I think one is up against the fact that, generally speaking, British industry then, and to some extent now, is run by people who are not actually terribly well educated. They take a fairly narrow view. They find it very difficult to admit that doing anything different from what their fathers did is right. So it was probably necessarily a fairly slow and difficult process. But I think I am disappointed that it really didn't get further.

TRIBE: Was it a problem with respect to the Civil Service, for example: at that time there were relatively few specialised economists, or indeed anyone with any kind of economic or commercial training, in the Civil Service. That changed again by the later 1960s . . .

CARTER: Yes, I think it probably was. And of course it would still be true that although there were quite a lot of economists around in the Civil Service, the senior positions tend to be occupied by itinerant amateurs who are in the Ministry of Defence one moment, and the Department of Trade and Industry the next.

TRIBE: This also coincided with a period of rapid industrial concentration, which one might naturally assume would be favourable to the ideas about innovation, or the use of science and technology.

CARTER: Yes. But we weren't saying that the position was uniformly black. If you look at the passage where we set out what we regard as the characteristics of the scientifically progressive firm, there were some firms which would score quite highly on many of these issues – but it only took one or two weaknesses. For instance, we identified some firms which were full of technological ideas, but absolutely devoid of the business sense or economic sense

---

[2] Delivered at the Annual Conference in Scarborough; see B. Pimlott, *Harold Wilson*, HarperCollins, London, 1992, p. 304; for the policy implications, see p. 526.

to bring them into use, and therefore things became abortive, or they went bankrupt, or things like that. On the other hand, you had got others who were really persuaded that the important thing was not what you produced but how you marketed it, and that if you tried hard enough you could sell anything, however out of date; and there are examples of firms in that position who actually did quite well for a period. The printing industry, for instance. The British printing machine producers had quite a time selling to the Third World until eventually of course they were totally overtaken by new technology, new forms of control and so on, and they were caught selling a really archaic product. So you know, getting all-round excellence was the problem; and getting all-round excellence implied having people at the top with a good deal of vision of what all-round excellence means. It was no good being single-minded about one aspect of it.

TRIBE: You co-operated with Bruce Williams;[3] how did that come about?

CARTER: Well, we knew Bruce of course, and he had a long-standing interest in the subject, I think, and being a member of the Committee confirmed it. Strictly speaking, I was Chairman and he was Secretary, but it didn't make any difference. We were really a kind of duopoly, we did things together. We wrote practically the whole lot. One of us doing the first draft and then the second one tearing it to pieces, and so on. And we looked after the research staff together. We had occasional quarrels but no more than usual in the best-regulated households!

TRIBE: The Science and Technology Committee came out of the Belfast meeting of the British Association. Was it 1953 in Liverpool, also at the British Association meeting, where the work on uncertainty that you did came out?[4] I would imagine there are many modern economists who would simply be unaware of this 1950's work on uncertainty and expectations. Would you see this as an early flowering of an idea, as another area of delayed reception?

CARTER: Yes, I think so. The trouble about anything on the subject of uncertainty is that it very easily gets up a blind alley. I got into this subject because I had to review one of Shackle's books for the *Economic Journal.*[5] But anyway, I knew Shackle pretty well and once you knew him he would send you copies of absolutely everything he did, and it was rather difficult not to get interested! His original work was very novel. It was pathbreaking. I criticised it then, and have always criticised it since, as being somewhat devoid of a serious examination of how people's minds actually work. How is a business

---

[3] Bruce Williams (1919–) was a Lecturer in Economics at Adelaide 1939–46, running the department for Keith Isles during much of the period. In 1946 he moved to Belfast with Isles, and then in 1950 was appointed the first Professor of Economics at the University College of North Staffordshire (now Keele University). From there he moved to chairs in Manchester during 1959–67, and then returned to Australia to become Vice-Chancellor of the University of Sydney, retiring from that post in 1981 (interview with Bruce Williams, The Athanaeum, London, 24 March 1995).

[4] Charles Carter *et al.*, *Uncertainty and Business Decisions*, University of Liverpool Press, Liverpool, 1954; and also edited with J.L. Ford, *Uncertainty and Expectations in Economics*, Basil Blackwell, Oxford, 1972.

[5] C.F. Carter, 'A Revised Theory of Expectations', *Economic Journal*, vol. 63 (1953), pp. 811–20.

decision taken? It certainly isn't taken in a way which economists had carelessly supposed, of people forming the mathematical expectation of the results of different courses of action, because they wouldn't have known how. But equally, I think the Shackle set of ideas, although it had something very important in it, was rather difficult to relate to somebody down the street who was running a company. So in a way I think what I was concerned with was trying to get a somewhat closer association with mankind and the ordinary business of life than Shackle had done; and I chased him about this for many years. He was a wonderful man. He always almost smothered everybody in compliments. He was terribly complimentary about anything you said, how pathbreaking it was. He then went on to indicate that he was going to take not the slightest notice of it! He never changed his mind at all! And right to the end of his life he was still defending pretty well what he had first thought of. So he was a hard man to talk to! But I thought then, and I still think, that there is a vast field here. One of the things which I have done during my life is manage investment funds – starting in my Cambridge days when I assisted the Bursar on the College investments, and in later times having to deal with the investments of charitable trusts. I am still responsible for the investments of one trust which is about £18m., and I am on the committee which is responsible for another trust which is nearly £140m.; so I do know something about the ways in which those decisions are made, which are of course rather pure decisions under uncertainty. Therefore I am very interested to analyse my own process of thought in reaching decisions. One of the troubles about Shackle's earlier work was that, if you believed what he said, it was not very logical to hedge; and it obviously is logical to hedge, so you have got to have a theory which allows for it! You can study the way in which investors' minds operate, and the way in which that then affects the market, with its rather exaggerated changes of sentiment, and so on. It seems to me there are great fields here in which economists could do some very useful work.

TRIBE: A great deal of financial economics now seems to be studying movements of the market and trying to deduce what is going on from market movements, rather than the way in which decisions are formed.

CARTER: That, of course, is, at least superficially, a more scientific exercise, because you can study the statistics of the markets, whereas studying what goes on in people's minds is very difficult; but it is also very much more fundamental.

TRIBE: Did this kind of approach and this interest lead you towards the Oxford work? What became the Oxford collection *Studies in the Price Mechanism*, and therefore into contact with Philip Andrews.[6] Was that the connection which brought him to Lancaster?

---

[6] Philip Andrews (1914–71) was the founding Professor of Economics at Lancaster, joining the University in 1967. He was an Official Fellow of Nuffield College, Oxford from 1946 and the founding editor of the *Journal of Industrial Economics.*

CARTER: Philip invited me to be on the editorial board of the *Journal of Industrial Economics.* That is where I first knew him. And he did that I think because of the work for the Science and Industry Committee. We shared among ourselves the refereeing of papers, and I used to meet him when he was with Elizabeth Brunner in Oxford, and that is where I really got to know him. It always seemed to me for all the oddities of what he did, Philip Andrews had very much in mind studying what people actually do, and not what some theoretical economists think they might do.

TRIBE: The work of Warren Young and Fred Lee[7] has revealed quite a lot of animus against Philip Andrews in Oxford – essentially on the grounds that he was not really an economist, that he was just concerned with the nuts and bolts. Second, if you look at the *Journal of Industrial Economics* in the 1950s and 1960s, it seems to be by contemporary standards a fairly untheoretical, or descriptive, approach to business organisation compared with, say, American literature of the same time.

CARTER: Yes. I think Philip probably held the view that a great deal of description had to go on before you were really ready to theorise very far. I mean that there was a gap in real knowledge of what was actually going on and you needed to try to fill that. On the other hand, I was rather disappointed sometimes by the solid quality of the things which got submitted to the *Journal.* I don't think the people working in the field at that time were terribly impressive.

TRIBE: But what I was struck by in the *Journal of Industrial Economics* was the relentlessness of non-algebraic, non-graphical, non-theorised articles; most of the articles at that time were case studies.

CARTER: I think that is true, yes. Well, that fitted in with Philip's predilections very much, I think.

TRIBE: You made a point earlier about Belfast being a springboard. How did the move to Manchester come about?

CARTER: Well, we had been in Belfast for eight years and I got an approach from Harry Johnson, who had held the Chair there and was just about to move, asking whether I would be prepared to be considered. I wasn't wildly anxious to move from Belfast, because it was a wonderful place to live and a great place to bring up children. But I was really only interested in opportunities which were plainly those of advancement. I sound rather bad in putting it that way, but I did apply for one Chair in Edinburgh and . . .

TRIBE: That would be the one that Peacock got?

CARTER: Yes. They discerned quite rightly that I wasn't a Scot, and I didn't get anywhere! But the Stanley Jevons Chair at Manchester had great prestige and it seemed to me it was something you didn't turn down. So it was by invitation essentially. And I thought after eight years in Belfast it was about time

---

[7] See F.S. Lee and P.E. Earl (eds) *The Economics of Competitive Enterprise: Selected Essays of P.W.S. Andrews,* Edward Elgar, Aldershot, 1993.

to move. And so we went to Manchester. I was rather overwhelmed in Manchester by all the other things I did. In fact I have a feeling I rather neglected my students. At least I hope I didn't, but I spent an awful lot of time on the train to London!

TRIBE: At that time it was a very prestigious department. Lewis had left by that time, and Johnson was leaving. But what is striking, and Dennis Coppock[8] brought my attention to this, is that no one ever stayed very long; and although it was actually a prominent department, it didn't seem to attract people who stayed for a particularly long period of time. Someone like Prest, for example, who seemed quite committed to the place, then eventually went to the LSE as well.

CARTER: Yes. Quite. I think there were faults in Manchester. Maybe a problem of size, or of structure. To start with, there was the Faculty of Economic and Social Studies, which really consisted of a set of warring departments. I mean the economists and the sociologists felt they were both competing for the same pot of gold; and there wasn't very much sense of Faculty unity, and certainly not very much output from the cross-fertilisation that there probably ought to have been. Among the economists, well, you see in Belfast we had a department which had two Chairs of Economics. Shortly before I left Stanley Dennison joined us, and that was quite a good move, but the holders of the Chairs, provided they agreed with each other, were in a position to exercise a position of leadership and draw the whole thing together. Manchester was very difficult to get hold of indeed. This was true of the University as a whole actually. I mean it had rapidly become apparent to me that the machinery of the University and the Senate and all that had absolutely no connection with what actually happened! Everything was cut and dried before it got to the Senate. Where it was cut and dried nobody knew! But it was. And it was true in the department that there was a lack of sense of community. We were a lot of individuals beavering away. I think probably a lot of us were spending our time on the train to London, and we didn't exploit our advantages anything like to the extent we should have done. I think I only realised that really after I had left.

TRIBE: You were appointed Vice-Chancellor of the new University of Lancaster.[9] How did you see the role of a new university then?

CARTER: Well, there were a number of basic ideas, but one of the important ones in the early years was to make undergraduate degrees less specialised. That arose partly from my Belfast experience, where the undergraduate degree had been made up in a very large number of different ways. But in Belfast it was just a question of adding units which had nothing actually to do with each other. We thought we ought to allow people to do combinations of subjects,

---

[8] Interview with Dennis Coppock, 29 April 1994, Stockport, Cheshire.

[9] The government announced the establishment of the University of Lancaster in November 1961, making it the only one of the new universities founded after the Robbins Committee began its deliberations in February 1961.

but in a way which enabled them to see the inter-relations better. We also were concerned to try and find ways in which students of the arts and social sciences could have some idea of the processes of thought of the natural sciences, and vice versa. That is always a very difficult one, but we did quite a bit on it. We also wanted to establish a reputation in fields which would be of direct interest to employers, but which had not appeared in the university field before; the first of which was Operational Research, and we had the first Chair of Operational Research in the country. That approach to business studies was really important.

TRIBE: So did you start off across the board, from the sciences, the humanities and the social sciences?

CARTER: Yes. We had a wide spread of subjects, in contrast to Essex, for instance, which had quite a narrow one to begin with, I think. We had Biology, Chemistry and Physics. We had Engineering quite early on. We had a whole range of arts subjects, including some like Classics which were regarded as terribly old-fashioned. And we had business subjects, Operational Research and Marketing, others which were really labour relations and had got a fancy name; and we actually regarded it as important to have all these. I mean it is no good saying things will interact if they were not there, and we were anxious to have a big range. So we were always anxious to grow as fast as possible and, well of course, all things seemed to be possible in the early 1960s, but we got a bit frustrated with not getting enough money out of the UGC. But nevertheless, we did grow quite fast and have gone on growing since.

We started Economics at Lancaster by appointing Stan Sturmey, who was an applied economist. I don't know whether he is still extant; he went to GATT and worked for GATT for a great many years. We added Philip Andrews after a few years and Elizabeth Brunner. No, I am afraid that the kind of economics we tried to develop was very much the kind I was interested in! I mean, we really had no pretensions to try and rival the famous economics departments. We didn't think it was a very likely spot at which to do it. What we did want to do was to provide an economics training for people which would stand them in good stead in a wide variety of related jobs. We had a very strong Accountancy Department, and it was important that the accountants should know something of what their accounts were about.

TRIBE: So would this have been one of the first university-level business schools?

CARTER: Yes, that is true. The distinction was that we had a Business School which was composed of separate departments in separate subjects. Whereas most people think of a Business School in terms of a School of a generalist nature, and we thought that in a subject like Accountancy for instance, if that was really going to be a worthwhile academic subject it had to be done with a very real research background, and not just as a useful tool to teach, and that this needed a specialist department to do it in. I think actually this was the right way to start. Some of our rivals set up business schools of a much more general nature. Over the years the departments in Lancaster have drawn closer together and now do what are really business degrees together, but they still have a very considerable weight in their own right. The OR Department is, as I see from the *Journal* of the OR Society, which I still get, still a major influence. I was, I think, essentially still pursuing a Marshallian approach you know!

11

WILFRED BECKERMAN

Wilfred Beckerman was born in 1925. After war service in the Royal Navy he entered Cambridge University in 1946 and completed the Economics Tripos in two years under the special regulations for ex-servicemen. In 1948 he entered graduate study in Cambridge, and was appointed to his first job in 1950 at the University of Nottingham, which had recently gained full University status after many years as a University College. Beckerman spent two years here, before moving in 1952 to the Organisation for European Economic Co-operation in Paris, where he stayed until 1961. This was followed by a period at the National Institute for Economic and Social Research in London, and then from 1964 until 1969 he was a Fellow of Balliol College, Oxford, latterly also the Economic Adviser to the President of the Board of Trade 1967–69. He was Professor of Political Economy at University College London from 1969 to 1975, when he returned to Balliol and where he stayed until retirement in 1992. The following is an edited version of an interview conducted in Oxford on 19 July 1994.

TRIBE: You served in the Navy before going to Cambridge?
BECKERMAN: It was conscription; you had to go into something. And I was 18. I knew I was going to go somewhere sooner or later; so I joined the Navy – when I saw there was this opportunity, in order not to go into the Army, that's all. I mean I wouldn't have minded the Air Force, but I didn't like the idea of being in the Army. You don't join as RNVR, of course. You join as an ordinary seaman. I was commissioned after six months. I was made a midshipman and *then* the distinction arises. Are you an officer in the RN? Or in the RNR (the Royal Naval Reserve, which was for Merchant Navy Officers who had switched to the Royal Navy during the war). Or you could be in the RNVR, the Royal Naval Volunteer Reserve which meant you were really temporary, that's all. You weren't a professional sailor. You hadn't been one before and no doubt you weren't going to be one after, although there were one or two people who liked the life and stayed on. But most of us weren't going to stay on after the war.
TRIBE: What was your educational background?

BECKERMAN: Well, I was at Ealing Grammar School, Ealing County School, I think it was called. I don't think it exists any longer. It was a state school of course, but it was a selective 'grammar school'; a very, very good school. I hadn't thought of becoming anything in particular. I just got rather interested in economics because I got interested a bit in politics. I started reading a bit of Karl Marx, and then I thought, this is all economics, and so I started reading some economics. It was through politics I got interested in economics – it wasn't a schoolboy ambition or anything.

TRIBE: So how did you end up in Cambridge?

BECKERMAN: My parents lived there. I left it until very late to decide where to go, and I wandered around a few Cambridge colleges whilst on leave around about spring the year I was demobilised – in 1946. I remember going round to about four or five colleges and saying, 'I would like to come here and study economics.' In those days the admissions procedure was not like it is now. At that time the Senior Tutor or somebody would come and have a look at you and talk to you, and they realised within two minutes, as one does in this country, that I was of working-class origin. I would always make a point of turning up in my Naval Officer's uniform, with medal ribbons. But they didn't care a damn about that, there were millions of people like me, and anyway he could see in two minutes that I was of working-class origin. They were already full up. All the colleges were, and they weren't going to make room for me. And then I got to Trinity, and it transpired in the course of the conversation with the Senior Tutor there, whose name I remember clearly because I had such great respect for the chap, Rattenbury, that my parents lived in Cambridge and so I wouldn't require rooms in college; and so he said, 'Oh, well, that's OK then', and he let me in. So that was why I finished up in the biggest and richest and most prestigious college in Cambridge! Just sheer luck!

TRIBE: Can you tell me something of your war service?

BECKERMAN: Well, I was an Executive Officer on destroyers, after the first six months. During my first six months in the Navy I started off like everybody else – with a bit of marching around, learning which is the front end of a boat and what is north, south, east and west. All that sort of basic stuff you do in the Navy. How to tie knots. Which still comes in very useful, you know. We often go punting here in Oxford. I have taught my wife how to do a round turn and two half-hitches when we pull up in the boat! It comes in very useful, this sort of thing. Then I spent a couple of months on a training cruiser, and then a couple of months shore training down at Brighton, at the King Alfred establishment there. And then I became a Midshipman. Because you could not become a Sub-Lieutenant until you were 19½, I think, and I must have been just nineteen when I was commissioned. And then I was sent off to my first ship, which was a destroyer. And I was on destroyers all the time for the next couple of years, with the exception of one frigate, but, as you may know, it is practically the same sort of thing. So I was an Executive Officer on destroyers. You know, there are not many officers on destroyers. Basically you drive the ship. You stand on the bridge and you say, 'port 20, steer 310', or something like that. You keep a look-out because look-outs often went to sleep, so if you don't look out nobody is looking out, and you have other special jobs. When the ship comes into harbour you are in charge of the fo'c'sle, or the quarterdeck, or midships. Or when you come to a buoy, if you're the fo'c'sle officer you have to see that you are moored to the buoy. I was very proud of my last ship, which was an 'O' class destroyer called the *Onslaught*. The speed with which we used to get two shackles onto that buoy was terrific. Practically singlehanded I did it with the Chief Stoker, who worked the winch to make the cable come up. And you had a whaler, the chap jumps on and hooks a little rope around the buoy, you pass it to the shackle at the end of an anchor cable, and then you fix the other cable to the buoy. It was a quite complicated job and we did the whole thing in about one minute flat! I used to be very proud of that. The last thing I ever did in the Navy really well was that! And then you have other jobs, there were all sorts of other things that had to be sorted out. Somebody was in charge of the wardroom and wine stores; and somebody was in charge of ship's correspondence; and somebody was the navigating officer; and somebody was the Asdic officer; and somebody was the radar officer; and somebody was the torpedo control officer – and I think I did every one of those jobs on different ships. It is rather like the British Civil Service, you move around and nobody knows much about anything, and you bluff a bit and you manage – and it is a wonderful experience. I would not have missed it for the world! On my last ship, the war was over and they were cutting down drastically on complements, and so there were only about six officers left, and I was the senior one apart from the RN people who were staying on; and so I was doing every job. I was the correspondence officer, the fo'c'sle officer, I was the Asdic officer and everything.

TRIBE: How did you find the change to being a student in Cambridge?

BECKERMAN: Oh, no problem at all because whenever I was on leave from the Navy I was already studying economics, reading it. So I knew where the library was and that sort of thing and I knew Cambridge you see, I lived there. So it wasn't as if I was adapting to a whole new lifestyle. I came up late because I wasn't due to be released until, probably in the normal course of events, November–December. But once I had been admitted by Trinity, as I was also the correspondence officer of the ship I was on I knew to whom I had to write, and I wrote to the Admiralty and said, 'Look, the term starts on the 5 October and could you give me early release'; and they were very efficient and we got a signal back, 'Signal: release Sub-Lieutenant Beckerman straightaway', and I was released straightaway, and I went back to Cambridge straightaway, and I got there, I think, just a couple of days before term started.

TRIBE: In October 1946?

BECKERMAN: Yes. It must have been a couple of days before term started, because I remember waiting outside my supervisor's room to see him with other people to arrange our tutorials.

TRIBE: Who was your supervisor?

BECKERMAN: First year was Maurice Dobb. It was very funny that my two supervisors in Cambridge were two very well-known communists! As far as I know, MI5 have never checked on whether I had been converted!

TRIBE: How did you find Maurice Dobb?

BECKERMAN: Oh, wonderful man. He was just too nice, that was the trouble. He was too nice. But he was very, very good. Not sufficiently critical. I mean, he would tell you when you made mistakes, but he didn't make me feel sufficiently guilty about it! I think he ought to have rubbed my nose in it a bit more; so that I might have worked harder! But he was a frightfully nice guy. He would never rise to the bait. I would occasionally want to talk to him about something else. Tease him a bit about what was going on in the Soviet Union or Yugoslavia. He was just too gentlemanly.

TRIBE: Which other students were there in Trinity at the time?

BECKERMAN: Well, Angus Maddison, who is still a very close friend of mine, my oldest friend; I met him queuing up outside Maurice Dobb's, which is why I remembered that I must have come up in time to check in. He wasn't at Trinity, he was at Selwyn. But they didn't have an economist there, and he always had this historical bent you see, even in those days. He was a very smart guy and he knew his way around and he knew that Maurice was not just an economist but was writing *Studies in the Development of Capitalism*, and a great big book on the Soviet economy,[1] and was an historian as much an economist, and so Angus wanted to be supervised by him. And that was where we met, and we have kept in close touch ever since. I contributed to the Festschrift for Angus which was published a couple of years ago, and we still keep in touch. In my first year I didn't do Part I, I did Prelims which was a second-year exam. You were allowed to take your degree in two years if you were an ex-service-man. And you could pick whichever two years of the course that you liked. I did Prelims straightaway and I was tutored together with some Greek student. But he wasn't very good and he rather reduced the speed at which we could go. And it is possible that Maurice supervised me separately towards the end of my first year, but I just don't remember. This was nearly fifty years ago.

TRIBE: Did you go to the lectures for the Part I then?

BECKERMAN: Well, I must confess that I went to lectures mainly for the wrong reasons. I went to the lectures mainly because it was a nice place to keep warm. It was very, very cold in those years. There was a fuel crisis early in 1947. I didn't actually live at home. We had another little flat which was over a tobacconist's shop and I lived there – and, I mean, it was just so bloody cold. And I couldn't get any coal. So I went to lectures partly to keep warm. They

---

[1] M.H. Dobb, *Studies in the Development of Capitalism*, Routledge and Kegan Paul, London, 1946; M.H. Dobb, *Soviet Economic Development since 1917*, Routledge and Kegan Paul, London, 1948, which was based in part upon his earlier *Russian Economic Development since the Revolution*, George Routledge, London, 1928.

were nice places where I could keep warm and write letters, although there was usually somebody making a noise talking which interrupted a bit. Or I went to lectures to chase the girls! It was a good place to pick up girls! I just wasn't a very good student. I still hardly ever go to lectures. I just find it very difficult to listen to other people talking for a very long time. On the rare occasions when I have been to lectures in the last ten or twenty years I have listened to them very, very intently, to get every word. But that is because I only go to lectures when I am really deeply interested in what they are going to say and it all means much more to me. As you know yourself, when you already know quite a bit about a subject, listening to people or reading about it means a lot more to you. In those days I didn't know very much about it and it didn't mean a lot to me and some of the lecturers were very, very bad. Anyway, I didn't go to the Part I lectures, and not all of the Prelim lectures. I went to Dennis Robertson. He was terrific.

TRIBE: Was he very theatrical? I have heard or read that recently.

BECKERMAN: No, I don't think he was theatrical at all, but he was amusing and had a nice style. Very clear and very thorough. He had good presentation. I don't think I went to any of Kahn's lectures until I was a graduate student. I used to go to Joan Robinson; they were terrific. Her lectures on money or whatever she was talking about. They were very, very good. I think I may have tried a couple of Ruth Cohen's lectures. I went to Dennison's lectures a bit for Part II, because they were the only lectures available that were related to one of the compulsory papers. There wasn't much to read in the various fields in which I was going to take exams. I went to Dobb, and to Brogan. Brogan's lectures were very interesting. He spoke very fast, but they were quite interesting; and I went to his class on politics. Mrs Holland's lectures on Public Finance were rather boring, I'm afraid, and she had this habit of looking all the time at something back up at the top of the lecture room. She never looked at us. I don't remember understanding or paying much attention. Amongst those I took seriously were Carter's classes on Statistical Methods. But that was in my second year when I was reading for Part II. For Prelims I didn't do much. I am sure I went to Robertson for Prelims. Oh, and I went to Shove on Development of Economic Thought. There was a paper on that for Prelims – there was a paper on Principles of some sort, there was a paper, a mixed paper, on History of Thought and Economic History. I went to Habakkuk on Modern Economic History. But I didn't go to any of them very seriously. I wasn't a very diligent student to be quite honest. I don't suppose I really started studying until after I graduated!

TRIBE: What about the reading? I have got here a list of the recommended reading,[2] but how far did the lectures in fact reflect that?

---

[2] The list of recommended reading for Pt. I before coming into residence, *Cambridge University Reporter*, vol. LXXVI, no. 39 (11 June 1946), pp. 920–1.

BECKERMAN: Well, I would have read Cairncross.[3] And I would have looked at all the books on your list. Cairncross, and Benham.[4] I remember Benham very well. Henderson. Withers, I don't remember. Crowther, *Outline of Money*. Dennis Robertson – *Money*. Joan Robinson – *Introduction to the Theory of Employment* – certainly. Austin Robinson – *The Structure of Competitive Industry*; *Monopoly*. That's right. They were the books.[5] I wouldn't have bothered about Ruth Cohen, *The Economics of Agriculture*. Dobb on *Wages*, yes. Richardson – *Industrial Relations*, doesn't ring a bell. Cole – *Condition of Britain*, no. Abrams, *Condition of the British People*, no. *White Paper on Employment Policy*, Yes. I would have known a bit about that. The main book was Marshall's *Principles*, of course. I mean that I would have certainly read and re-read that two or three times. *Social Structure of England and Wales*, yes I knew about that. Hicks – *Social Framework*, was that out then?

TRIBE: 1942.

BECKERMAN: 1942. Was it? Right. I remember reading it very well but I don't remember reading it at that stage, but I suppose it must have been then. The Beveridge book I would have known. *Economics of Overhead Costs*?[6] I knew about it. Smith, *Wealth of Nations*. I would have looked at it because we had this paper in Prelims. Ashley – *Economic History*. Faye. Yes, I would have looked at those things. But I loved books, and I had a lot of these books, I probably had my own copy of practically all of them. I was always in debt to bookshops.

TRIBE: How Marshallian was the teaching then, if you say you read Marshall two or three times?

BECKERMAN: Yes, it was very Marshallian. Dobb had a lot of time for Marshall as, of course, did Dennis Robertson. I don't seem to have kept my old copy of Marshall's *Principles*; it is amazing, I would have thought I would have kept it.[7] I have got my copy of Pigou.

TRIBE: *Economics of Welfare* is that?

BECKERMAN: Yes. 12 December 1946, Cambridge. Which I heavily annotated and marked, you know; funny childish handwriting I had in those days! Queries which when I see them again now I realise I had got it all wrong! And then other books. This book for some reason I got very early. Oh somebody gave it . . . I got a member of my family to give it to me as a present, Christmas 1945 – Abba Lerner, *Economics of Control*. It looks as if I read some of it very, very carefully. Very heavily annotated with my then rather childish handwriting. I didn't rely entirely on the official reading list. I didn't read most of it. I knew about most of the books on the list and I looked at them several times,

[3] A. Cairncross, *Introduction to Economics*, Butterworth, London, 1944.
[4] F. Benham, *Economics: A General Textbook for Students*, 3rd edition, Pitman, London, 1943.
[5] Cambridge Economic Handbooks.
[6] J.M. Clark, *Studies in the Economics of Overhead Costs*, University of Chicago Press, Chicago, 1923.
[7] The interview was conducted in Wilfred Beckerman's study.

and no doubt consulted them for essays, like a lot of my students at Balliol. I consulted most of them for essays but I didn't read many of them.

TRIBE: How did you prepare for your weekly tutorial with Dobb in your first year? You must have had had a weekly essay?

BECKERMAN: I would have got it mainly out of Marshall, and two or three of these other books. As you probably know, there weren't many decent textbooks in those days. For macroeconomics there was nothing really. In my first year I relied a lot on Marshall and an American book by Boulding which I notice isn't on your list. But I used it. I think it was called *Economic Analysis*.[8] It was a proper American textbook. That was about all there was. And there was a book by Stigler, I think it was *The Theory of Price*.[9] That was it. I think I used them, rather than the things like *Supply and Demand*[10] and whatnot, which I probably would have looked at but I think, now you ask me about these things, my impression is that these books in the Cambridge Economic Handbook Series like *Supply and Demand*, and *Monopoly*, or *Competitive Industry*, I found rather waffly by comparison with the American textbooks. I love diagrams you see, and I quite like a bit of algebra, and I think I just found most of these Cambridge textbooks too waffly. I realised that Marshall was jolly good waffle, but I would have found the others too waffly, and I relied much more on Boulding and Stigler.

TRIBE: Did anyone else do that? That strikes me as relatively unusual for that time, compared to other people I have talked to.

BECKERMAN: Well, I don't think so. I am just looking at this list. Because I have got old books, I have got Dobb's book on *Wages* up there. I don't think so. I think people relied a lot on the lectures and maybe my contemporaries quite liked these Cambridge Handbooks. They just didn't suit me. I found them rather boring. I relied – as far I read anything – on these American textbooks.

TRIBE: Was Dobb still your supervisor in the second year?

BECKERMAN: No, Sraffa. Piero Sraffa. A wonderful man. Wonderful man. He didn't really teach me any economics. He wasn't very interested in the sort of stuff we had to cover. I totally sympathised with him. But he did teach me something which was invaluable, although I must say I hardly ever use it. He taught me how to write a rigorous sentence if I really wanted to do it; and of course the trouble is most of the time I don't do it. Piero taught me that. He was a genius for that. Wonderful! But he wasn't really interested in ordinary economics, and the only way I could get him interested in my essays was to tackle something which would be way above my head. You know, something at the frontiers of the subject which I ought not to have been playing with. I

---

[8] K.E. Boulding, *Economic Analysis*, Harper, New York, 1941; revised edition, 1948.

[9] G.J. Stigler, *The Theory of Price*, Macmillan, New York, 1946; originally published as *The Theory of Competitive Price*, Macmillan, New York, 1942.

[10] H. Henderson, *Supply and Demand*, Nisbet, London, 1922; second revised edition, Cambridge University Press, London, 1932.

should have learned the foundations before that. But that was the only way I could get him interested.

TRIBE: What sort of things, then?

BECKERMAN: Well, yes, I remember very clearly for example, writing an essay for him about Hayek on the feasibility of equilibrium in what nowadays one would call a game-theoretic situation, although Hayek of course wasn't using that terminology; the feasibility of equilibrium, the whole concept of equilibrium. Well, for somebody in the second year of economics, you shouldn't be wasting your time on that! But he got very interested in this. I remember, there were game-theoretic aspects to the question of whether an equilibrium existed; and so I wrote an essay for him on this; and you know he was very interested in that. Even then it wasn't really the frontiers of economics! I remember getting very interested in some critique I had concerning an argument about rent in Joan Robinson's *Economics of Imperfect Competition*. Oh, that was one of the books I used. I certainly read that carefully.

TRIBE: Was that partly because of all the graphs in it?

BECKERMAN: That's right. I loved that. It would be like Boulding. I liked all that. But I remember writing an essay for Piero in which I was criticising a whole chapter she had – I don't remember, I must have the book somewhere or other – on the concept of rent and he got very interested in that. That was the only way I could get him interested. Otherwise he would just go to sleep, you see. So I really didn't learn much economics from him. I remember writing something for him, when I was a graduate student actually, on the theory of capital and measuring capital, and after I had been working as a graduate student for a year on this subject. And he was at Trinity of course; and I used to see him now and again and one day he said, 'You had better come and tell me what you are doing', and so I wrote a ten-page paper on this which was the culmination of a year of work, and we never got past the second page. He just tore every line to pieces and I came out of there absolutely shattered and would have given up economics. I sat in my room for a couple of days thinking, 'Oh God, it is a bit late now, what I am going to do, I am no good at football.' And I was walking along the street and I bumped into I.G. Patel, you know, the very distinguished Indian economist who knew me slightly, I don't know how because he had been a year or two ahead of me, but somehow we knew each other slightly, and we chatted and I said 'I'm going to give up economics. I have just had this session with Sraffa and he just absolutely tore every sentence to pieces.' He said, 'Oh don't take it to heart, he did that to me as well. He's done that to everybody!' And I thought, 'Oh well, if he can do that to Patel . . .', who already had a great reputation – he had gone off to Harvard as a graduate student, he had wowed them all. The news had come back that they had never seen a graduate student like this for twenty years. So I thought, 'If he can do that to Patel, then OK, I will stick at it.' But I changed my thesis topic. I didn't continue with capital theory.

TRIBE: So you took your Part II in 1948? What made you think of graduate work?

BECKERMAN: Well, I was starting to get seriously interested in the subject and they thought that I was good enough, although I didn't get a First, I got a 2.1, but as I had done it in two years, and I took the full set of eight papers (in fact I took nine) – if you were doing the two-year ex-serviceman's thing you could do it on the five compulsory papers only. I didn't expect to get a First because there were some papers that I had no intention of doing any work on at all. There was a compulsory paper on industry linked to a course taught by Dennison. He gave these lectures on industry, and he had written some book about economies of scale that did not happen to interest me, so I wasn't going to do any work on that at all, and I didn't. There were a couple of other compulsory papers which I knew I wasn't much interested in. Labour relations. I wasn't the slightest bit interested in that. But there were some optional papers you see. I didn't *have* to do any of them, but I was interested in the subjects – particularly statistics and politics – so I did nine papers altogether instead of only five. Among the compulsory papers I really only worked on Principles and the Macro (the Money paper). I was very interested in that partly because of Joan Robinson's stimulating teaching. Oh, there was another good book that I used again for finals, a book by Tom Wilson called *Fluctuations in Income and Employment.*[11] I used that. It had just come out. I am sure I have got my copy of that somewhere around still. That was quite good. Yes, here it is, *Fluctuations in Income and Employment.* Oh no, I bought it in 1949. I had already graduated by then. January 1949. But no, that is my copy. I must have read it before buying it. I distinctly remember reading this for Part II. I didn't buy my own copy until afterwards.

TRIBE: You say you were in debt to book shops. Did you use the Marshall Library very much?

BECKERMAN: Yes, quite a bit.

TRIBE: How developed was it at that stage?

BECKERMAN: It was certainly adequately developed for my purposes. There were no problems. I never felt any constraint from the point of view of access to books or journals. You couldn't take books out as far as I can remember, except perhaps during the vacations. And that was why I bought a lot of books. Because I like books and, as you see, I have to write on them and mark them, so I had to have my own copies.

TRIBE: How did you finance your period as a graduate?

BECKERMAN: The college gave me an Exhibition and the Department of Education gave me a graduate grant for two years.

TRIBE: What was your initial topic? You said you worked on capital to start with.

BECKERMAN: Yes. Initially I wanted to work on measuring capital, measuring the stock of capital. I had already got vaguely interested in problems of

[11] T. Wilson, *Fluctuations in Income and Employment*, Pitman, London, 1942.

measuring productivity, partly because of my close friendship with Angus Maddison. I remember writing quite a big research paper, which I think wasn't bad, as an undergraduate; and Sraffa even asked whether I was thinking of trying to publish it. The paper was on the relationship between changes in capital stock and changes in productivity. I did a lot of work in the Easter vacation of my second year in the LSE Library. Quite an empirical piece of work. So I got interested in how to measure the capital stock. That was one of the reasons I started to get academic potential, you see. And so my first graduate research project was the measurement of the capital stock; which, of course, is ridiculous; you shouldn't be allowed to do it. Here in Oxford, I ran the graduate programme for three years, and we would never have let anybody do that. Much too difficult for graduates starting up graduate work. Something for Kuznets to do in his middle age. So I got interested in that, and Dick Stone was my supervisor. Now Dick was a wonderful man and I had enormous respect for him. He didn't pay very much attention to his supervisees though. I think I saw him three or four times in the whole two years I was his supervisee. Again, nothing like what students get these days, or what they demand these days, and he left me more or less to my own devices. I think I saw him twice in my first year of graduate work. And it was a hopelessly difficult task. *Hopelessly* difficult. You know capital theory, you couldn't find anything worse, you see. And then the idea of actually bringing it into a relationship with measurement problems! Hopelessly difficult! And I realised this at the end of the year. It was just hopeless. To do anything you had to be a top-rate economist, a top-rate mathematician, a top-rate accountant and philosopher, and God knows what else, and I wasn't any of these things – so I abandoned it. But I only had one more year left at Cambridge, and two more years to submit my Ph.D. thesis, you usually had to submit in three years. So I switched to a totally different topic – Anglo-Danish trade in the inter-war period.

TRIBE: That seems a very abstruse topic?

BECKERMAN: As I said, I was supervised by Dick Stone, who was also the Director of the Department of Applied Economics in Cambridge. Pretty well everybody there under his control had to work on one or other of two things. Either you worked on national accounting, which was where my measuring the capital stock fitted in his grand scheme; or you worked on demand analysis. As I had given up the capital stock topic I became a demand analyst. Measuring demand curves – my work on Anglo-Danish trade was actually econometrics: the estimation of demand curves for Danish butter, bacon and eggs, and the Danish demand curve for British coal – maybe I measured that as well. But any rate the chief thing was our demand curve for their butter, bacon and eggs. The reason why I picked Denmark was, well it is difficult for me to say, but I mean – you will think I am a terribly frivolous character, as I may well be – I had a Danish girlfriend and this was a wonderful pretext to go and spend some time in Copenhagen collecting statistics! I met her when she was an *au pair* girl in Cambridge. We had got on very well and I wanted to go and spend some time with her over in Denmark. It just happened to fit rather well because Anglo-Danish trade had a very simple structure. They sold very little else to us, and they were nice simple primary products, and so you could measure the elasticities quite well, and the impact on Denmark of changes in our demand was big enough, so that you could follow it through. And we were the main market, so the supply elasticity was very relevant; so it all fitted very well. So that was why I finished up doing Anglo-Danish trade in the inter-war period!

TRIBE: When did you complete that thesis, then?

BECKERMAN: I actually finished it in three years. Well, I finished the Danish thing in two years, but I would have submitted the thesis in 1951.

TRIBE: Who were your examiners?

BECKERMAN: Both Nobel Prize winners. No, sorry, it is not true. My supervisor, Dick Stone, won a Nobel Prize. And one of my two examiners was James Meade, who also won a Nobel Prize. The other examiner was Charles Carter. But I completed the whole operation within the three years of becoming a graduate student. It took me two years to do the thesis. In my third year I moved to Nottingham, where I was a lecturer in economics.

TRIBE: Brian Tew's appointment to the Chair there occurred about the same time, didn't it?

BECKERMAN: He had gone there before me of course. It was him who hired me.

TRIBE: How many of you were there on the staff at that time?

BECKERMAN: There weren't many. But it was very, very good! It was a small department, and it contained a sort of sub-department which was called Industrial Economics, but I think that was because it was a hangover, I suspect, from the old days. I never really bothered to check up or ask, but I suspect that there had been staff already installed there who had been teaching traditional industrial economics or something beforehand, and when they re-organised the place they set up a proper economics department and brought Brian back from Adelaide to run it. The industrial economics group included Ivor Pearce, who was brilliant as a proper theoretical economist, and another chap whom I happened to know because he was at Trinity with me; but he didn't do graduate work at Cambridge, he went straight to Nottingham. Ivor Pearce was the star of the place, of course. He had gone into industrial economics because he was also a qualified accountant. He was much older than us. Already in his late thirties. The Economics Department – leaving aside the industrial economics – consisted of Brian Tew, a chap called André Gabor, who was a frightfully nice Hungarian. He taught basic economic theory. There was me, and I just gave lectures on international trade, although I also gave classes in basic theory; and then we got Stanley James there, who came about nine months after me to teach economic statistics. I had known him slightly in Cambridge. He was at Trinity and he worked for Dick Stone in the

Department of Applied Economics after he had graduated. He was a first-rate mathematician. I play bridge with him. He lives in Oxford. Stanley was a very, very good mathematical economist. I wrote an article in 1953 co-authored with him which I couldn't have done without his help.[12] And Ivor Pearce in his first, and perhaps best article on factor price equalisation,[13] got Stanley to help him with the maths, although later on Ivor became so good at maths that he could do it without anybody's help. But Stanley didn't stay on. He went into the Civil Service not long after I left Nottingham. I have never asked him why. So it was a very small department, but I enjoyed it enormously! Enormously! Stanley and I spent most of our time playing chess, bridge, tennis, fencing, badminton, swimming. We kept fantastically fit. And during that two years I wrote six articles which were published in the top journals. So you know, all this business about fitness and whatnot, it helps! It was my most productive period in terms of my output per unit of time. I wrote six articles. They weren't all published in that two years. Some of them came out in the subsequent period. I would come home late at night and I would get an idea and I would work half the night.

TRIBE: So why, then, did you go to the OEEC?

BECKERMAN: Oh well, that is very simple. I was engaged to get married to a French girl whom I met just before I left Cambridge, and I couldn't possibly expect anybody to marry me on my salary then. I had never been so poor in my life. I was poorer as an Assistant Lecturer in Nottingham than I had been as a graduate student in Cambridge. It was awful. When my students here complain about the grants not being big enough, my God, at least in Cambridge I used to supplement my income by working on farms and whatnot in the vacations. But I couldn't do that somehow in Nottingham as an Assistant Lecturer, there was nothing like that going. And I was so poor that I couldn't afford to buy newspapers. I used to read the ones in the Senior Common Room and then if I hadn't finished them I would take them home at night. Appallingly poor. Well, I couldn't expect a young lady who was used to a reasonable standard of living and was earning three times as much as me in her job in Paris to come and live with me in utter poverty in a virtually empty flat. It was a nice flat, but it was in the worst part of Nottingham. It was right opposite the gas works, the stink around was terrible. If anybody in Nottingham asked, 'Where do you live?' I used to say, 'Oh, you go up the Middleton Boulevard until the smell becomes unbearable and that is where I live.' I couldn't get married under those conditions.

I was offered a job by Robert Hall.[14] Brian Tew apparently had a high opinion of me. Wonderful man, Brian Tew. When he knew I desperately

[12] W. Beckerman, S.F. James, 'Interdependence of Consumer Preferences in the Theory of Income Distribution', *Economic Journal*, vol. LXIII (March 1953), pp. 70–83.

[13] S. James and I. Pearce, 'The Factor Price Equalisation Myth', *Review of Economic Studies*, vol. XIX (1951–52), pp. 111–20.

[14] Director of the Economic Section of the Cabinet Office.

needed to earn some more money he wrote to Christopher Dow, who was then deputy to Robert Hall, and I went to see Robert Hall who interviewed me himself. Not like that these days. After half an hour Robert said, 'Yes, OK, we will hire you.' Offered me a salary which was slightly over twice what I was earning in Nottingham. I was earning in Nottingham £500 a year and he was offering me something like £1100 or something. Wonderful for me. He said, 'Would you like to go and talk about your work to Christopher Dow, my Deputy, who is just down the corridor?' And I went along to see Christopher, whom I had never met before, and chatted to him, and Christopher said, 'Well, why are you doing this, you are obviously going to do all right academically?' And I explained to him I needed to earn the money and so Christopher, with his wonderful logic, says, 'Oh, if it is money you want to earn this isn't the place to go, why don't you go and work for an international organisation where you can get paid a lot more and then you can save up and come back to academic life?'

Now, actually, I had already been interviewed by the Economic Commission for Europe in Geneva by Teddy Jackson. The people you had in those days! You had Teddy Jackson, Hal Lary and Tibor Barna: these were the people who interviewed me in Geneva. They eventually did offer me a job, but the offer came too late. The UN is a great bureaucracy. It took an awful long time for my appointment to go through the machinery so their offer came too late. Meanwhile, you see, Christopher said, 'Why don't you go to work for an international organisation? I have the Deputy Secretary General for the OEEC coming to see me in a few minutes; if you like, hang around I will ask him if he would like to have a talk to you.' So, OK, it seemed to be very logical! Oh sure, what can I lose. So anyway the Deputy Secretary General for the OEEC was Sir Harry Lintott, an ex-mathematician. Also a terrific guy, first-rate chap. After he had seen Dow on official business he then talked to me, and he had obviously been briefed on me by Christopher or Robert Hall, I don't know, on my background. And he said, 'Yes, well, it looks as if we ought to be able to give you a job. I will arrange for you to come across for an interview.' About a week later I got a telegram from the OEEC Personnel Department: 'Come for an interview.' I was interviewed, believe it or not, by Marjolin himself, the Secretary General. Imagine that sort of thing happening these days. He was a marvellous man. One of the greatest men I have ever met. And we had a really interesting discussion. A technical discussion about economics. He really understood the concepts, and everything. Didn't look as if he was in a hurry; he had time to talk to nobodies like me you see, relative nobodies. And then a few days later I got a telegram offering me the job. And I took it. So I finished up in the OEEC. And Christopher was quite right: the salary, I don't know, I have never worked it out, was about five times what I was getting at Nottingham. Yes, it would have been five times that. It was £2,500 a year. Tax free as well. So I went to the OEEC.

TRIBE: What did you do there?

BECKERMAN: A series of different jobs. At the beginning I was really thrown into the deep end. I worked for a very eccentric character called François Walter, a Frenchman. The Economics Directors before that had all been English. One after the other. Donald McDougall and Cairncross and Reddaway, three in a row. And then they got some Belgian called Kirschen, who was dynamic. I liked him, an engineer, was very interesting, but didn't know much economics. So he had underneath him a Head of Division, that was the structure: I mean Kirschen would be at director level, A7 I think; and A6 would be the Head of Division, François Walter, who was a wonderful guy as a human being, really *sympathique*, and he was one of the few Frenchmen who knew Keynesian economics. He was one of these small group like Pierre Uri and a few others who, before, during and immediately after the war, had got on to Western economics and Keynesian economics, and understood it. He wasn't very well organised about it, but he understood it. He was completely disorganised. Had no idea of how to work in an office and shortly after I arrived we had to write the Fourth Annual Report of the OEEC, which was mainly an economics report and which had to be written mainly by François Walter – which meant that *I* was writing most of it! That was the second most useful thing I have learnt in my life, which I have used far more than what I learned from Sraffa. As I say, I hardly ever used his knowledge – how to *really* analyse whether something is logical or not. But from Walter I learned how to write fast; and boy, that stood me in good stead for the rest of my life! Because he was totally disorganised.[15] He would say, 'Beckerman' – (well, we talked in French to each other because my wife was French and I was fluent in French) – so he would say the equivalent of, 'Beckerman, for this meeting tomorrow let's give them drafts of Chapters 1, 2 and 3.' And I knew it was a waste of time. We would do a rushed hasty job and, of course, it would be torn up by the committee, and then we would have to do it all again. Instead of saying, 'Right we will give you Chapter 1 next week, and Chapter 2 three weeks later, and Chapter 3 a couple weeks after that', so we could do a carefully prepared job and think about it. No, Walter would say, 'Right, well, tomorrow we will come back with revised drafts.' So we just tore up the first drafts and threw them all away. And then hastily wrote new ones. Crazy. But I learnt to write fast.

I remember one occasion, coming to a meeting, with the British delegation. It was a special meeting, I forget why. The British delegation was Christopher Dow and Robert Neild. Robert Neild was in the Government Economic Service for a short time in Robert Hall's outfit, and Walter and I were going up in the lift to the meeting and Dow and Neild got in at the same time. Now the previous evening I had been working with Walter on the draft for this meeting in his flat, because he lived not far from where I lived in west Paris;

---

[15] See Angus Maddison's description of Walter and the OEEC in his 'Confessions of a Chiffrephile', *Banca Nazionale del Lavoro Quarterly Review*, vol. 47 (1994), pp. 132–3.

and it was going on all night so we didn't want to work in the office, we worked in his flat, and then about two o'clock in the morning Walter was already lying on his bed sort of talking a bit and I realised this was a waste of time and I insisted we pack it up. He really wasn't awake any longer. I was still awake but he wasn't awake, and so he agreed we could pack up and so I toddled off home about two in the morning. The next morning we all got into the lift by coincidence at the same time, and Walter said, 'Oh yes, zee draft would 'ave been finished, but Beckerman, 'e wanted to go to bed at two o'clock in zee morning!' So I said, 'Yes, tell them! A whole night's work wasted! Blame it all on Beckerman, he was too tired!' So I did all sorts of things. I got a bit fed up with this after a while and, thank God, Angus[16] arrived and was able to share the work with me, and shoulder a lot of the responsibility. He arrived about a year later, 1953.

But I got fed up with this disorganised work, and wanted to do something serious; and so I asked the then Director of the Statistics Department, who was Milton Gilbert, if I could transfer into his outfit. I could see there was some interesting research going on that Gilbert had initiated when he arrived in 1953 on international comparisons of real products. You know, the research that became the great big international comparative project directed by Irving Kravis. I could see that there was some serious research going on, and I wanted to do some serious research instead of all this quasi-journalism that I was doing under Walter. It was journalism really. And so I moved over into some sub-section of Gilbert's Statistics Directorate, where we did research, and I had a lot more spare time. In fact I published articles in three of the top journals in 1956. In that year I published an article in *Econometrica*,[17] an article in the *Economic Journal*,[18] and an article in the *Review of Economics and Statistics*.[19] You know, I was working on these things when nobody was looking – pulling stuff out of the drawer and hoping my boss wouldn't turn up and look to see what I was at. So you know, I had these academic interests still very much at heart, and was much happier doing a quiet research job. I actually wrote the Gilbert and Associates' book on *Comparative National Products and Price Levels*, which was the sequel to Gilbert and Kravis. I wasn't involved in the Gilbert and Kravis study, which was the first pioneering comparison of five countries. I wasn't actually involved in that. But then Gilbert decided to extend it to a sequel covering nine countries, and I wrote the whole book, except one chapter that Stephen Marris wrote. But the book was signed 'Gilbert and Associates'. Since Gilbert didn't even write the bloody letter of transmittal and the acknowledgements at the beginning – I had to write that

---

[16] Angus Maddison.

[17] W. Beckerman, 'The World Trade Matrix Multiplier and the Stability of World Trade', *Econometrica*, vol. 24, no. 2 (July 1956).

[18] W. Beckerman, 'The Economist as at Modern Missionary', *Economic Journal*, vol. 66 (1956), pp. 108–15.

[19] W. Beckerman, 'Distance and the Pattern of Intra-European Trade', *Review of Economics and Statistics*, vol. XXXVIII, no. 1 (February 1956).

for him – at the last minute, when I sent off the proofs, I thought of changing it. I had written an acknowledgement for him saying 'How much I acknowledge the assistance of so and so and so and so and Wilfred Beckerman in writing this book.' And I thought, 'He's never going to look at this, he didn't even look at the original, I'll change it round and I'll sign the book Wilfred Beckerman and say how much I was indebted to the contribution made by Milton Gilbert.' He wouldn't have known! But at the last minute my nerve failed.

Anyway, the fact is that he was the intellectual inspiration behind the work. He worked out the whole system: how you should make real expenditure comparisons between countries. There were an enormous number of conceptual problems to be faced, such as what weights do you use, and how do you price non-comparable goods? How do you make sure that the shoes you are pricing in France are comparable with the shoes you are pricing in England? Machinery and housing? Enormous conceptual problems, particularly the quality problem – the proper way of adjusting for differences in quality. Gilbert really worked it all out. He was the mastermind behind it. He had been very much involved in the Gilbert and Kravis study you see. Then Kravis went back to America; he was only over for a year or so to do this. So when we got onto the sequel Gilbert had already done all the intellectual work, and he wasn't very interested in the nitty gritty. He was a bit like me. He was a chap after my own heart, you know, once you have sort of done something, solved the problems and worked out the ideas, to hell with fiddling about with all the details, you go on to something else. And so he didn't make much input into the sequel. Nevertheless, he deserved the credit. It was true I wrote it, apart from the Marris chapter, but I was just sort of writing up the results from the actual work that had all been done. It was all Gilbert's conceptual work behind it. We were just applying it really. So he deserved the credit. Yes, he was such a lazy bugger too! We used to spend half our time playing chess.

TRIBE: So you came back to the National Institute?

BECKERMAN: I came back in 1962.

TRIBE: And then you came to Balliol?

BECKERMAN: And then I came to Balliol. Well, you see, both moves were supposed to be only temporary. When I went to the OEEC I intended to go only for two years in order to save up enough money and then I would go back to England. Brian Tew assured me that I could go straight back to a Readership, because I would be giving up a salary which would be bigger than anybody on the Selection Committee, including the Vice-Chancellor. He thought they would be impressed by that and by that time, as I say, I had already had six articles accepted for publication in major journals. I was bound to have got a Readership in those days. So, if I saved enough money I could buy a house or something, and I was intending to come back after two years. But I found I quite enjoyed it there; and I loved Paris, especially after this first crazy year working for Walter. I was then able to do work on these little articles in my spare time, so life got a lot easier, I stayed on. And in 1961 I was asked by the National Institute to come and do their long-term forecasting study, because I had done a lot of work for the OEEC on the Eighth Annual Report. This was a medium-term forecast – quite a pioneering piece of long-term forecasting. We forecast the evolution of the European economy for several years ahead. And I had also been consultant to a great big work by Dewhurst, Coppock and Yates on 'Europe's Needs and Resources'. Again, a long-term forecast. So the National Institute knew about this and asked me if I would come and direct this big study for them, *The British Economy in 1975*.[20] So I accepted, for two years. And I got two years' leave of absence from the OECD, thinking I'd go for two years to do this study, and then come back again. But once again, while I was in England I was asked whether I would be interested in the Fellowship at Balliol. It wasn't an ordinary tutorial Fellowship in economics that I was offered originally. It was a Senior Research Fellowship. It was a P.D. Leake Senior Research Fellowship in Accountancy. Now, I am not an accountant but Dick Stone's Chair in Cambridge was the P.D. Leake Chair in Accountancy, so I knew perfectly well that whatever the appointment was called you still had a lot of latitude as regards what you actually worked on. So I applied on the grounds that I was going to do some more work on national accounting, which was my intention. My formal position at the OECD was Head of the National Accounts Division. For although I was doing various sorts of research work really, I was also responsible for producing the OECD's annual national accounts Yearbooks. Of course, I had three or four assistants who did most of that for me, and a couple of other people who worked with me on interesting projects. So I was qualified for the Balliol post. I was agonising about whether to take it or not. It was a very difficult decision to take, because it entailed an enormous cut in income. But in the end I never regretted it, and so that was how I finished up not going back to the OECD. I had been on leave of absence for two years, but I never went back.

TRIBE: So how did the connection with the Board of Trade come about?

BECKERMAN: That was on account of Tony Crosland who was the President of the Board of Trade.[21] I never really found out exactly how it came about. I am pretty sure I know what happened. I never asked *him*. It was out of the blue. I was in Greece at the time doing some work for the OECD helping the Greeks with their long-term plans, and I got a telegram from my wife saying something like, 'Come back quickly, they are offering you the job as Economic Adviser to the President of the Board of Trade.' So I came back, and went in to see Crosland and we chatted for half an hour. He asked me my views on this, that and the other. And at the end he said, 'Fine. OK, right, we will be getting in touch with you.' So I got up to go and I said, 'How long will

---

[20] W. Beckerman and Associates, *The British Economy in 1975*, Cambridge University Press, London, 1965.
[21] Crosland was President of the Board of Trade from 1967 to 1969.

it be before you let me know whether I have go the job?' And he said, 'Oh no, you have got the job, that is settled.' I think what happened was that Tony Crosland had gone into the Board of Trade only about a month or two months before, something like that. He realised that although there were people inside the Board of Trade who were supposed to be qualified economists and were supposed to be giving him economic advice, he realised – and these are my words not his – that these economists didn't know a demand curve from a telegraph pole. Unlike his predecessor, Douglas Jay, Crosland knew that he wasn't a professional economist. He had known a lot of economics. If you look at Ian Little's book *Critique of Welfare Economics*, you will see that at the beginning Little says he is indebted to Tony Crosland for going through the draft very carefully.[22] But Tony was a sufficiently great man to know his limitations. He knew that he hadn't kept up with the subject and he wanted a real professional economist, and not these two or three civil servants who had probably dabbled in economics twenty years earlier. So he needed a professional economic adviser, and he wanted somebody who was quantitative. Now by that time I was regarded as probably one of the most quantitative economists in the country. And I was on the whole sympathetic to the Labour Party. Tommy Balogh knew me; I was really his successor at Balliol, you see, and we got on very well. I am not 100 per cent sure, but I am 90 per cent sure, that Crosland had said to his pals, like Nicky Kaldor and one or two others, 'I need a proper economist, someone who is quantitative, who is basically in sympathy, politically in sympathy, and can you suggest anybody?' And they suggested a few names and I was presumably one of them; and I think that is how it happened. And so he offered me the job on the basis of what people had told him.

TRIBE: So this was the beginning of the post when Crosland appointed you?

BECKERMAN: Yes, there hadn't been any such post in the Board of Trade.

TRIBE: Has it been continuous since then?

BECKERMAN: Yes, but it changed form. There was a gap after me for some time and then Crosland left the Department. Not long after I did. Moved into Environment. Became Secretary of State for the Environment. And I think there was nobody there for a while and then they got in Alan Peacock. But I don't know whether already they had re-organised it so that he had a five-year contract, and he was the head of the Economic Advisory Service in the Board of Trade, whereas I wasn't, you see, I was quite separate. There was still an Economic Advisory Service in the Board of Trade, but I was quite separate. I advised the President direct. I had direct access to him, but, of course, everything that the 'economists' said was copied to me, and I could comment on it, and they would consult me and so on. So I was on very good terms with them.

---

[22] 'I am also specially indebted to Mr. C.A.R. Crosland, at whose insistence many improvements of style and exposition have been made'; I.M.D. Little, *A Critique of Welfare Economics*, Oxford University Press, London, 1950, 'Preface', n.p.

TRIBE: Was there any initial friction brought about between the economists who were there and someone coming in from outside – who really hadn't been in the Civil Service?

BECKERMAN: Well, a bit to begin with. Not so much between me and the economists, but between me and the Permanent Secretary to the Board of Trade, Sir Richard Powell. He was dead against getting an economist in to start with. I suspect that he tried to sabotage the level of my appointment, if not the appointment itself. For example, at this interview I had with Tony Crosland, I raised the question of my salary and he told me that the salary would be £X,000. Nothing happened for ten days. I didn't get any letter from their personnel department for ten days, and I thought that was very odd, particularly since Crosland appeared to be anxious that I start work as soon as possible. And then I got this letter in which they offered me a salary significantly below what Crosland had offered. And so I wrote to him. But, on advice, I wrote directly to him at his private address saying in effect, 'I am very sorry I can't take the job. I would love to work for you, tremendous opportunity, but there is a limit to how much sacrifice I can expect my family to incur just because I would like to work for you in this job.' It had all been kept quiet from him, how much they were offering me, and it looked rather like sabotage; they were getting the result that they had expected. I was turning down the job. Anyway he was absolutely furious about it apparently. And so there was some friction between me and Sir Richard Powell. There were some excellent, first-rate chaps in the Board of Trade with whom I got on very well, but there was a lot of friction between him and me. We always argued at any meeting. He had almost every misconception about economics you could possibly have. For example, he believed that only output that is, in turn, an economic input into something else is worthwhile; so no value in consumer goods, let alone things like education, health, and so on. They do not, he believed, add to output. He just couldn't understand that, in the end, what you want from economic activity is to raise the standard of living. What is so good about it going indirectly rather than going in directly? We were always arguing, you see. But, thank God, he reached retirement age about six months after I arrived, and was replaced by a completely different sort of chap. Anthony Part. Completely different sort of person. Excellent. Very lively and receptive. So some people there were very receptive. The good people were always receptive to economic advice. Tony Part was receptive and he trusted me after a while when he found that I did actually know what I was talking about on things that he consulted me about. The Deputy Secretary in charge of the whole of the trade side, Bill Hughes, was another wonderful man. He was an ex-classicist. He didn't pretend to know any economics. But he knew when to ask for advice and he understood it when he was given it. So I never had any problems with him *at all*. First-rate man.

The people with whom I had the friction with were one or two old hands who had reached Under-Secretary level. They thought they knew what they were doing and didn't want this economist bastard screwing up all their schemes for helping industrialists. They all become tools of pressure groups. The Ministry of Agriculture were tools of the farmers, and at the Board of Trade they became tools of their pet industrialists. Terrible things they would try to get up to. One of the worst cases was when an Under-Secretary wanted to get the government to agree to subsidise the building of hotels. He brought along his calculations, he showed how much they got from receipts from hotels from their customers, what they paid in room rents, he compared that with the capital cost of the hotels and he said, 'Look, there is a terrific rate of return here, 40 per cent!' He did not seem to realise that the hotels do actually use people to do work, and you use materials and services and so on, that you have got to knock all this off before you find what the rate of return on the capital was – he hadn't any idea of that! So of course I tried to scupper his scheme, you see. And so he didn't like me. Here he was, he was getting on well with the people in the hotel industry; and here was this bugger Beckerman mucking it all up! So these people didn't like it. I didn't care. I had nothing to lose. It wasn't my career. That was what Crosland got me there for. To stop some of these people doing crazy things. So it was mixed. I don't think I ever had any problems with the really good people there. There was a slight problem with Sir Alan Neale for a time. He wasn't Sir, he was Alan Neale then. He had been an Under-Secretary, and he was a very clever chap indeed. His knowledge of economics was rather limited, but he was a world authority on regulating monopolies, and had written a most scholarly standard work on antitrust legislation in the USA for the National Institute.[23] I think he was a bit dubious and nervous about his position at first. When I was brought into the Board of Trade part of the deal was that he would be promoted from being Under-Secretary to becoming Second Permanent Secretary in order to keep him happy and give more weight to the insiders. He was head of the Economic Services inside the Board of Trade. So the relationship wasn't too good at first, but it got better because I liked him, and I think he realised that I did know what I was talking about on the subjects I was consulted about – and we played bridge regularly, at the Reform Club! So it was OK. Then he went off to the Treasury.

TRIBE: A point made to me by Sir Henry Hardman was that there were . . .

BECKERMAN: Oh yes, I knew him, yes. Great chap. He was at the OECD for a bit. He was the head of the Economics Committee at the OECD that I used to work for under François Walter for a while.

TRIBE: He was saying that there was a group of older economists who met regularly at the Reform Club up to quite recently. He was talking about Harry Campion[24] and others, that generation.

---

[23] A.D. Neale, *The Antitrust Laws of the USA: A Study of Competition Enforced by Law*, 2nd edn, Cambridge University Press, London, 1970.

[24] One of the founders, in 1941, and then later Director, of the Central Statistical Office; see A. Cairncross, N. Watts, *The Economic Section 1939–1961: A Study in Economic Advising*, Routledge, London, 1989, p. 31.

BECKERMAN: Yes, well, practically every senior professional economist was a member of the Reform Club in those days. There was a little club within it called the Political Economy Club, or something. I only went along to a couple of the meetings. There would be two or three good people there, but there would also be a lot of members of the Reform Club who thought they were economists and weren't, you know. Didn't know anything about it at all. They would talk an awful lot and I just got bored, so I only went to a couple of these meetings. Campion was a member of the Reform Club, I used to see him nearly every day at lunch there. He would be there with his little coterie, with a couple of other statisticians. I don't remember their names now. I thought they were generally rather an obstructive trio; suspicious of any change, any innovation; it was always too difficult, you couldn't change this, you couldn't do it this way. Always negative. Most of the economists in Whitehall were members of the Reform Club. Tommy was a member. Nicky was a member.[25] Christopher Dow was a member, everybody. Donald McDougall was a member. John Jukes was a member. It was known as the Treasury Cafeteria. So one could meet and discuss things. And one did so all the time without having to meet officially . . . There was no point in having an official organisation. There was also a dining club set up by me, actually, with Ralph Turvey – who was also a member of the Reform Club – soon after I joined the Board of Trade. It was a dining club just for senior economists in the government service. We didn't want to have the top boys in. We didn't have Nicky in, because Nicky would have dominated the conversation, you wouldn't have got a word edgeways in. Or Tommy, the two of them together would have been just arguing, haggling all the time. But there was Ken Berrill, Wynne Godley was in, and me, Michael Posner, Turvey, Fred Atkinson, Alan Williams was a member. Leonard Nicholson, he was a member. Kit MacMahon was a member in his capacity of being at the Bank of England. So that was once a month. It was a dining club, but every month somebody would have to introduce a topic and then, after the food, we would seriously discuss the topic. I am not aware of any other organisations.

TRIBE: So you are talking really about the late 1960s?

BECKERMAN: Late 1960s, that's right. I went to the Board of Trade in October 1967 and that was the situation. There was the Political Economy Club or whatever it is called inside the Reform Club, which in my day wasn't worth going to. It may have changed. I think it went through a better period a few years ago, I am not sure. There were these three statisticians, Harry Campion and whatnot, but not many people talked to them. They talked mainly to each other. And there was this dining club once a month. They were the only ones I know about. The top economic advisers in the relevant departments used to meet once a week and we arranged this informally. We became known as the Council of Economic Advisers, copying the American system,

---

[25] Tommy Balogh and Nicky Kaldor.

which was formally created about six months after I went in, but that was of no importance whatsoever. Everybody forgot it. We were this group of top economic advisers to the Labour Government at the time and we met regularly every week at a working lunch, where we swapped views. What is going on in our department, and so on, and how do we view problems which would be common to all of us so that we weren't giving advice which was needlessly inconsistent or contradictory just because we hadn't sorted it out with each other.

TRIBE: So what you are saying in effect, then, is that the economists in government, because of their backgrounds and the fact that they had worked together before being in government, actually carried that into government and the co-ordination occurred because of their relationships, professional and personal relationships developed over the years before?

BECKERMAN: Yes, that's right. We had all known each other before. That was how we were recruited. As I said, I was recommended to Tony Crosland by people who knew me. That was certainly the case with Michael Posner, and all the other people. Oh, Robert Neild, he only stayed two years in government and then he pushed off to Sweden. Yes, that was how it worked. Of course it doesn't mean that we had much *influence*, apart from Kaldor and the two others in the Treasury – Berrill and Posner. And maybe that's a completely different story. We may have all been giving the same advice, but I suppose that means that the government was being equally consistent in rejecting much of it! If they had been getting conflicting advice, it would have been more difficult to have rejected all of it without being grossly inconsistent!

12

BERNARD CORRY

Bernard Corry was born in 1930 and was an undergraduate at the LSE from 1948 to 1951. After two years in the RAF doing National Service, he returned as a postgraduate student in 1953. After a brief spell teaching in Durham, he returned to an Assistant Lectureship at LSE in 1958, coinciding with a period in which the 'Young Turks' were challenging the established economic order (see the interview with Richard Lipsey on pp. 206–224). Although he was responsible for the teaching of economic thought at LSE, he joined the M²T seminar. He is now Emeritus Professor of Economics at Queen Mary and Westfield College, London. The following is an edited version of an interview conducted in his office on 10 January 1995.

CORRY: I did my Higher School Certificate in 1948, and Higher Schools was very different from A level. People would say it is about the same level, but I did five subjects, which you had to if you were doing 'Commerce'. You did four if you were doing Arts or Science. And I studied, in the Sixth Form, Geography, French, British Constitution, which was a sort of Government paper, Economic History, and Economics. Five separate papers. And I got a State Scholarship to the London School of Economics.

TRIBE: What sort of text did you use at school?

CORRY: We used a book by Silverman, but our main school text was Benham. Later on there was I think about a fifth edition of Silverman, and Austin Robinson in the *Economic Journal* reviewed it and said, 'The candidate can no longer be sure that they will fail if they use this book.'[1] But I do remember in the local library in East London coming across Keynes' *General Theory*. I didn't know how to pronounce it, and for years I called him 'Keanes'. But I did read bits of it and I didn't quite understand it. My Economics teacher at school was a history master, Victor Cohen, a very influential man. He produced I think, looking back, several professors in about four years,

---

[1] 'It is no longer absolutely certain that anyone who reproduced it perfectly would fail in a first-year examination.' E.A.G. Robinson reviewing the 13th edition of H.A. Silverman, *The Substance of Economics* (1950) in the *Economic Journal*, vol. 62 (1952), p. 366.

mainly in social studies. Some of them, like Philip Foster, the sociologist, and Peter Hart, both well-known figures.

TRIBE: Which school was this?

CORRY: This was Leyton County High School in East London. People call them grammar schools today, but we never heard the word, and we called them High Schools. When I went up to LSE I think I wanted to do sociology. I wasn't sure what it was. But I did sign on for Economics. And I did a bit of sociology. Well I started, but soon gave up, Morris Ginsberg's course on social philosophy; I really didn't understand a word of it. And that put me off almost for life, I think, although I have come back to it in the last fifteen years. So I was more concerned with Economics. But the most influential person was Karl Popper. Now the structure of the degree then was a funny one, and it relates to current educational thinking. I had done well enough in my Higher School examinations to go up to university with an Intermediate B.Sc. (Econ.). If you did well you got your Inter, which meant that theoretically I could do my degree in two years. Now today people say it is impossible to do a degree in two years, but I think a lot of people could do so. People who didn't have Inter did a three-year degree at LSE and the first year was what you would now call a Part I. But because I was so young and you couldn't graduate then until you were 21, so in fact I did the programme there. I spent three years really on a two-year programme. So in the first year of the degree proper we had 'Economics Principles' from Lionel Robbins, twice a week. We had a course they called 'Topics in Applied Economics', which members of the department gave; for example, Richard Sayers gave two or three lectures on banking, Ronnie Edwards on the structure of industry, and so on. But the course that I remember the most, and influenced most people I suppose of my generation there, was Karl Popper. We had compulsory papers in Economics; and then we had options – and everybody incidentally had to do two languages as well. But the options I picked were Elementary Statistical Methods, which Roy Allen taught; and after giving up social philosophy I switched to . . . I think the course was called 'Logic and Scientific Method', but I wouldn't swear to that – and the lecturer was then *Dr* Karl Popper. He got his Chair I think about two years later.

Now I wasn't being a precocious youth, but I wasn't unfamiliar with Popper, because once again in the local library I had come across *The Open Society and its Enemies* – the two volumes. And that had shaken me a bit because I thought I was a Marxist. I had read a bit of Karl Marx; I had joined the Socialist Party of Great Britain, because I liked their badge, it said 'The world for the workers', I used to wear it to school and the teachers got upset. So I wasn't unfamiliar with that line of enquiry. Anyhow, Popper lectured twice a week. But of course you'd worried all the time about whether history has a meaning. Are there laws of history? What is a science? Is Economics valid? All the questions we were worrying about, and Popper seemed to give absolutely clear answers to everything. The hypothetico-deductive system we used to chant; and falsifiability not verificationism, we used to shout! Some of my friends who weren't taking Popper, like Michael Swift, now dead, an anthropologist, were getting a very different line of course, because they were more influenced by people like Ed Shils, and the Chicago School of Sociology. I think Michael read Rex Tugwell, and people like that. And he used to say, 'It's all not so simple', but we thought, well, that just showed that Economics, because it was accepting Popperian canons, was streets ahead of these daft things like Anthropology and Sociology and so-called Political Science.

When I was an undergraduate there weren't exam papers in specific bits of economics. In my finals I took nine papers. First of all the ninth paper was a general English essay. Now that may sound very odd. It wasn't anything to do with economics. You did a three-hour essay to test your 'presentational skills'. And the topics might be something like 'The Future of Democracy', or 'Should we abolish the House of Lords?' or 'Culture must be for an elite. Discuss.' I don't know if everybody ever failed it, but that was the ninth paper. Now on the other eight papers I did two Theory papers, two Applied papers. Economic History was compulsory. I still feel that was a good decision, I think forced by Robbins. That is five. An Economics essay. Now this isn't the general English essay, but we had a three-hour economics essay when you had to answer one or two questions. And there would be something like, 'The Future of the Gold Standard', or 'Inflation', just general headings. 'The Quantity Theory' – I think that was the one I answered, in a Popperian framework. And then I did my two options, which was my Elementary Statistics paper and my Popper paper, Logic and Scientific Method. You had your general principles course from Robbins, and these topics in Applied. And you had a statistics course that Roy Allen took us through, all the things that became his elementary book, I guess. And then odd people in the department would give courses of, say, ten lectures. So, for example, I remember fifteen lectures from Ronnie Coase on public utility pricing. I was totally impressed because he never seemed to have any notes, and he just sat warming his bum on the radiator; and just walked in and talked. Ralph Turvey, who had just come back from Sweden full of period analysis; he was my tutor actually. Your written work was really done for your tutor. He impressed me enormously. I mean, as a father figure, like Victor Cohen my school teacher had been. He had a roll-neck sweater as I recall, so I bought one and I think he wore corduroys, so I bought a pair of corduroys; and he used to say to me things like, 'Don't you read Swedish?' He said, 'Now in your first term you will write a book on consumer theory.' Now don't forget I had just come from school. Although I knew some economics, and I felt that when I listened to other people in the classes I knew as much as them, even though they had taken the Inter there. So I did my book on consumer theory and the first book he gave me to read was Samuelson's *Foundations*, which had just come out. I had to read the section on 'Consumer Theory Post Indifference Curves.' And then the second term, he said, 'Now write me a book on the theory of production'. So what I am supposed to read? He said, 'Well, Schneider.' So after that I said, 'Well, what about some applied work?' And he said, 'Write me an essay on location theory. You read German'; well, actually, I did but not very well; and I remember he said, 'Well, the best book is Torg Pallander, *Betriebsstandorttheorie.*' So I would go to the library with a dictionary and try to get through that. He had also, I think, been to America, I am not sure of this, I think he had been, and he was the first person I saw who in a sense was doing modelling. He actually started putting a Keynesian system in equations. Not fancy ones, because I don't think he knew any calculus, but I mean he could do y as f of x. Fairly advanced in those days. And he used four quadrant diagrams, which obviously was the Pallander Swedish influence. We didn't use ISLM much. In my second year I had to do a synthesis of macro for him – as a book, because he called these long essays 'books'. And I began to get the idea, because it used to puzzle me that anything could happen in economics. What would happen if interest rates went down? And you thought, 'My God, I just don't know!' Well, I think, actually that is the correct answer today. Looking for certainty. It seemed as though these models actually could, as we would now say, 'sign the derivative'. And I found that a great leap forward. And I am thinking now about Chris Archibald's famous paper on monopolistic competition: can you sign the effects? And that was thought to come from this formal modelling; I don't mean this too mathematically.

And then we had Henry Phelps Brown, who gave the Economics of Labour. But that once again wasn't for a paper called Labour Economics, it all meshed in and you went to the lectures or you didn't. And we didn't have classes in these separate topics, because they weren't exam papers. We had a Theory class a week, and an Applied class a week. And for my Applied class I had Alan Peacock. No, I first of all had Ronnie Tress. And that was terribly impressive once again. You must realise that neither the Theory nor the Applied class were in a sense technical. After Ronnie Tress we had Alan Peacock. And I remember, because I was a bit of a show-off, and I actually read an article in the JPE by Lawrence Klein on estimating macro models or something, and so I had to give a paper on forecasting. You would do it in words, or you could do. 'What is consumption going to be like next year? Well, like it is this year plus or minus a bit.' There was no 'modelling'. But I learned the word 'parameter'. I wasn't quite sure what it meant, because I remember saying, 'The parameters of the system are . . .' and I wrote numbers on the board; and everybody said, 'What the hell are you talking about?' So I was beginning to get a bit into technicalities, but there was still this emphasis on the generality exemplified in the exam papers. Whether that was due to Robbins I don't know. Anyhow, that is the degree I took. Then I graduated. I then went into the Air Force.

TRIBE: Was that deferred National Service?

CORRY: That was deferred National Service, exactly. I came from a poor home. My father was a merchant seaman who, when he left the sea in the early 1930s, when I was born, found it difficult to get work; and then got a job as a labourer for Waygood-Otis, you will see relics of it in this building. And then, of course, got work in the war developing the Central Line, which was used as air raid shelters because it only went, I think, to Liverpool Street, something like that. And then he died when I was quite young, 15 or so. My brother was the first one to stay in the Sixth Form, never mind about going on to college. We knew nobody at all who had got a degree apart from, I suppose, the teachers who taught us. So why go to university? And relatives of mine and, I suppose, all my friends, apart from one or two, left school at 16. To go to the High School you had to guarantee you would stop on until you took what was called School Certificate. Your parents had to sign that.

TRIBE: When was that? When you entered at 11?

CORRY: Yes. And it was to stop kids leaving before they got School Cert.

TRIBE: So you *could* leave at 15 in effect?

CORRY: Well, if you went to what was then called the Senior School or the Technical School. There was a lot of choice. I find my young colleagues here, as well as the students, misunderstand completely education before the 1946–47 reforms. I was born in East London, but in the Borough of Leyton, which was part of Essex. It wasn't part of the London County Council. And Essex had tremendous opportunities for 11 year olds in East London. It wasn't the Secondary Modern *versus* the Grammar. If you got the 11-plus you went to a High School, as I did. Or you might even get a place at one of the Independent schools, like Bancroft for example, or Chigwell. Or you could go to a Technical School, which produced all the great apprentices. Friends of mine who went into printing and coopering, and so on went to, for example, South East Essex Tech., which is now East London University. Or they would go to South West Tech., which I think is also a part of that University now. Or if you didn't do that there were things called Central Schools. There was one called Tom Hood in Leyton. And then if you didn't do that there were the Senior Schools. There was actually a four-tier system. How universal that was I have never known.

Anyhow, I didn't know anybody who had been to a university. My Mum was a widow, and working, she worked at Mills Equipment and in the evening in an off-licence, then she became a dinner lady. I was an embarrassment down the street. Pressure from other families: 'Why isn't he at work? And, 'Where are you?' 'The School of Economics.' 'But we thought he was at a university?' And I was terribly embarrassed. Now one of my friends from another part of Leyton went to University College, London. That sounded much smarter. And I honestly didn't know the status. Even some of my teachers at school would ask about it, when I went back to prize days, or something like that. So I really had no idea what you did with a degree to come back to the observation you were making just now. And a relative said, 'What will you do with it?' And I said, 'I don't know, but I'm sure I'll earn £1,000 a year.' Now that was really talking big. You know, twenty quid a week. I don't think *I* believed it. And then my headmaster said to me, 'What are you going to do?' And I said, 'I will be a trade union official.' I mean, I didn't know what you did, because there weren't things called economists, I guess, when I was an undergraduate.

It didn't affect me there going to Careers Advice, because I had made up my mind to do military service. But it did when I came back to LSE, because I got a university studentship to do a Ph.D. – in those days you didn't have to arse around with Master's, because the Master's was a failed Ph.D. The Careers Advisory Service didn't have much clue about occupations for professional economists even then, let's say, 1953 to 1956. One or two openings, perhaps financial journalism. You had Whitehall, but it wasn't a Government Economic Service; so, I mean, it was a very odd thing. And firms like Unilever might employ an economist, but it wasn't to do much, so there wasn't really much idea of doing it as a professional. And economics at LSE when I was an undergraduate, I don't think it was a big group. I mean, economics itself was a many-splendoured thing. I did a thing called Analytic and Descriptive and I think there were about thirty per year. But don't forget there were evening streams as well then. Often ex-service people who couldn't perhaps afford to be full-time students, even though they got the ex-service grants – my brother did – would be evening. For one of my years, it may have been because I couldn't get up in the morning, I volunteered to go to the evening classes in Theory and Applied. That may be how I switched from Tress to Peacock, I can't remember. And there may have been twenty or thirty of them, although the dropout rate was higher. So that was Analytic and Descriptive, and they in a way were regarded perhaps as the elite, because Robbins was in charge of them. Then there was another group that did Money and Banking, and the head of that group was Sayers. So that is two groups. There was a third group called Industry and Trade, and I have a feeling the boss of that was Ronnie Edwards, helped by Harry Townsend, and they produced their famous book of case studies. There was also a group doing international economics headed by James Meade.

TRIBE: When you had classes, how many people were in them?

CORRY: I remember there being about twenty or twenty-five in the Theory or Applied classes. From the word go, you had to give papers, they may not have been very advanced, but you see, quite rightly I suppose, I went into the first year of the degree and many people around me had done the Inter there. I had studied Economics at school, but I don't suppose doing two years' Economics at Leyton County High School for Boys was like doing one year of it at LSE. The books may have been dated, and the guy that taught me was a historian, though he did his best. He never used a diagram, for example. I learned that from the books. Benham's *Economics*.[2] Frederic Benham was a terribly important textbook, and I managed to acquire a copy of Stigler. We did have Benham at school, it was issued to us and I think it had diagrams in it. Robbins once said to me that Benham was much more interested in his bridge than his economics. Apparently he became quite a famous bridge player.

Going into the first year, what is Robbins going to recommend? He didn't really go in for recommending much, but I do remember he came in once and held up Samuelson's elementary book and said, 'I have been reading this. It is worth reading.' And a book that I used, and actually this sounds perhaps incredible but it is a true story, I read bits of it for my Higher Schools – Stigler's *Theory of Price*. That was regarded as a smart book at LSE for grown-up microeconomics. No, it wasn't called that, it was called the *Theory of Value*. So, I suppose that was the advanced textbook. The general one was Samuelson. Benham was OK for the beginners, for the intermediate. What about macro? Well, there weren't macro textbooks. This is being unfair. But there was a book they called in the trade 'Deadly Dullard'. Dudley Dillard's book on the *Economics of J.M. Keynes*. And there was Alvin Hansen's book *A Guide to Keynes*.[3] But there weren't macro textbooks. For example, when I had to do my survey for Turvey he gave me to read things like Hicks' ISLM paper, bits of the *General Theory*, Torg Pallander, which was the first used of the four quadrants, which was translated later by Frank Brechling. I don't know if they were published, but I have Brechling's translation of it somewhere in my papers. It is the most remarkable article. It was in *Economisk Tidsjrift*, an amazing review of the *General Theory* using four quadrants.[4]

TRIBE: What I noticed yesterday, looking through the 1950s in the *LSE Calendar*, was that Turvey's macroeconomics course around about 1954 becomes almost entirely led by articles. By 1956–57 that sorts itself out and there are more books. Which suggests . . .

CORRY: . . . that there weren't textbooks. It is particularly true in macro, I think. Louden Ryan was regarded as an important figure, because he was doing analytic work and he had come from Trinity College, Dublin. Another important influence in macroeconomics was David Knox; I went to a course of his called 'The Trade Cycle'. Eight lectures I think. I have forgotten where Knox had been educated; I think, Toronto, although he was from the West Indies. And we went along to this course as theorists. Or at least those of us who were interested in the economic theory. Robbins' elite. And the first thing he put on the board, which we should have known from Sir Roy Allen, was a scatter diagram of C and Y, and put a straight line through, and said, 'The problem is, is it the intercept or is it . . .?'; and we thought, 'What is this

---

[2] F. Benham, *Economics*, Pitman and Sons, London, 1938; the 1955 fifth edition represented the most systematic post-war updating, the 1960 sixth edition introducing newer material but remaining substantively the same.

[3] A. Hansen, *A Guide to Keynes*, McGraw-Hill, London, 1953.

[4] T. Pallander, review of Keynes' *General Theory* in *Economisk Tidsjrift*, December 1942.

guy on about?' He then started talking about the consumption function. Whether it was linear or whether the MPC declined, and so on. And we really hadn't been introduced to that sort of linking together. The statistics was one thing. Applied economics was . . . what was the number of spindles in Manchester? – rather boring, factual lectures from Arnold Plant; or policy, industrial policy. Should the textile industry have a levy to develop research? It was that sort of stuff from Ronnie Edwards; we didn't have, I suppose what we would now call Applied Econometrics, that sort of thing at all. I am not sure if there was a course in the *Calendar* on econometrics. But it was very much held back at LSE. How much this was due to the influence of Robbins we won't know properly until Sue Howson completes her investigations.[5] Sir Roy Allen, of course, was in the Statistics Department. Never in the Economics Department. I don't know whether that was by choice or design. Even though, if you talked to many people who still remember Roy Allen, they still think of him as an economist. *Mathematical Economics: Introduction to Mathematics for Students of Economics*,[6] the article on the theory of value with John Hicks. But he was a Professor of Statistics; and taught very bread and butter statistics. We used to take it in turn to go, because it was so boring to go to two lectures a week. You know, on basic chaining, index numbers, that sort of thing. Cycles and trend by graphical methods.

I was talking earlier about classes and undergraduates for applied economics, when we had Ronnie Tress. Ronnie, of course, had been in government service in the war and I think had been behind the scenes in the estimation of national income. He didn't publish much when he was an active academic, but he had published something using Ragnar Frisch's circular flow diagrams, a couple of papers in *Economica*, on the visual representation of national income statistics.[7] Well, his classes would consist for example of, 'Next week, you two, recent vicissitudes in the balance of payments.' And you were supposed to come in with balance of payments tables, and then you got all these numbers and said, 'Look if the deficits have gone up or down on that . . .' sort of thing. In other words, familiarity with the data. But although you were perhaps using theory to explain it, it was a bit off the cuff and *ad hoc*. Now today, I suppose, you have to come and say, 'Well, this is our model of how the international economy works; now will it explain this British data set?'

But the situation with statistical analysis was very problematic in those days. People like Frank Brechling, I guess when he was doing his paper on regional unemployment rates,[8] used to go down every night to *Teddington*, to the

[5] Susan Howson is working on a biography of Lionel Robbins.
[6] R. Allen, *Mathematical Economics*, Macmillan, London, 1956.
[7] R.C. Tress, 'The Diagrammatic Representation of National Income Flows', *Economica*, n.s., vol. 15 (1948), pp. 276–88.
[8] F.P.R. Brechling, 'Trends and Cycles in British Regional Unemployment', *Oxford Economic Papers*, vol. 19 (1967), pp. 1–21.

National Physical Laboratory![9] As did Bill Phillips working on the 'Phillips Curve'. Because the University of London system hadn't got going, and LSE had few computational people. And it took a long time. You might have two hours of the Research Assistant in a month's time. And you couldn't run everything against everything. You really had to say, 'Could you just do the following two things?' So you spent an awful lot of time with your colleagues, perhaps we had more leisure time then, discussing what would be, to use our old-fashioned language, a crucial experiment. It probably turned out there was no such thing as a crucial experiment, but we did use to discuss for hours, because I used to share a room with Chris Archibald, and we used to spend hours on questions like that. 'If Dick [Lipsey] could only do one thing, what should he ask June [Wickens, the Research Assistant] to do?' It was quite remarkable.

TRIBE: So the time that you are thinking of is the mid to late 1950s?

CORRY: I was a graduate student from 1953 to 1956. I worked under Robbins. I wanted to work on Welfare Economics which I had been interested in as an undergraduate, very much indeed. The New Welfare Economics, as it was then called. And I thought you could distinguish efficiency criteria from distributive . . . that people believed in those times. I think Melvin Reder had just produced a book which influenced me.[10] And I thought about that a bit when I was in the Services; I didn't think about much, other than getting my rifle clean. Then when I came back I realised quite soon that a lot had been written and shied off the subject. I made a mistake, I think. And Robbins was very good to me, and I think he could see that I was just a bit lost, although I had this damn studentship and he then said, 'My boy, look at the history of thought.' Now, I had never studied it as a subject as an undergraduate because there wasn't a paper in it. Had I been to courses in it? Robbins didn't teach it, really. There was a long course, which I think I didn't survive, by Fritz Hayek. Because when I first went up to LSE Hayek was there, before he fled to Chicago. And he gave a course – it may have been the General History of Thought. Oh, I can see my notes now, because of course, my notebooks were school books I had pinched from school to write in, you know, to save money. I think it may be apocryphal, you can never remember whether you were there, you half-remember it, but he came in and wrote something on the board, and we all looked blank and I looked at Klappholz, and Hayek said 'Does anybody not speak Greek?' I then remember long periods on sixteenth-century Italian monetary thought. Scaruffi and God knows who else, and then I think he got onto the school of Salamanca, you know. Whether it went on I don't know, but I can't remember much after that. Anyhow, we knew that there was no exam on it.

---

[9] Those familiar with the film *The Dam Busters* (1955) will recall the Teddington tank for the study of wave motion which was used in testing Barnes Wallis' 'bouncing bomb' idea in 1943.

[10] M. Reder, *Studies in the Theory of Welfare Economics*, Columbia University Press, New York, 1947.

So here I am, back with this scholarship wanting to do welfare theory, but the thing is, it has all been done, and then Robbins got me going and he said, 'Just write an essay.' I hadn't written for two years, I guess. And the first essay he gave me was a history of the quantity theory. Well, I just did it chronologically because I had lost analytic skills I think. And I do remember, I actually did look at a ten-volume work on the economics of Confucius. It taught me something about infinite regress in studying economic ideas! Money is tight, price is high. You know, I can quote it all now! I did a massive long thing, in those days handwritten, I didn't have a typewriter. And I used a bit of Hugo Hegeland, *History of the Quantity Theory*,[11] and I went up to Friedman, I suppose. But it got me back into the game. I then did an essay, which I thought was much better, on Adam Smith's monetary theory. But of course the big influence in my economics, apart from Popper and methodology, was Keynes, quite clearly, about unemployment. I wasn't interested in the theory of what really does determine prices and allocation; I didn't think it was serious, compared with unemployment and growth and poverty. And so then, after reading Keynes properly, I got this idea – because I was still influenced by Marxist ideas – that there could have been a Keynesian revolution after the Napoleonic wars, and it was just a class thing. The establishment won. But it was all there. And that gave me a research agenda. Because I then went through that literature, about which very little had been written, but of course there were clues in a book that was very useful for me, Viner's *Studies in the Theory of International Trade*,[12] the first two chapters which had footnotes on people like Lauderdale. So I got the names and I wrote a plan. I knew my chapters already. I could see it all. Then I spent two of the happiest years of my life, two happy years just in the British Library, reading all this stuff. I hadn't really finished my thesis but my scholarship was up.

So what do you do? I was about to get married, I had no money, and I went to the Careers Advisory Service. Nowadays, the Careers Advisory Services on the campuses in Britain I think are superb, particularly in the new universities. But in those days – in a sense there wasn't a lot of unemployment because we weren't producing many graduates, I guess. The ex-servicemen and women when *they* came on the market, there was a lot of unemployment. My brother hit the market in 1950 and you got killed in the crush. You see, we are now talking about 1956. I went to see this careers advice guy who, I think like so many of them, was an ex-officer, who hadn't got a clue about young people, the graduate labour market, or jobs; and I think they used to just spend their time being wined and dined with one of their clients at lunchtime and come back pissed. The first time I went to see him he said, 'Ah,' he said, 'Economics. There is a wonderful job on the *Winnipeg Wheat Gazette* for a financial analyst. Do you like travel? You will have to go to Canada.' So I got

---

[11] H. Hegeland, *The Quantity Theory of Money*, Göteborg, 1951.
[12] J. Viner, *Studies in the Theory of International Trade*, Allen and Unwin, London, 1937.

in touch with them and they said, 'Are you a half-wit? We made it absolutely clear that we wanted Canadian citizens.' Back I go to this guy. And then the Atomic Energy Authority want an economist. They have just started up and they have got a big new building just off Tottenham Court Road. I march along there. In I go. The first question is, 'What is the difference between fission and fusion?' I said 'I am sorry, I've no idea', and they said, 'We made it absolutely clear we wanted . . .!' Back I go to this bloody office at LSE, I am getting quite desperate and then I nearly got a job with what was then called the Federation of British Industries, they wanted an Assistant Economic Adviser to Arthur Shenfield, who was then the Economic Adviser. I think I did quite well at the interview, but then I went for another one with their high-ups, and they asked me if there was any difference between Labour and Conservative fiscal policy. Well, the economists at the time were talking about Butskellism, so I said that, and I could see Shenfield thinking, 'You've had it, mate!'

So I didn't get that job. And I was getting quite desperate. And one evening I was going from the LSE Library to the then student bar, which was called *The Three Tuns*, just opposite the main building; I was pretty desolate, and then I saw one of my old teachers, Alan Peacock, who I guess was then in Edinburgh. And he said, 'What's up with you?' and I said 'Listen, I am getting married, I have got no money and I haven't got a job.' He said, 'Do you want a job?' and I said 'Yes!' He said, 'There is a temporary Assistant Lectureship going in Durham, if you apply you might get it.' Well, quite frankly, I wasn't sure where Durham was. Anyhow, I did get the job. Austin Laing was on leave in Hull, with the White Fish Authority; Durham then was part of the University of Newcastle, History of Thought was compulsory and they had nobody to teach it, as he did. Although I had never taught it. I had got this bit I had done for my Ph.D. but that was, if you like, macroeconomics 1780 to 1850. So I really had to mug up the History of Economic Thought to teach it there. I was a temporary Assistant Lecturer. So, as soon as I got there I was applying for jobs.

TRIBE: That was a one-year post?

CORRY: Yes, but Laing stayed at Hull and Durham gave me tenure. But then I got a note from Robbins saying that there was an Assistant Lectureship at LSE, it was in Industrial Economics, because the man who taught Industry and Trade, who's name escapes me now (Alan Fox?), had tragically died young. I thought, 'I know I work in the North East and I could waffle on about the pits and so on, but I don't know much about all this,' and so I didn't apply. Robbins then wrote back, and said I think you have misunderstood my letter. I didn't say you wouldn't get it. So I applied. I go down for an interview. I was strongly questioned by Ronnie Edwards about coal-cutting methods in the Durham pits. Whether they were short-wall or long-wall. I knew a bit about it, since I actually bothered to go down pits; I had joined an industrial group there. Anyhow I got the job. I chucked tenure in Durham to become an Assistant Lecturer at LSE. Actually I was brought there really, I realise, to teach the History of Thought. Robbins, I guess, was getting busy on a lot of other things, and he was running everything, as well as from the Economics Department. So I went there to teach the History of Thought, which was compulsory. Almost as soon as I got there a lot of things happened. I knew Archibald from undergraduate days. Archibald had just come from New Zealand to an Assistant Lectureship. I didn't know Lipsey. Dick had finished his Ph.D. and had got on the staff. I didn't know Maurice Peston. Maurice, I think, had just finished his military service. And so I immediately got to know this mob, because I shared a room with Chris Archibald and was invited to what became known as the M^2T: Methodology, Measurement and Testing. It had been going for a year. I must confess I found their discussions methodologically a bit naïve, because I actually had been a student of Popper. I don't think any of them had been. Klappholz may have been.

TRIBE: The de Marchi essay suggests that in fact Klappholz was the conduit between Popper and the seminar.[13]

CORRY: Could well have been. The main rapporteurs were Archibald and then Steuer. I don't think Professors were invited, but I believe Bill Phillips was allowed in. And I think they had been thrashing out methodology for a year. And they had come along with a broadly Popperian stance. And very influential, although he wasn't an economist, and didn't go to the M^2T, was Joseph Agassi. Very nice, mad guy who went to the United States. By the time I got into M^2T they were beginning to want to test economic theory, so they'd got beyond the methodological stage. They all knew the Ten Commandments and could get on with it. And almost everybody had a research project testing. No piddling around like today on a minor thing. The whole of economics was being tested in one year! Archibald was going to test the theory of short-run profit maximisation, just like that. Was getting data on whether total receipts were less than total variable costs in America in the 1930s; because one of his research assistants was Miles Kennedy – who was an accountant. Lipsey of course was following up Phillips. Klappholz never played that game, because Kurt never got involved in any statistical work, and never has done. He stayed with methodology, and wrote the paper with Agassi.[14] Which basically says, 'Do anything, but be critical!' It was a very liberal sort of thing. The History of Thought was not respected by the Young Turks. They often used to say to me, 'Look, here you are one of us. Why are you doing it?' I had done a couple of things, but the first big paper I suppose of any use I did was the one on Malthus and Keynes in the EJ.[15] I remember I couldn't get them to read it,

---

[13] N. de Marchi, 'Popper and the LSE Economists', in N. de Marchi (ed.) *The Popperian Legacy in Economics*, Cambridge University Press, Cambridge, 1988, p. 158.

[14] K. Klappholz and J. Agassi, 'Methodological Prescriptions in Economics', *Economica*, n.s., vol. 26 (1959), pp. 60–74.

[15] B. Corry, 'Malthus and Keynes: A Reconsideration', *Economic Journal*, vol. 49 (1959), pp. 717–24.

really. They thought – along what they considered Popperian lines, and perhaps it is – that the history of theory is irrelevant to the current status of theory. So, on the one hand, I was teaching it, and great reforms were about to appear in that subject at LSE, as I will come on to in a moment. On the other hand, I am in with these Young Turks. I have always been interested in macro rather than micro. Kaldor's theory of the share of wages or profits, whichever way around you want to put it in the national income, had come on board, and we were beginning to teach it. And I got out volumes of statistics and I think I had some research help, maybe from Joan Wickens. And I ran regressions. The share of profits as a function of the I/Y ratio, and $X - M$. What the hell do you do with government, you know? I suspect in the end I was just running an identity, because I had got high r's! I presented these as papers on tour. You are asked to go to Manchester. Well, you can't give a paper really I suppose on Malthus versus Ricardo, so that was my tour paper for a bit. So we were into the applied work, and then any visitors that came to the school were always invited to the M^2T. Quite famous Americans, that the Young Turks tried to, I wouldn't say tear to bits, but show up methodologically. They were always presenting applied work on, I don't know, measuring productivity growth; and then people would say, 'What theory are you testing? All you are doing is empirical work.' They must have thought, 'What a lot they have got here!' And of course, as I said earlier, there wasn't a lot of econometrics known. Bill Phillips knew a lot. And Phillips was rather cautious about doing high-powered work, because Phillips was very aware of data limitations.

I had come to LSE to teach thought mainly, that was my field. It was a compulsory subject for the third-year A & D. We had a third-year seminar. I think almost the first year I had Laidler, who was one of my tutees; Sammy Hollander, Alan Budd. Bright guys, you know, giving very good papers on Marshall's Representative Firm, or something. Robbins had reverted for the syllabus to set books, and it was Smith–Ricardo–Marshall. And I ran the seminar as well with Klappholz. I think, for a time Lipsey did, because Robbins' view always of young people was that you should teach something you didn't know anything about, to broaden you. To Archibald: 'Have you done anything about international trade? No? Right, give ten lectures on it.' It was very much like that.

Then things happened to the teaching structure. I told you that the structure of the degree that I took was an Intermediate plus two years. Then when they reformed it, soon after I graduated – Maurice Peston, I think, was the first year of the reformed degree – they brought in a Part I and a Part II formally. So you didn't need this Inter beforehand, although people then had A level when they went up to do it. And Robbins was for a two-year Part I and a one-year Part II, because his heart was in the PPE, although he himself didn't take PPE, he took B.Sc. (Econ.). But don't forget Robbins' Special Subject was never Economics, it was Government, and his tutor was Laski. And I think increasingly the Young Turks felt that one year wasn't enough to develop good economists. I have a feeling that people like Laidler all did that one-year programme. So you did two-year's compulsory economics, political ideas. The Oakeshott course, I think, was compulsory. Wonderful course. Economic history. I think that was compulsory. And then you did one year of your Special, and I think it was five papers. And then they were beginning to get them in areas, History of Thought was one. So that was under review, and then the wave of opinion was a one-year Part I and a two-year Part II, and that is what it reverted to, and remains today. The other thing was that the Turks, I think it was mainly the Turks rather than Robbins, wanted to abolish the History of Thought; and as a compromise we had a paper which I taught called 'The Development of Economic Analysis'.

TRIBE: When would that be? You were teaching History of Thought in 1958–59?

CORRY: I started as soon as I came there to teach it. At least the seminars. I would say about 1960. Like other people, I don't have any notes from that period. There was a reform of the B.Sc. (Econ.), part of it was that the History of Thought went, although Robbins then started that famous course that overseas visitors in particular started to go to. But the paper for specialists was called the Development of Economic Analysis. I think I wrote the syllabus, I may still have the class sheets, and it very much was, if you like, Blaug; although Blaug wasn't yet out, but that was a godsend, that book. It was very much how my thinking then would have been to have written the subject up. And we may have done some Physiocracy, but I remember more vividly the twentieth century; because I certainly taught Myrdal and Lindahl and the Swedes, and compared them with Keynes, and so on. The classes were difficult to do. Devlatoglu, who had written on Montesquieu, also did some of the classes, he was a lecturer there. So that was going on, and I think that slightly upset Robbins as well. And it was in that background that the Turks began to think about graduate education. So with changes going on in the undergraduate programme, wanting to bring in more maths and stats. I guess it may have been in Part I where that basic maths came in, Roy Allen's book. Where students of economics had to begin to do some compulsory maths and stats. Don't forget, when I was an undergraduate it was an option. Elementary statistical methods was not compulsory for economists. It was an option.

Outside economics the only compulsory paper was Economic History, to teach it we had the great T.S. Ashton, who taught financial history, it was like Gayer, Rostow, Schwartz[16] verbally. 'On July 5th 1867 the 'ouse of Overhead Gurney fell. Then the price of wool went down.' It was all empirical. One day he came in, 'July 4th 186 . . . I have forgotten me notes, I can't go on.' Just reading out! And then we had Jack Fisher who we thought was wonderful.

---

[16] A. Gayer, W.W. Rostow and A.J. Schwartz, *The Growth and Fluctuation of the British Economy, 1790–1850*, 2 vols, Oxford University Press, London, 1953.

Because, in a sense, he spoke our language. He had been in the Air Force in Africa and he would swear in lectures. He used to say, 'You have your bloody breakfast afterwards like I do!' And it was rumoured that he had his famous seventeenth-century seminar in a pub! He was one of the lads. And he actually talked about the economic development of the Commonwealth. The development of wheatlands in Australia, and so on. There was an awful lot of it, although these were different years, I think. And then there was the history course that, looking back, I suppose was the greatest – the economists hated it and I think petitioned against it – and that was Lance Beales. Beales is a highly regarded figure. He only died recently. But was never given a Chair. He lectured on the development of social policy. Really the rise of the welfare state, and it was all words and you couldn't take notes. I didn't have the nerve, I was too shy . . . but the tougher guys petitioned. Because I remember he came in the next week and said, 'I gather that the economists want facts.' And for an hour he read out statistics and then he said, 'That is the last bloody fact you are getting.'

13

SIR ALAN PEACOCK

Alan Peacock was born on Tyneside in 1922 but received all his early education in Dundee and attended St. Andrews University, his studies being interrupted by war service in the Royal Navy. On graduating in 1947 he became Lecturer in Economics at St. Andrews, but then moved the following year to a post at LSE, becoming Reader in Public Finance in 1951. At 34 he was appointed to the Chair of Economic Science at Edinburgh and was subsequently founder of the Economics Department at the new University of York where he remained from 1962–77. His final full time academic appointment was as Professor of Economics and later Principal and Vice Chancellor of the independent University College at Buckingham (1978–84) where he negotiated the Royal Charter which conferred full university status. His interests in economic policy led to his full time appointment as Chief Economic Adviser at the Department of Trade and Industry (1973–76) on leave from York, membership of the Fowler Committee on the reform of the state pensions system (1983–84) and Chairman of the Committee on the Financing of the BBC (1985–86) as well as to many assignments as an economic consultant in countries as diverse as Colombia, Fiji and Russia. On returning to Scotland in 1984 he co-founded the David Hume Institute. He was elected a Fellow of the British Academy in 1979 and knighted for public service in 1987. The following is an edited version of an interview conducted in the David Hume Institute, Edinburgh on 23 October 1995.[1]

PEACOCK: I grew up in Dundee. You must remember that Dundee was hit very badly by the Depression. I was at school in the middle of Dundee and there was a big contrast between the relative stability of the Dundee High School and what was happening in the jute industry. I was puzzled by this, and that was certainly always in my mind. I was always interested in politics, I would read the *Observer* at the weekend, because it was the only national newspaper that my parents read. They believed implicitly in

---

[1] Alan Peacock has recorded his own reflections on British economics during the second half of the century in his 'Introduction' to D. Greenaway, J.R. Presley (eds), *Pioneers of Economics vol. 2*, Macmillan, Basingstoke, 1989, pp. 1–10.

anything that J.L. Garvin wrote! I also discussed politics with one or two of my friends at school. I went to university in 1939, almost exactly when the war broke out. My father was of the view that the war was going to be a long one, and that I might as well get a year at university before I was hauled into the Services. I was 17 at the time. I had an incomplete University Entrance: I was allowed into university only as a non-graduating student because I didn't have enough Highers. In fact the reason I didn't have enough Highers was that I had myself arranged my Leaving Certificate and I had removed Mathematics – much to my regret in later life – from my studies, and entered Music, without my parents knowing. So I finished with English, History, Chemistry and Physics; but since I didn't have Maths. I couldn't enter the science side of the university, and on the Arts side I didn't have Latin, since I had done German instead of Latin. But there was a let-out: I could read two Modern Languages instead of Latin or Greek, so I did two subjects for one. I started with French, German and Geography at the Dundee part of St Andrews.[2] It was just really to see how I would get on; and in fact I got on really rather well. I did very well in German, quite well in Geography, not so well in French. It was the first time I'd ever worked; I don't remember ever doing a stroke of work at school! There I remember playing cricket, and writing and playing music; I don't remember ever having studied in depth, but at university I learned to work. I had no idea at that stage what I was going to do. But then it became clear that I might get another year in; I was 18 and could be called up at any time, and I decided that I really was interested in Politics, and the nearest thing to it was Political Economy. My parents agreed with this and sent me to St Andrews for my second year, in which I read Political Economy, History and Philosophy. What I can say for the system is that I am very glad that I didn't have to specialise immediately; and I'm infinitely grateful that I was able to study Modern Languages. I became very interested in German language and German literature, and that has remained with me. Then I came to study Political Economy. If you were to go on to read Honours then you had to choose another subject for Joint Honours, and I chose History. I did very well at History, but I did not do particularly well in Political Economy.

TRIBE: Was Nisbet teaching on his own by that time?[3]

PEACOCK: Well, he had lost his Lecturer, a chap called Blair, who obviously was a very clever man indeed; he was killed in the war. Blair had read very widely, and I later had the chance to look at some of his personal books. He had made his own annotation of editions of Wicksell and others that showed he was very good. Nisbet was left with two Assistants: one was a lady called Isobel Menzies, who was really a psychologist and who later worked at the

---

[2] The present University of Dundee was affiliated to St Andrews as University College, Dundee until 1954 when it became an independent institution with the title Queen's College, Dundee.

[3] For details on Nisbet see pp. 40–41.

Tavistock Institute. The other Assistant finished up in the Board of Trade. They were as green as they came and knew it, but Nisbet did the bulk of the lectures and these were dictated. I was totally confused about the nature of Political Economy at that stage. The History of Thought seemed to have some kind of continuity, and Nisbet clearly knew something about it; but the rest of it – National Income, Production, and so on – that seemed to be very confusing. History of Thought, on the other hand, was the spinal column of the subject.

In my second year I had to write a longish essay, and I had no idea what to do. The first thing I tried was something on co-operatives, because I was quite interested in the co-operatives in Dundee. But I couldn't get any information on them, so I wrote something on the smallholding movement in agriculture. Trying to think of one book of the time which I read, found useful and which gave me some indication of the relevance of economics to modern society, I would say that Crowther's *Outline of Money* impressed me most – together with Robertson's book *Money*, with its 'Alice in Wonderland' approach to economics. And Henderson's *Supply and Demand* – I began to see that there was some kind of analytical framework, as distinct from a scholastic progression from Adam Smith, or even before.[4]

Nisbet had graduated with a double First in Glasgow in Economics and Law. He had come top of the Civil Service examinations. Josiah Stamp[5] was one of the examiners, and was so impressed with Nisbet's style and his knowledge that he suggested to W.R. Scott[6] that Nisbet would be far better off if he became an economist, since he would be lost in the Civil Service. Nisbet had at that time accepted an invitation to join the Chambers of Macmillan;[7] but after some deliberation he decided to follow a career in Political Economy, rather than the Law. I think that was a fatal decision. He would have probably made a very good civil servant, and possibly an excellent lawyer, dealing rather with pleadings and the rather more esoteric branches of the law. But as an economist he had none of the analytical interest and ability of an Alec Cairncross, who followed him rather later at Glasgow. The other problem that he faced was that he was a first-class golfer, of almost professional standard. There is a wonderful statement in his inaugural lecture in which he refers to having visited St Andrews and 'capitulated to its amenities'. That, I am afraid, is what he did. His passion in life was golf. He was also a very kind man, and he had a great gift of being able to insinuate his students into the job market. You can talk nowadays to heads of industry, people like Reid, who was head of ICI and then went to British Rail, politicians like Macgregor, Allan Stewart and Michael Forsyth; I am sure that they had, as I did, a great affection for

---

[4] Robertson's and Henderson's books appeared in the Cambridge Handbooks series.
[5] See p. 16, fn.7.
[6] Professor of Political Economy in Glasgow; see pp. 39–40.
[7] The Macmillan who was Chairman of the Committee on Finance and Industry, 1929–31: see P. Clarke, *The Keynesian Revolution in the Making 1924–1936*, Oxford University Press, Oxford, 1990, Part III.

him. He used to write, in beautiful copperplate, references which were models of their kind; and he worked assiduously at placing his students. And yet, I often ask myself, what had they actually learned from him? I don't know. I think they had to learn their economics on the side if they were to become economists.

TRIBE: How long were you at St Andrews before you were called up?

PEACOCK: Well, I spent the year in Dundee, and then a year and a term at St Andrews. I then sat for a War Degree, a Pass degree, which I passed and then I went into the Navy in April 1942 for three and a half years. I was astonished to find myself back at St Andrews in October 1945, but the universities were able to recall students who had not finished their studies under a Class B Release. I didn't expect to get out until 1946 at the earliest, but was glad to find myself back, for in the meantime I had married. I had had quite a busy and not unadventurous time in the Navy; I had been in the Naval Intelligence Service and had kept my German going, and my last five months in the war were in Kiel as the Assistant Prize Officer. I had to seize ships in Prize and turn them over to the Royal Navy. I had been expecting to stay in the occupation forces, or, maybe be sent out to the Far East, but then of course the war collapsed in the Far East and when my order of release came through it notified me that I was to be released as an 'Art Student'! There was absolute horror at the naval base, wondering why I should be released so early; and I told them that it was a new Labour Government, and they loved art! When I got back to St Andrews I took nearly a couple of years over Honours, and it was during that period that I had to teach myself.

TRIBE: You mentioned earlier your involvement with the College of the Sea.

PEACOCK: Yes, and it still exists, as a correspondence college for sailors. As I said, my tutor was Pigou, but I only wrote something like six essays for him. It was a little bizarre, bucketing around the Arctic writing essays on what determines relative wage rates, and getting back little comments from Pigou saying, 'I think you are quite good at describing individual trees, but I fail to see the wood.' Criticism was couched in elaborate metaphors. But at least I was able to keep going a little. I did once give three lectures in the Navy on economics, mainly, I think, on the structure of the economy, a social accounting approach.

TRIBE: But that would have been quite new at that time. You knew enough to do that.

PEACOCK: At the end of the war I had applied to go to Clare College, Cambridge, thinking that there was no point in going back to St Andrews. But I didn't qualify because I had no Latin, and when the chance of returning early to St Andrews came through I thought I might as well make the best of things. I always tell the story that I became a lecturer in part because Nisbet was a bit wary of appointing people from other universities. I was appointed as a consequence of Nisbet looking around the Honours Class and asking himself, 'Who is hungry, who might do quite well, and is a non-golfer?' A great problem in the department was that all three members – they had lost a member and were after a replacement – all three were ardent golfers, and the important thing was to get down on to the first tee at the Royal and Ancient by 12 o'clock on Wednesdays; but Political Economy had to be taught from 12 until 1 p.m. on Wednesdays, and I always maintain, although that was a necessary but not a sufficient condition, that was how I became an economist! I must say I worked bloody hard at it for my first year. I gave a course of lectures on 'The Theory of Value'; I was expected to follow a Marshallian line of argument, one talked about supply and then demand, and then about the 'scissors'. I puzzled my way through this, stated it in the form of about twelve propositions, and then set out to elaborate them and gave out a reading list. I suddenly found that in the Faculty of Arts there were no facilities for reproducing the reading list. So I sweethearted a friend of my father's in the Extra-mural Department at Dundee, and she produced it and I gave it out to the students. But I had done so without the permission of the Professor, and I was of course later suitably apologetic. I think I sent him a copy, and he was horrified to find this advance commitment about what I was going to say! When I later went to LSE I first gave the course for non-economists in Economics. Honor Croome had taught this course and she was having her fifth child, I think, and that was why I was appointed. When I went to Lionel Robbins and showed him my syllabus for the course, he was a little puzzled about why I was doing so, although he went on to say that he was of course always interested in teaching ideas. I replied that as Head of Department he perhaps wanted to see it and approve it. 'Approve it?', he said. 'This is Liberty Hall, Alan! Put it in the *Calendar!*' So the contrast between the hierarchical system in Scotland and LSE was very striking.

TRIBE: How did the move from Scotland to the LSE come about?

PEACOCK: I realised by then what the professional ethos was: that I would not only be expected to lecture, but that I would be expected to make some contribution to the subject, although I wasn't quite sure what it would be. I had in those days a strong scholarly bias, almost a rabbinical fervour for reading; but it wasn't closely directed reading. I had some idea that I might write something on German economic thought, and I was interested in von Mangoldt, and actually, later on, I asked Lionel Robbins if I might work on a Ph.D. on von Mangoldt, but he dissuaded me from that. 'The best thing you could do', he told me, 'would be to go on writing articles of the sort you are writing on national insurance.' But at St Andrews I had no direction, nobody to talk to about this, except Graham Moodie, who was Lecturer in Politics, who had read PPE and who later on became Professor of Politics at York. I thought that I had to do something about my situation, and that I therefore should try to get a job elsewhere. I was asked to apply for a job at Glasgow as a Lecturer, and I went to see Macfie and talked to one or two people there; but my wife said, 'Why don't you apply for this job at LSE?' She comes from London, and she had some interest in returning there, although she too was a student at St Andrews, it wasn't that she had any great prejudice against St Andrews. I made an application, sent a telegram, and I then confessed to Nisbet what I had done. He was very gracious about it. I also confessed to Malcolm Knox, the Professor of Moral Philosophy, who was furious, and said that I was a better political scientist. There was a lectureship going in Newcastle, and he said I ought to apply for that; but I didn't. To my surprise I got an interview at LSE, it was a very stiff interview. The Board consisted of Carr-Saunders, the Director, with Hayek, Robbins, Plant, Paish, Sayers, Meade, Phelps Brown – the top brass. James Meade, I remember, noted that I was becoming interested in social policy, and I had been asked to lecture on the subject to graduate medical students taking the Diploma of Public Health. He asked me, 'What is the optimal expenditure on national health?' A terrible question! And I replied, 'Professor Meade, I really don't know the answer, I would have thought that is an entirely political question, based upon an initial value judgement. I don't think the economist has anything to say about that.' And then Frank Paish said, 'Tell me about how you organise your lectures,' so I told them. And then Lionel Robbins and Hayek noted that I had an interest in German economic thought, and began questioning me in detail. That was the end of the interview, and I had no idea what had happened. But I had been asked by the brother of the wife of the local minister where I lived – a very remote connection! – to go and have dinner in the Reform Club. He said, 'You must come to the Political Economy Club.' And I went to the meeting of the Club, and to my horror met all the people who had interviewed me! But a few days later I got a letter offering me the job, and nobody was more surprised than I was. Years later I asked James Meade why he had asked me such a horrible question. He said, 'Well, I think you answered it correctly, but I'll tell you why it was in my mind. I was very friendly with a man who believed he could find the optimal expenditure. He had worked out demographic projections of incidences of morbidity and mortality, and from that he had worked backward to expenditure coefficients; but when I asked him where opportunity cost came into this, he had got very worried, and a few years later he shot himself!' I have always maintained that I got the job because I had a broad education and broad interests, I had the kind of scholarly interests which Lionel Robbins and Fritz Hayek held dear, I was probably regarded with some scepticism by James Meade, Phelps Brown and Frank Paish, but later on they became my firm friends and a great help. And I may add, on LSE, I have never come across a place where, whatever they taught as economists, people were more concerned and helpful to individuals without being paternalistic, and where academic politics was at a minimum. That was partly Carr-Saunders' doing, which I found delightful at the time; but when I came to Edinburgh I was an innocent abroad and it became clear that there was something in my education which was sadly lacking!

TRIBE: You were promoted Reader in 1951, when you were only 29.

PEACOCK: I was already lecturing in Public Finance and also in Social Policy.

Two Readerships were advertised at LSE: one Readership in Economics with special reference to Public Finance, and one on Social Policy. I was approached by Richard Titmuss to apply for the Social Policy Readership. I thought about it and decided against it, but Richard was a very persuasive man, I got on very well with him, although latterly I disagreed very profoundly with his views on social policy. But he never held this against me. The ultimate appointee for the Readership in Social Policy was Brian Abel-Smith. I applied for the other readership, and had the initial advantage of being an incumbent, but I have always felt how lucky I was. The three who were interviewed were Douglas Hague, myself and Duncan Black. I have always thought that Duncan Black should have got the job. But Duncan was not well known, he was a very reserved character, working more on the theory of committee decisions, and public choice theory had not been integrated into the study of public finance at that time; and his work on public finance had been written in 1939, on the incidence of income taxes, and it was partly a discussion of Italian literature, and so he was really not in the mainstream. In those days there were two grades of Readership, and what I was getting was equivalent to a Senior Lectureship elsewhere, with the prospect of promotion (in terms of salary).

TRIBE: Could you tell me how you came to translate Stackelberg's *Grundlagen?*[8]

PEACOCK: Simply because Hayek wanted it done. He needed someone who knew German, I had an interest in Stackelberg's work, and I was very hard up! It was a very difficult task indeed, but I think it is quite a reasonable translation. It was worth doing. But simultaneously Terry Hutchison was translating Schneider's *Einführung in die Wirtschaftstheorie*, which is a different sort of book, but which was much more in accord with what was happening in Britain at that time, in the way of the teaching of economic theory. That is borne out by the review of both books by Frank Hahn, which appeared in the *Economic Journal* shortly afterwards, and I think I agree with Hahn.[9]

TRIBE: Read today in the context of the available literature of the time, Schneider's work seems very advanced at a pedagogical level; it is a good textbook, but it did not seem to catch on at all. Likewise, neither did the translated works of Eucken and Stackelberg seem to have had much of a reception.

PEACOCK: Well, I think that Eucken and Stackelberg appeared to many British readers to have a rather convoluted style. Stackelberg in the eyes of some people made too many concessions to his audience by not employing enough mathematics in the way that Schneider did. Schneider, you must

---

[8] Translated by Peacock as *The Theory of the Market Economy*, William Hodge, Edinburgh 1952.

[9] F. Hahn, 'Review of E. Schneider, *Pricing and Equilibrium* (1952) and H. von Stackelberg, *The Theory of the Market Economy* (1952)' *Economic Journal*, vol. 53 (1953), pp. 407–10. Hahn praised Schneider's presentation of modern microeconomic analysis, but expressed reservations with respect to Stackelberg's textbook, which, he argued, was neither so clear nor as up-to-date as that of Schneider.

remember, was a mathematics schoolteacher at one time, and had taught Schumpeter mathematics. It was just at the time when the battle had been won to include mathematics as an essential part of the training of an economist. You must remember that there was a very good rival work available at that time, a book which I certainly found extremely useful when I began teaching, and that was Stigler's *Theory of Price*. And if I had to make a bold statement about this, I would say that it was Stigler's *Theory of Price* and works of that kind which in fact spoilt their market.

TRIBE: But Stackelberg's *Marktform und Gleichgewicht* was not included in this translation activity; although it contains theorems which have been very influential for the theory of oligopoly, it has never been translated and little is known about Stackelberg outside Germany.

PEACOCK: One very important inhibition of course was that Stackelberg was a Nazi. There are various interpretations of what this means; he came from a very prominent family in Eastern Germany who had lost their land after the First World War, and there was a great deal of bitterness over this, especially with respect to the Russians. This is often given as an explanation of why he fell into the arms of the Nazi Party. He was never a Nazi in any positive and malevolent sense, and he was defended very strongly by the Eucken *Kreis* and the Social Market economists after the war. They claimed that he had virtually joined them, if only clandestinely, in 1943 or thereabouts. As you know, he died in Spain in 1944, so we are not able to add any further autobiographical content to this particular defence. I was very much influenced by this defence, and it made me willing to translate Stackelberg, which was at the time regarded by many as rather making concessions to the former enemy. And I might say that there was a similar prejudice against Schneider who became Professor in Denmark during the war. He was regarded as an out-and-out Nazi, and he had gone on record with statements favourable to the Nazi regime, particularly their employment policy. Some Danish academics were very upset by his appointment, and he was deported from Denmark immediately after the war. So you must remember that there was an atmosphere of prejudice at the time, whatever their particular qualities as economists might have been. There is another very interesting aspect to this: why then did Hayek support these translations? Well, it's very curious, it all goes back to Ragnar Nurkse: he came to Edinburgh in the late 1930s, was very interested in music and formed a friendship with an Edinburgh publisher called William Hodge. William Hodge had studied music in Leipzig, and had wanted, I understand, to become a professional musician. But his family were against this, and he had settled down to become head of the publishing firm. Nurkse induced Hodge, supported by Hayek, to publish the first translations of a whole series of economists: the first translation of Morgenstern, *The Limits of Economics*, Haberler's *Prosperity and Depression*, Machlup's early work; and Hodge then went on publishing translations of German economics, but eventually had major problems selling them. In fact Hodge gave up publishing economics in the mid-1950s because the translations were simply losing money.

By the time I reached LSE, although lip-service was paid to having a working knowledge of French and German so one could read works in foreign languages, this was, I think, honoured more in the breach than the observance. It was a formality getting through the examinations, and texts in foreign languages in economics had all but disappeared. If you look at the 1930s I think you will still see reference to German and Austrian works in the original. I suppose that by the 1950s people had neither the knowledge nor the incentive to learn these languages.

TRIBE: One thing that has always puzzled me in respect of Eucken, Röpke and others concerns their great vagueness with respect to public finance. Your own first book on national insurance[10] is a very detailed account of the administrative organisation of social security and insurance, its economic implications, distinguishing clearly between health and educational expenditures, transfer payments and straightforward payments for services; but so far as I am aware, there is no work at all in the early German Social Market tradition which looks at this quite central problem for the organisation of a social market. Röpke made dismissive remarks about the Beveridge Plan as a mechanism for pumping the national product around, but this was as close as any of them got to considering the impact of taxation and benefits on the economy.

PEACOCK: Well, you must remember that in those days I was very much a Keynesian liberal. As a junior St Andrews lecturer, my token act of defiance was to lecture on Keynes, who was virtually proscribed. I was very much taken with Keynesian analysis, and I was very much influenced by the growth of macroeconomics, particularly the work of James Meade. My differences with other Keynesians, so far as they mattered, were not so much over the objects of policy, for I accepted Keynesian analysis of inflation and deflation. I didn't accept the idea of underemployment equilibrium and stagnation, but I accepted the Keynesian macroeconomics framework. My concern at that time was how did you achieve economic stability without at the same time having a growing public sector, using public sector investment rather than controlling private consumption? This was, of course, James Meade's view as well. There was a lot of misunderstanding of Keynes by Röpke and others – one could almost interpret it as deliberate misunderstanding. Schneider got me to write a piece in the *Frankfurter Zeitung* attacking Röpke's views. One of Röpke's allies, Muthesius, had written a review of a book by Tom Wilson in which he said, 'Here is the answer to Keynes, Keynes had never really understood the nature of inflation', which was, I thought, a misrepresentation of Tom Wilson's position, which furthermore I thought was very close to mine. So I wrote an article showing how Keynesian analysis could be employed to

[10] *The Economics of National Insurance*, William Hodge, Edinburgh, 1952.

explain inflation. Röpke wrote a reply to me, which is, I think, of a rather confused nature. I point this out because I had given a lecture at Cologne in 1950, saying that you could equally apply Keynesian analysis to anti-inflation policy. The lecture was attended by a number of social market economists, including people like Müller-Armack, Schmoelders and others, and they were absolutely astonished at this kind of interpretation of Keynes. They had never read Keynes' *How to Pay for the War* or some of the post-Keynesian discussion. Later on, there was some acceptance of James Meade's position; and his *Planning and the Price Mechanism* was actually translated and published by Mohr and was regarded by some of the social market economists as being more akin to their position. But I do agree that I had a problem in trying to make contacts with German economists, and I did make some effort. One hindrance was that I had already advanced in Britain, not by British but by German standards, in the economics hierarchy. Germans of my generation, who had fought in the war, were still *Assistenten*, and they had to keep their mouths shut. It was only later when I met Herbert Giersch and others, that I discovered that there was much more sympathy than I had at first encountered with the idea that the purpose of theory was not simply to present some particular economic philosophy, stick to it at all costs and see that your *Assistenten* kept in line. This was a matter for disquisition and discussion, possibly change, and the purpose of the theory was also to see how far it could be actually applied to policy. But even today I find in Germany relatively few economists who are interested in what you might call the institutional aspects of economics: how do you adapt the institutions to make these changes, what is the economist's contribution? What has happened in Germany is very interesting; they have accepted that theory has to be tested, and the whole emphasis has been placed upon testing, entirely an academic exercise. The idea that economists might be involved in the evolution or even the invention of new institutions – that idea has gone completely, if it was ever there.

TRIBE: If you compare pre-war and post-war German economists, people like Stackelberg and Schneider in the pre-war period look far more modern than any of their post-war counterparts.

PEACOCK: Yes, they were very good theoreticians – they were really the mathematical economists of that period, although they wouldn't be so regarded today, their mathematics might be regarded as old-fashioned and rather primitive. They were genuinely interested in reaching conclusions which were based upon logical analysis; but you very rarely find in Schneider or in Stackelberg any kind of sense of how the analysis related to the situation as it is, and how institutions might be changed. But then, you don't find a very great deal of this in Britain at that time, although there is much more in the United States; much more possibly in Italy.

I was astonished at the credit I got at the LSE for having this kind of interest. You mention *The Economics of National Insurance*, which is a plea in the end for a negative income tax; it now seems very crude alongside for example,

Tony Atkinson's latest Lindahl lectures, but the book is at the beginning of the discussion. I remember when it appeared, Ralph Turvey, a contemporary whom I regarded as quite brilliant, astonishingly good at formulating analysis, and others, said that they had never come across this way of looking at the issues, it seems to tell us something about policy and policy problems. But maybe it was because I had an interest in politics, I was at the stage when one thinks that one might, in a minor way, reform the world, and my kindred spirits at LSE were James Meade and Frank Paish, a very underestimated economist, who was always looking for ways to translate his economic ideas into institutional change, into some way the government could act.

In 1955 I took three months' leave, and I went to calculate the national income of Tanganyika, which I was asked to do by the then Colonial Office. As I was getting on the plane I read that the Chair in Edinburgh had been advertised. I didn't give it a moment's thought, went out to Africa and came back. In May 1956 I was just about to move into a small house in Hampstead Garden Suburb, we had just about scratched together the money, the price was enormous – £4,150; we were about to close the contract and on the Monday morning, before the contract was to be signed, I got a letter to my home address offering me the Edinburgh Chair – just like that! So I went to see Lionel Robbins and said, 'I suppose this is your doing!' And he said, 'Alan, I was asked, but I am afraid something I have said may have indicated that they might approach you.' Having ascertained that it wasn't a way of getting rid of me, I thought about it, and decided to go up to Edinburgh. I think they had approached Charles Carter before me, but I can't be sure. He was then Professor in Belfast, and had turned it down.[11] I decided to accept, with mixed feelings, but I think it was the right thing to do. It would have been a long time before I got any promotion in the area of Public Finance, which was not then one of the accepted major disciplines and, although I wasn't overambitious, I thought that the change was probably a good idea. So I went, and then began all my troubles!

TRIBE: It is evident from the *Calendar* that you threw out the old teaching plan; as you said earlier, you put yourself in bad repute with James Thin, the University Bookseller, because of their being left with a stock of unsaleable books.

PEACOCK: That is the kind of quip one makes. Ainsley Thin was a friend of my predecessor Alexander Gray, who was himself very kind to me. I was given a lecture by the Professors in the Faculty of Arts to the effect that the main obligation of the Professor was to the first Ordinary Class. His job was to introduce the subject in the old Scottish tradition, stand up in front of 450 students and make clear the importance of your subject. In the days when there was only one Professor this was an important obligation with which I agreed. I went to see Alexander Gray, who retired at 76, a most delightful man;

[11] See the interview with Charles Carter, p. 170.

he asked me where I had been to school, and when I said it was at the Dundee High School he said, 'So was I!' He asked when I left, and I said 1939; he said, 'Good God, I left in 1898! Christ, man, you're a bairn!' Problems arose because his was a single chair department, with seven or eight members of staff. There were enormous obligations accumulating, because both lawyers and accountants had to take one year of Political Economy, and they had to be provided with tutorials.

TRIBE: When you say accountants, do you mean externally for the professional body?

PEACOCK: Yes, in those days the Scottish Chartered Accountants had to attend one year at university, studying Accounting, Law and Political Economy. That was an enormous burden. And I discovered that the staff–student ratio was way out of line with some of the other disciplines, even allowing for the level of the teaching involved. Initially, I was able to recruit only two staff; all the other members of staff, with only one exception, were Edinburgh graduates. They had all had an enormous amount of teaching to do, had been able to undertake very little research. There was a problem concerning the proper place for the teaching of economic history; I had great difficulty in gaining any say in the appointment of a Professor of Economic History; in the end I did, and I helped to appoint Sandy Youngson.

TRIBE: You inherited a tripartite teaching structure, from the Ordinary Class to Honours. It would seem that to modernise the teaching you would have to get rid of that, but how far was it embedded in the system?

PEACOCK: Oh, that was embedded in the system, I couldn't do anything about that. There was a First Ordinary Class and then Second Ordinary, and this entitled you, if you got through two subjects at that level above 60 per cent, to a Pass degree. And then there was Honours. You could start your Junior Honours in your third year, if you were not going to take the Pass Degree. It was like a pyramid: at the bottom you had 450–500 students in the Ordinary Class studying economics for a year, that would go down to about 100 who would go on to do an Ordinary Degree, and then they might go on to teacher training, or some of them went on and read Law, got an Ll.B. after they had completed their M.A. And then at the top end you would have a batch of Honours students, no more than about a dozen in the third and in the fourth year. I had some very good students indeed; Edinburgh had some kind of cachet, although some had come almost by accident. I always had an Assistantship open for an American, or at least for an overseas candidate; I had David Kopf from Princeton through a link with Will Baumol, whom I knew very well, and Fritz Machlup. I had Frank Shupp, now a well-known econometrician, now at Illinois. This system worked very well indeed. Then we tried to get members of staff to take a term off and go elsewhere; one went to Illinois, another to Michigan, we tried to keep people turning over so that they had something like a sabbatical. But it was very hard, because of the rigidity imposed by the teaching programme.

TRIBE: Was that the attraction, when the opportunity at York came up?

PEACOCK: Well, the trouble with Edinburgh was that in the long run I would have probably been able to work the system. We would have been able to develop a respectable training – in those days I was very much concerned with the standards of teaching and research – but I wasn't a very good academic politician. I tried to get a second Chair, and I failed. The Principal had no interest whatsoever in Economics. When I was asked out of the blue to go to York, I didn't think about it at first; but I was made certain informal promises, and when I went to York they were, broadly speaking, fulfilled. And I learned, perhaps rather late in life (I was 40 by then), that I am much better at starting things than coping with the steady state.

I had the advantage in that I was the only founding Professor at York who had already been a Professor; so that gave me something of an inside track. I must confess that this was all Lionel Robbins' doing, since Lionel was Chairman of the Academic Planning Board for York. Given that we were a small department, it seemed sensible to focus our efforts, so I decided that we should concentrate upon Public Finance and related fields, appointing people who could contribute to that, but who were also able to teach something else at the same time. Jack Wiseman came from LSE to run the Institute of Social and Economic Research, and he taught on public utilities. Even John Williamson, who was appointed as a specialist on international trade and invented the 'crawling peg', got interested in public finance. The tendency was that those interested initially in public finance often got interested in other things. The other thing was to make it international; and I had very strong links with Italy, which was very strong in public finance. Along with links with the United States and Japan we were able to build up graduate work very quickly. With the most fascinating and peculiar results: I am told that some 50 per cent of Professors of Public Finance in Italy have been through York! And they vary from Communists to right-wing Catholics. The V-C was very keen on this, for otherwise we would have had to look for massive funding, and we wouldn't have got that. Fortunately the Rowntree Memorial Trust, as it then was, did give us the money to start the Institute, and were quite supportive of research bearing on public finance but related to social policy; we were lucky in that.

TRIBE: Where does the title 'Economics and Related Studies' come from?

PEACOCK: Well, this was a compromise. There was understandable worry that we were trying to push Economics beyond its legitimate rights with respect to university finance, given the number of students and the allocation of research money. But this was accepted for example by the historians, who were quite prepared to see economic and social history linked with economics. Our original Reader in Economic and Social History was Bob Coats, who was trained as an economist. He left after a couple of years when the Chair of Economic History at Nottingham came up. The teaching of social and economic statistics was agreed by the mathematicians to differ rather

204

from what they meant by statistics. 'Related Studies' was a way of preventing everything being placed under the umbrella of 'Economics'.

TRIBE: Was there any problem of a single Honours degree at York?

PEACOCK: From the beginning I was a little sceptical of a single Honours degree. Of course, it didn't preclude you from taking other subjects, if you were taking English, you might take History courses, and you would certainly be expected to take another language, although more as a tool. Originally I proposed a rather broader-based degree in economics, or in social sciences specialising in economics. I also wanted to offer specialisation in economics with other subjects. But that concept of gradual specialisation towards the third year, which I had practised in Edinburgh, was not the way the historians or those in the English Department thought, although they did introduce the idea of major and minor subjects in a degree. Equal combinations were, however, rare. We started an equal combination in Economics and Maths, but that obviously was not going to work; and we compromised on Economics as a subsidiary to a Maths degree. That was a fascinating development, because we found that the mathematicians had great difficulty understanding mathematics as applied to economic questions. Somehow or other it did not fit into their pattern of teaching, and they somehow did not see the relevance of even very simple principles, for example, the multiplier. For some of them it was a great revelation that maths could be applied at all in this particular way. But I don't think we had any great quarrels about that. On the whole, we did not have quarrels about the content or even the form of degree courses, but we did have quarrels over the power structure, who should decide? In the York constitution the last thing wanted was a professorial dictatorship. Lionel Robbins insisted that we didn't have a Senate – the function of the Professors was to decide who was to be appointed, because they had experience but no further expectations. The curriculum was to be decided broadly by all members of the teaching staff; which is widely accepted now, but which was not widely accepted then.

TRIBE: To what extent do you think that the strength of York in economics is related to the original design?

PEACOCK: I think that the strongest residue from the original intention is a collective commitment to scholarship and the exchange of ideas. It is not a 9 to 5 job, and this is reflected in the kinds of things people do and write. And there is still a strong interest in policy problems; the Health Economics side grew very distinctively out of public finance, in which there was a great interest in applying public expenditure analysis, and after all in public finance we were very much more concerned with the expenditure side, rather than taxation. The optimal taxation revolution practically by-passed York. We didn't believe in it, Jack Wiseman and I for philosophical reasons; but, on the other hand, you have people there like Peter Lambert who are fully familiar with this, and who specialise in measuring the degree of progression in taxes.

14

RICHARD LIPSEY

Richard Lipsey was born in British Columbia in 1928, and studied at the Universities of British Columbia and Toronto before coming to Britain to study for a doctorate at the LSE in 1953. Lionel Robbins was still active in the LSE at that time, and other members of staff included Ralph Turvey, Frank Paish, Terence Hutchison, Bill Phillips, James Meade, and Henry Phelps Brown. By the later 1950s a group of 'Young Turks' had formed, among them Corry, Lancaster, Archibald, Klappholz and Agassi, whose principal institutional monument was a seminar on 'Methodology, Measurement and Testing' – hence M²T. Lipsey, Lancaster and Archibald jointly and severally published a number of innovative papers in economic theory at this time, but Lipsey subsequently became chiefly known as a writer of student textbooks, beginning with his *Introduction to Positive Economics* (1963), which during the expansion of university economics teaching in Britain during the 1960s was rapidly adopted as the standard textbook. With Chris Archibald he also wrote *An Introduction to a Mathematical Treatment of Economics* (1967), which likewise served as the standard modern textbook in mathematical economics for many years. In 1963 Lipsey was appointed founding Professor of Economics at the University of Essex, a new university distinguished from all others by its dedication to the construction of a graduate programme in the social sciences at a time when no other university in Britain had such a programme.[1] In 1970 he returned to Canada, and is currently based at Simon Fraser University. A selection of his papers, together with an intellectual biography which enlarges on some of the issues raised below, has been published in three volumes by Edward Elgar.

The following is edited from an original interview in London on 1 November 1994 followed by a telephone conversation on 28 January 1996, plus various additions and revisions in correspondence.

TRIBE: Could you tell me a bit about the way you started off in Canada? You went to the University of British Columbia, and graduated in 1950?

---

[1] See the interview with its first Vice-Chancellor, Albert Sloman, pp. 225.

LIPSEY: Yes, I was born in Victoria, and went to a high school in Victoria. The University of British Columbia had a two-year Arts College in Victoria at the time. Some 300 students. It was wonderful: classes of 10 or 15, and so you did your first two years of Arts, and then went over to the big factory at Vancouver, then 10,000 students, which was big for those days. I went through right after the war with all the veterans. It was a wonderful time: men and women five and ten years older than us kids; they had seen the world. I started off life to be an astronomer, but got seduced by this social science that talked about having laws about human behaviour; I became fascinated by this idea when I did a course in economics. It was a four-year degree, I took the course in my second year, got an A, and I just thought economics was the greatest thing I had seen.

TRIBE: What textbooks did you use at that time?

LIPSEY: John Ise – it was readable Marshall.[2] It was the structure of Alfred Marshall, but, you know, written for less sophisticated readers. A really nice book. Very liberal. I would imagine he was a social democrat.

The fellow who taught me economics was a political scientist, a Canadian. And there were two or three of us who got A's and we used to sit up all night talking about economics, and how it shed light on the world; I had a vision in my mind of a general equilibrium model in the first year! It was all demand and supply curves, they were all crossing and you put your finger in here and something happened there; and I could see the whole economy working in mechanical, neo-classical demand and supply curves!

TRIBE: That is all very Smithian, isn't it, because the metaphor of the Invisible Hand comes from a model of planetary motion, and that would fit in with your early interest in astronomy?

LIPSEY: Yes, that's right, it was. It was very Smithian, and it's Newtonian; and you see, coming in from astronomy and having read a certain amount of popular high school-level astronomy that whole Newtonian conception of the world grabbed me. It was about the principles organising our understanding of space and time, which is really a methodological issue; and so I was always interested in methodology right from the beginning. I didn't come into it like my veteran friends, who had been through the 1930s and whose interest in economics had been fired by unemployment and recession. I became really interested in this subject that purports to have laws of human behaviour. So my interest was always methodological, which shines through everything I have written.

At the end of the second year I went over to Vancouver and I did an Honours B.A., which was altogether four years, the last two years you specialised, you did almost all economics, but we did a bit of history and it was a fairly intensive degree. I did a whole course in the history of economic thought.[3] I also did a course on all the great social and economic thinkers – e.g.

---

[2] J. Ise, *Economics*, Harper, New York, 1946, revised edition, 1950.

[3] Unlike the US semester system, courses lasted the entire academic year and one did five or six courses each year.

Sombart, Mackinder, and Schumpeter. I read Schumpeter's *Theory of Economic Development* as an undergraduate. So it was a fascinating and broad course, and with all the veterans there, we had a Political Science Club and used to argue about economics and politics with the professors. So it was a very exciting time. And in this general course we were given Robbins' *Nature and Significance of Economic Science*; and I read that, and I thought this was wonderful, until I came to the chapter on empirical work and that was straight Austrian methodology, Euclidian, which says basically that the assumptions appeal to our common sense, we know they are right and all the deductions must be right, the facts illustrate the theory but they don't test the theory; and if the facts disagree, the facts must be wrong. We know the theory is right because its assumptions are intuitively correct. And I read this and I said, 'There has got to be something wrong with this. This just doesn't make sense to me.' So I scratched my head and one of my first lifetime research programmes became: 'What is wrong with that chapter in the *Nature and Significance*?' So that stuck in my head until I got to England. So I got my B.A. I got First Class Honours. I thought I was going to win the Governor General's award for the top average of marks in the whole 10,000 students, but I missed it by about one mark. I had had enough of the ivory tower, and I took a year out and I worked for the government, the Provincial Government.

TRIBE: Was that just one year out? Because according to your *Who's Who* entry it has you down from 1950 to 1953.

LIPSEY: Yes, that's true, but some of that was in vacations. I started work in 1950 after I got my B.A. as a Research Assistant with the Department of Trade and Industry. I did a lot of work on surveys, all kinds of interesting things. Then at the end of my first year I decided I wanted to go and do my M.A. They gave me leave of absence, and I went back and worked in the department during the summer vacs, which in Canada are four months. They treated me like I was a full employee, I got the annual holiday, so I was an employee of theirs until 1953, when I quit to go to England. So I had the full year, and then two long four-month summers with the B.C. Government. And that taught me that, whatever else I wanted to do, I didn't want to work in the Civil Service!

TRIBE: What sort of work did you do there?

LIPSEY: Well, it was assisting more senior guys in research, and I was picked up by a very good senior fellow called Jack Meredith who really trained me well. We did a couple of big surveys. We did a market survey of the Okanogan Valley: we went around and talked to every firm in the Okanogan Valley about where they bought and where they sold, and so on. And we did a number of general economic surveys, some of which involved going out and collecting data in the field, which I had never done before; which was lots of fun. We did a market survey of one area where we went and knocked on every tenth door, and asked the housewives, 'Where did you buy your last pile of groceries?' That was fun. When I started there the Deputy Minister interviewed all the new staff and he said to me, 'Tell me which is bigger, GNP or NNP?' And I said, 'GNP.' And he said, 'Always give me GNP, never report the NNP!' So I thought, that tells me all I need to know about the government! The man who had taught me this general course about Mackinder and Sombart was Bill Merritt, who was a great advocate of Harold Innis; and I decided that I had had enough of the theory and I should get to work on history. So I went to Toronto where Harold Innis[4] was still teaching, it was still a big historical school. I did a two-year M.A. at Toronto, and did an awful lot of economic history, together with a certain amount of theory. Most of the theory I already knew, because I had such a good B.A. And then at the end of that two years I had as professor Nat Wolfe, who came from England; he persuaded me to apply to Oxford, I was successful, and was admitted to Wadham College. I also at the same time applied for a Frank Knight scholarship at Chicago, which I got. And at the very last minute I saw on the noticeboard a Sir Arthur Sims Fellowship to study anywhere in the UK, and I put in for that. I was interviewed, had already accepted the Frank Knight scholarship at Chicago, and, lo and behold, I got offered the Sims Fellowship. So I had a real problem, in that I had to choose between Chicago and the Sims Fellowship, with which I could go the LSE. How I decided was that Chicago still demanded French, and LSE had dropped their language requirement, and I am no linguist! It took me five years to get through three years of compulsory language, so I went to LSE in order to avoid having to pass in French! That was the difference in becoming a Chicago economist and an LSE economist! Your whole life turns on this silly little thing.

TRIBE: I didn't know that Chicago required that.

LIPSEY: There were still major language requirements in the 1950s. We had to do French for our Honours B.A., and for the Ph.D.; most of the American universities were in the process of dropping it in the 1950s. Some of them of course still had two languages, but most of them had dropped that. And I would say by about 1960 they had all dropped the pretence of the language. But through the 1950s the better ones still had it. And the idea of struggling through French texts was just too much for me! Anyway, I did the right thing, but it was for the wrong reasons.

TRIBE: So the Wadham College place you had, but dropped as well?

LIPSEY: Yes I dropped that, in favour of the Frank Knight Scholarship. I had got mixed reports about Oxford, and the college system worried me; it seemed that I might have been a bit isolated, and I got an awful lot out of mixing with other students. I can't remember who was at Wadham. But Nat Wolfe, who

---

[4] Harold Innis was Head of the Department of Political Economy from 1947 until his death in 1952, at which time he was President of the American Economics Association. During his tenure the Department began graduate work at Ph.D. level, extending the influence of Toronto through subsequent appointments to Canadian universities. See I.M. Drummond, *Political Economy at the University of Toronto: A History of the Department, 1888–1982*, Faculty of Arts and Science, University of Toronto, 1983, pp. 81ff.

became professor at Edinburgh, I think this was his first year teaching and I was his star pupil, and that is where he had been, I guess. I was married then to my first wife, and she very much wanted to go to England, so that in so far as it was any pressure from her, it was England rather than the States – but to LSE, not to Oxford.

TRIBE: So you went in 1953–54?

LIPSEY: Yes in the autumn of 1953, I came to the LSE.

TRIBE: What courses did you take?

LIPSEY: Well, the first term was devoted to learning chess, which I didn't know, and to learning the ACOL system of bidding in bridge. My father was a grand master in bridge and I played a bit of bridge using the Culbertson system, and the British were the champions of the world at the time, and ACOL was very flexible, a good system. And so I spent almost all my time in the graduate lounge with George Morton and a couple of other staff who frequented it, playing bridge and learning chess. I went to a few lectures. One was James Meade on 'Apples and Blankets' in what became his book *Trade and Welfare*. Max Corden was there, and he thought it was wonderful. I just couldn't stand it. I thought it was the most boring stuff I have ever heard! And of course James is a great man, it was my failing, not his, but I just couldn't stand these bloody 'Apples and Blankets'! And I went to hear Lionel Robbins. I maybe went to six lectures altogether, because I heard Lionel twice. Wonderful stories and things, but he was wandering and chatting, and it was fun. But clearly I wasn't going to learn much, and I had done a pretty good course in history of thought, and so I didn't go back to that. And then I wandered in to Helen Makower, who happened to be talking about customs unions, she was expounding Viner's trade creation and trade diversion model, and I scratched my head and said, 'All my Austrian economics tells me there is a demand side to this as well as a supply side.' So I went home, and it was my first term as graduate student, I wrote what became the article, my first publication, in *Economica* two years later on trade diversion and welfare,[5] and it took me quite a while to figure it out. About three in the morning, very drunk on a bottle of sherry, but I finally got it drafted to say, 'This is what is wrong with what I heard in the lecture.' And I just sat on it for two years. Fortunately I told Harry Johnson, whom I had just met, that I had this piece, and two years later Harry said to me, 'You know, you ought to publish that'; and I said, 'Why, do you really think so?' So I sent it in to *Economica* and it subsequently occurred to me, although I didn't know this at the time, that Harry had had submitted to the *Review of Economic Studies* an article by Franz Gehrels saying exactly the same thing, but Gehrels didn't get it quite right.[6] If Harry hadn't told me that I should publish it I would have just had it sitting on my shelf.

[5] R.G. Lipsey, 'The Theory of Customs Unions: Trade Diversion and Welfare', *Economica*, n.s., vol. 24 (1957), pp. 40–6.

[6] F. Gehrels, 'Customs Unions from a Single Country Viewpoint', *Review of Economic Studies*, vol. 24 (1956), pp. 61–4.

TRIBE: Surely it was pretty advanced in 1953 to be talking about customs unions, since Viner had only just published his essay on trade creation and diversion?[7]

LIPSEY: Meade hadn't come out,[8] and I didn't hear it from Meade. Viner's book had come out in 1950 and Helen Makower was lecturing at a fairly advanced level on Viner's book; and I was just lucky that I went to the lecture as she was expounding the theory, and scratched my head and said, 'I don't think that's the whole story.'

TRIBE: You are still working on this sort of area aren't you, because of the NAFTA work . . .[9]

LIPSEY: Yes, so that started me off on that because, well, all Canadians are interested in trade: scratch a Canadian, you find a trade economist there somewhere! So I have always been interested in foreign trade, but I never thought of really doing anything on it. This was just pure chance. But that got me interested in it and then the thesis grew out of that. My thesis was 'The Theory of Customs Unions: A General Equilibrium Analysis', which is not general equilibrium as is now understood. Basically, it was putting in a balance of payments constraint. People like Makower and others had been looking at the cost and the demand structures without putting in any balance of payments constraint. And I said, 'Look, if you put a balance of payments constraint in here you're not sure what is going to happen; because what on the surface looks like is going to happen may be turned around.' And so what I did was just close the model with a balance of payments constraint and have what was a general equilibrium model of the effects of customs' unions, and that became my thesis. I put it aside when I got appointed to the staff, and I picked it up and finished it in 1958, three years after I was appointed to the staff. I remember Helen Makower saying to me, 'You know you should publish that'; and I said, 'I don't think it is good enough.' And that was the end of it, and I didn't publish it. And then, about 1970, people were still working on the problems that I had been dealing with in my thesis, and there was this LSE reprint series, and I was asked if I would let it be reprinted. So it was published in the LSE reprint series in 1970.[10] But that was twelve years after I finished it. I think that was a mistake: I think I should have published it in 1958. But I didn't think it was good enough.

TRIBE: At that time you were involved in the staff seminar. I get the impression from the work of the staff seminar that the economic issues you were dealing with were against the British trend, more microeconomic than

---

[7] J. Viner, *The Customs Union Issue*, Carnegie Endowment for International Peace, New York, 1950.

[8] J. Meade, *The Theory of Customs Unions*, North Holland, Amsterdam, 1955.

[9] For example, *Taking the Initiative: Canada's Trade Options in a Turbulent World* (with M.G. Smith), Observation no. 27, C.D. Howe Institute, Toronto, 1985; and with R.C. York, *Evaluating the Free Trade Deal: A Guided Tour through the Canada–US Agreement*, Policy Study no. 6, C.D. Howe Institute, Toronto, 1988.

[10] R.G. Lipsey, *The Theory of Customs Unions: A General Equilibrium Analysis*, LSE Research Monographs, no. 7, London, 1970.

macroeconomic in character. This impression is also reinforced in your text-book, *Introduction to Positive Economics*; it is striking that it is very strong on the micro side, while the macro is relatively neglected, it is more descriptive than theoretical.

LIPSEY: I think I was always interested in micro. I didn't know what macro-economics was. I was taught all micro as an undergraduate. I didn't know what the multiplier was until I went to Toronto and did an M.A. course in money and banking. When I first had to teach the classes, a back-up of the main lectures in the LSE as an assistant lecturer, I had to go to Kurt Klappholz's lectures in order to learn what the full Keynesian model was. I went to every one of Kurt's lectures. So basically my training was micro, and my interests were micro, and when I did the Phillips' Curve article I was interested in what the micro underpinnings of it were. I didn't get it quite right, but the key thing was the second part of that, where I tried to give it a labour market interpretation.[11] So my interest was always micro. And with *Positive Economics*: particularly to appreciate this you have got to read Samuelson's Third Edition, which was The Book at that time. That was the world leader at the time, and Samuelson was all macro, when you come to micro he says in effect, 'Here's a few curves, I'm sorry, kiddies, you have to learn them, I don't think they're much fun.' That basically was the tone. And so what I set out to do in *Positive Economics* was to say, 'Look micro is not only fun, it is useful, it is relevant, it sheds light on the world.'

TRIBE: That comes through because the other British competitive textbook would be Stonier and Hague,[12] or Cairncross. Cairncross's textbook originated in his accounting lectures in the late 1930s; I asked him what the background of that was, because it looks very much like the Jones and Cunnison textbooks of the 1920s,[13] which start with production and then move on to consumption. He argued that this tradition was nothing to do with it. But it is very marked, if you look at these older textbooks, like Benham and Cairncross: they are mostly organised around production, and then they make the move to consumption, in a pre-micro/macro fashion.[14] Samuelson's textbook was quite different to this.

LIPSEY: But he was *the one*. Up until then it was micro. The book that I read, as I said, was a 'readable Marshall'; so it was Samuelson who turned the whole profession in one swoop around from a micro orientation to a macro orientation.

TRIBE: So when you wrote your textbook you mainly saw the Third Edition of Samuelson as the dominant alternative?

---

[11] R.G. Lipsey, 'The Relation between Unemployment and the Rate of Change of Money Wages in the United Kingdom, 1862–1957: A Further Analysis', *Economica*, vol. 27 (1960), pp. 1–31.

[12] A.W. Stonier and D.C. Hague, *A Textbook of Economic Theory*, Longmans, Green & Co., London, 1953.

[13] J.H. Jones, *The Economics of Private Enterprise*, Sir Isaac Pitman & Sons, London, 1926; J. Cunnison, *Economics*, 2nd edn, Methuen and Co., London, 1928.

[14] F. Benham, *Economics: A General Textbook for Students*, Sir Isaac Pitman & Sons, London, 1938 (sixth edition 1960); A. Cairncross, *Introduction to Economics*, Butterworth & Co., London, 1944 (second edition 1955).

LIPSEY: Well . . . one of them was the Third Edition Samuelson, which was the first time I taught.

TRIBE: Was that 1961? That was when you started that course built around *Positive Economics*?

LIPSEY: No, I had been back to Canada during the first years I was on the staff at LSE. Assistant Lecturers just gave discussion classes. I went back to Vancouver and taught Summer School just so I could go back and see my parents, and I taught out of Samuelson's Third Edition at UBC. That was the first time I taught, and I thought the macro in Samuelson was wonderful, but I was appalled at the micro, and that would have been about 1956. So that was one thing, and the other thing was the feeling that Cairncross and Benham were in some sense old-fashioned. Benham was full of mistakes, and Benham was as well used as Cairncross at the time, but it was very much in the Robbins' armchair tradition. You said, 'Can we believe marginal productivity theory?' and then you sat down and you thought of eight reasons why a businessman might or might not think in terms of marginal productivity theory. So the whole approach, which was Robbins' – 'argue about the intuitive plausibility of the assumptions' – seemed to me to be wrong; so another part of my textbook was to argue the positive economics as opposed to Robbins. And I saw Benham as a book that was very Robbinsian in style; and by that point I had decided in my own mind what was wrong with *Nature and Significance*, and so it was with a kind of revolutionary zeal that I wrote a textbook that said, 'We don't *have* to worry about plausibility of assumptions, we can look at economics in terms of deriving positive predictions about the world which are, at least in principle, open to empirical testing.'

TRIBE: De Marchi's article on the Seminar and the work done there points out that in the second edition of your textbook you modify your position with respect to Popper and the principle of falsifiability.[15] Would you agree with the image which de Marchi projects in that article of this very strong, semi-Popperian influence in the seminar, through Agassi and Klappholz? Reading Chris Archibald's work it seems that the style of arguing is quite distinct, much more related to a philosophy of science style of argument than that typical of economics at that time.

LIPSEY: I think I set up the M²T; I was certainly one of the three or four founding fathers, and given my interest in what the hell is wrong with Robbins, it was natural that I be one of them. We were all interested in methodology and we discovered Popper; we discovered Popper through Agassi, and Klappholz, but it was mainly Agassi, and I probably learned an awful lot about Popper before I ever read him. Just listening to Agassi. It was the first year we set up this seminar that Agassi came. It was Popper who answered my questions and my concerns about Robbins. So yes, there was a

---

[15] 'Popper and the LSE Economists', in N. de Marchi (ed.), *The Popperian Legacy in Economics*, Cambridge University Press, Cambridge, 1988, p. 158.

very strong Popperian bent to the seminar, no question. And Chris [Archibald] always seemed to me to be more inflexibly Popperian; I was never influenced to the same extent. Coming from my interest in the natural sciences, I thought that the world was vaguer than that: there is no definitive test. I remember when I gave a little paper that was never published on the loops in the Phillips Curve, and I did something which seemed to refute some idea. And then I said, 'Well, let's try again. Let's look at it and take another set of data.' And Chris put up his hand and said, 'But you've refuted that idea. Let's get on to the next idea!' And I said, 'I am not so sure I refuted that idea!' So I always had a feeling that things were a little less cut and dried than they would be in a simple naïve Popperian view.

TRIBE: You say loops there; there are a couple of striking diagrams in the first edition of *Positive Economics* which are electrical circuit diagrams. I have never come across anything like that in an economics textbook before. Obviously you get the circular flow . . .

LIPSEY: That is from Phillips. It was Bill Phillips, the water machine, and his view of the world, but I took very naturally to that. I always had a dynamic model in mind ever since I read Schumpeter. I felt Schumpeter inoculated me against the excesses of Hicksian comparative statics and Samuelson. I always had a dynamic view of a model in my mind, that the world was constantly changing, and I understood Keynes in terms of Swedish process analysis. This talked about processes that took place in real time, and disequilibrium phenomena. And of course there was a big effort in neo-classical economics to turn Keynes into comparative statics, and say, well, we can't talk about these dynamic things. So that circular flow model which is a dynamic disequilibrium model was just something I took quite naturally to; but I have to give Bill the credit for those diagrams.

TRIBE: What would have been the main introductory textbook used the late 1950s at LSE? Would it have been Benham and Cairncross, or Samuelson?

LIPSEY: Well, of course, as you know the people didn't assign texts in those days. They do now apparently. Ralph [Turvey] would get up and give the lectures and say, 'There are ten to fifteen books. Three or four of them are quite good. The rest of them are probably not very good. Here is a list of them. Talk to your friends and colleagues and fellow students and see what you think you should read.' And then he would give a set of lectures with no relation to any textbook whatsoever, and that was fairly typical. And the kids read typically, if they were bright, Stonier and Hague, or Louden Ryan;[16] he had a very austere, Hicks-style textbook full of indifference curves and everything, and not a word about the world. It was the then-equivalent of the modern mathematical textbooks where everything is done in closed form point sets. And then the students who wanted something a little more discursive would have read Benham and Cairncross. Some of them read

---

[16] W.J.L. Ryan, *Price Theory*, Macmillan, London 1958.

Samuelson, but by and large Samuelson, being an American, was regarded as a little suspect.

TRIBE: I haven't followed through the various versions of Samuelson, but you refer to the Third Edition. I have been looking at the First Edition,[17] and it is incredibly discursive. It has hardly got any diagrams in it at all, and no equations to speak of.

LIPSEY: If I remember even in the Third Edition there are about 150 pages of pure description of the American economy, saving, and government finance before you got even any analysis.

TRIBE: But in your *Positive Economics* you refer readers to Cairncross for a description of the UK economy. In fact, there isn't very much of this in Cairncross . . .

LIPSEY: That was one of those things: I should have picked somebody else! It just showed what little I knew! I was trying to say something nice about Cairncross. I had it in for Benham because I thought Benham was so full of mistakes, or this kind of Robbinsian stuff, that I really didn't like Benham's book. But I thought Cairncross was quite a nice book and it did have some descriptive material, so it was a kind of silly arrogant way of trying to say something nice.

TRIBE: But would there have been anything else really which was about the economy as a whole?

LIPSEY: No, you are quite right. There was a book, Phelps Brown had a book, *A Course in Applied Economics*, but that was really meant as a textbook.[18] But I don't think there was the equivalent of Prest, or Prest and Coppock in those days.

TRIBE: De Marchi says that the textbook is very much a product of the seminar. How close is the fit between the thinking that went behind the seminar and the drafting of the textbook?

LIPSEY: Oh, very much. I mean I saw, I think I say it in the Preface, I saw the textbook as expounding the views that we had all come to in the staff seminar. Very much so. I think I said I had just given a personal view. None the less, there are passages I can show you where I am taking Archibald on and saying, 'Let's suppose that we think we have refuted the short-run theory of the firm, now what do you think we would learn from that?' And I am even there trying to say that maybe things are a little greyer than a simple naïve refutationist view. But then I don't think Popper was a naïve refutationist. I think we were, originally.

TRIBE: Well, he excluded economics from refutationism.

LIPSEY: So all I did in that famous footnote, in the second edition of *Positive Economics*, was to say that I didn't believe there could be a conclusive refutation or proof, final, of anything. The fact that you couldn't prove anything

[17] P.A. Samuelson, *Economics*, McGraw-Hill, New York, 1948.
[18] E.H. Phelps Brown, *A Course in Applied Economics*, Pitman, London, 1951.

universal is Popperian, and the fact that you can't disprove anything conclusively merely says that you believe there are errors of measurement. Think of all the well-documented evidence showing the existence of witches that convinced contemporary observers. Well, you have got to go on making observations that refute a hypothesis. So I just saw it as a process of ongoing tentative decisions to accept and reject; and that goes away from a mechanical Popperian view. And I am sure that my ideas evolved, but I don't think I was ever quite as rigid as some of the people in the seminar. But I certainly shifted from being more of a believer in that you could, with some degree of finality, refute things, to believing that you could certainly collect conflicting and non-conflicting evidence; and that was useful, but that you didn't finally refute any universal theory.

TRIBE: One of the things De Marchi says is that you and your fellows in the seminar set yourselves up against the old liberals: Paish and Plant and Robbins. That seems to be overdrawn. But what was the situation in the School in the late 1950s, because there were some of the older people still there?

LIPSEY: Well, we loved and hated Lionel. We had a love–hate relationship with him. We all loved him because of his enormous belief in scholarship. The Wednesday afternoon seminar when you could talk about anything. The whole of economics was your province, no specialisation. It was a wonderful intellectual experience and I think we all loved Lionel for all those reasons. But Lionel was a very definite advocate of the Austrian methodology, and most of us at various times came to reject that. So we were very much at odds with Lionel in terms of his view of the world, and as you know in 1959 he wrote that article in *Revista* where he basically recanted his own view, but very quietly in an Italian journal.[19] But we think we were not without influence in that! I was on the best of terms with Paish, but what he did didn't seem to be particularly relevant to what I was doing. I don't remember any great battles with Paish; although on reflection I think that it is fair to say that we were left-leaning and found Paish's liberalism hard to take at times. Phelps Brown I, of course, obviously loved. There was a man who was really doing things, you gave him any economic idea and he'd figure out a way of measuring and gathering some evidence for it! So he seemed to me to be quietly, happily, the great propounder of all this stuff on empirical relevance. But we did see ourselves as revolutionaries, but as against the Robbinsian methodological position. You know, when I was a graduate student I remember going to Oxford–Cambridge–London joint economics seminars, and you would sit for hours and argue about whether some assumption was plausible or not, and it was the pervading method. It is not recognised I think as much in the books as it should be, because it was so much in the oral tradition; but it was the oral

---

[19] L. Robbins, 'The Present Position of Economics', *Revista di Politica Economica*, vol. 49 (1959), pp. 1347–63. See on p. 1360: 'I think it is a real reproach to economists in the present age that there is so much untested theorizing . . . one of the most urgent needs is the harnessing of empirical study to the business of discovering which constructions stand the test of fact and which prove to be irrelevant.'

tradition. I remember Michael Parkin saying when he read the first edition of my textbook in an afternoon that it changed his whole view of the world! There were a whole group of people who were sitting there unhappy; younger people unhappy with this idea that we should argue about the plausibility of the assumptions. And all it needed was to just *say* there was another way of doing things and the house of cards fell. So there was a certain amount of that going on; but there was certainly a lot of heat, and I think Lionel was the main person whom we saw that we were battling against intellectually. Yes, we were antagonistic, but there was still this great respect for most of the older members of staff, including Robbins and Paish.

TRIBE: How did the Essex appointment come about? It was a new university. You went off on a Fellowship to California, Berkeley. Was that actually the year, or just part of it?

LIPSEY: I had already decided to go to Essex. I decided to spend a year in the States and I had the choice between MIT and Berkeley; and I chose Berkeley in the end mainly because of the climate. And between deciding to do that, and actually leaving LSE in the spring of that year, I decided to go to Essex. So I told them that, when I came back, I would be going to Essex and not the LSE. They were two totally independent decisions.

TRIBE: So when were you formally appointed to Essex?

LIPSEY: Well I took up my appointment in the fall of 1964. I was probably appointed in the summer of 1963.

TRIBE: Had the University been open in 1963?

LIPSEY: No. The very first meeting took place in 1963: the whole of the staff – the five founding professors, the Vice-Chancellor, and the Registrar in the Senate House. We rolled up our sleeves and the Vice-Chancellor said, 'Gentlemen, let us proceed to build a University.' That was the most exciting moment of my professional life – 'Let us proceed to build a University.' And then there was a year of planning without any further staff, any teaching, and then the students came along in October 1964. I think all the rest of them were lecturers or readers. The trick was to pick up young guys like Peter Townsend or Jean Blondel who were going to be good, but I think I was the only person who left an established Chair. People used to scratch their heads and say, 'What are you doing! You left the LSE. You already had a Chair!' I got my Chair at LSE, in I guess about 1960, and Lionel wanted to spend more time doing the Royal Opera and various things; and he ran the Economics Analytic and Descriptive, which was the theory speciality in economics. With, I think, a little pushing from Bill Phillips, Lionel decided to let me run the Economics A & D once I got my Chair. So I took over the Economics A & D about 1961, and the very first thing I did was I held a meeting of all the staff, which had never happened before. There had never been a staff meeting other than just the professors. I had everybody; and I said, 'I think we should have a taught M.A.' We had been talking about this with all the Young Turks for a long time: the subject was changing, a B.A. wasn't enough. You had to have more professional training; and much to my enormous surprise in two agonising hours the staff decided they didn't want it; and each one of them had some reason why they didn't think a taught M.A. was right, the most convoluted reasons in some cases, and I was absolutely devastated. I thought, I can't believe this. I have been talking to you guys before. Here is the chance now to change the world, and they said no. So when I got the chance to go to Essex I said, 'Here is our chance to go and bring Britain into the twentieth century and have taught degrees, Masters degrees, that recognise the fact that you can't become a professional with just a standard B.A.'[20] So one of the big pushes out of LSE was that I couldn't do what I wanted to do there. And we put a taught M.A. in at Essex and the students voted with their feet. We had one of the biggest graduate schools in the social sciences almost immediately. So that was one of the big reasons for going. The other one was that Sloman was a very exciting man. Archibald, Corry and I had put in a paper to the Robbins Committee saying that we thought the new universities that they were proposing were all going to be too small.[21] If they went to 2,000/3,000 and had everything (i.e., all the main departments), then they would lose all the economies of scale, there wouldn't be specialisation, they would just be glorified arts colleges. And if they wanted something that really was recognising the technocratic needs, they needed something different. So when Sloman got the idea of having just four or five different departments so you could get the scale economies within 3,000 students, by having only seven departments, I think it was, that just seemed to me to be right. So I was really excited with this idea of a research-orientated university with a lot of specialist training. Sloman pursued me for about a month and I was very busy. This was in the spring of 1963 and he kept phoning and I kept finding excuses, and not answering the phone or forgetting to phone him back. And after about a month and a half of pursuing me, I said, 'OK. I will go and have lunch with you.' And I went to the French Club with him and had lunch and he talked for the whole time, and everything he said was everything I had thought about what was needed in education; and I came home and I said to my wife, 'We are going to Essex.' Just like that. It was just over lunch. He was, he is, a very charismatic character.

TRIBE: So how did you set about structuring the degree, the postgraduate work and the appointments at Essex?

LIPSEY: Well, Sloman, I guess, already had a bead on Blondel and Townsend, and he had me particularly go and see Peter. I talked to Peter and liked him; and I put a lot of pressure on Peter, because there was a lot of pressure on him to stay at the LSE and everybody said to him, quite rightly, 'You'll get tied up in administration, you won't write the books', and so I helped persuade Peter to move. And Blondel, I think, was going to move anyway, but I chatted to Blondel . . .

---

[20] According to James Tobin's obituary, Harry Johnson had had a similar project in mind when he went to Manchester in 1955; see *Proceedings of the British Academy*, vol. 64 (1978), pp. 443ff.

[21] Neither Corry nor Lipsey now possess a copy of this paper, unfortunately.

TRIBE: Where was Blondel before?

LIPSEY: He was a Reader at Keele. He had written at least one book on this . . .

TRIBE: *Voters, Parties and Leaders.*

LIPSEY: Empirical testing. Not testing so much as just measuring. The great thing he discovered before anybody else was that the marginal swing voter isn't the intelligent reader of the *Guardian*. It is the fellow that just votes with his emotions and how many pints of beer he had drunk![22] It is the uneducated guy who is the swing voter. And that was an absolute revelation! So that fitted very much with my view of the world: an empirical guy who didn't want to just philosophise. I wanted a philosopher too. We had Alistair McIntyre. But anyway I was involved in the choice of those two; and then there were two or three scientists and a mathematician, Proudman, and Donald Davie in English. So I guess there were six or seven of us at the beginning, and that was the first wave of professors. And then I became Dean and Chairman of the Department. I didn't do much economics for five years. So I guess I was involved in all of the appointments in all of the social sciences and what do you do? We just set out to find good people around.

TRIBE: Well, looking back on my own undergraduate experience of Essex, my impression is that it was a very rigorous training. There was a lot of computing, there was a lot of maths and stats. It seems now, looking back to that time, that no one today has such a broad and yet rigorous social sciences training.

LIPSEY: Well, probably not. We took MIT as our image, and we said we are going to have a training of professionals. In so far as we can, we will add a little culture as well: and I got them for two to three years to have a course called, 'The Use of the Novel as a Tool of Social Change'. I used to try and say, 'Look, it is all very well to criticise conditions from theory, but what really changes the world is if somebody writes a novel that really turns you on, like Ralph Bellamy's *Looking Backwards*.' So I got the English Department to teach a course to the economists saying, 'Here are the great novels that have changed the world.' I thought that was important. But it was very important that they really learned to be a professional, so maths, statistics, theory, we had twice as much theory. We did a course in both third and in fourth year on both micro and macro, so it was much more intensive, and in our own way that was true of the other social sciences. Peter Townsend's approach was more empirical, but I think we did our best to make it as tough and as rigorous as possible. And then we put the taught M.A. in. We just got this flood of M.A. students.

TRIBE: Did they get grants automatically?

LIPSEY: Yes, the students had grants for postgraduate work then. I think we may have had the second biggest school of graduates of social science in Britain in three years, second to the LSE.

---

[22] J. Blondel, *Voters, Parties and Leaders*, Penguin Books, Harmondsworth, 1963, pp. 71–2.

TRIBE: Was that simply because there was unsatisfied demand?

LIPSEY: Well, the students knew but the staff didn't. When the Robbins Committee began they went to the old redbrick universities and said, 'Wouldn't you like to expand? Wouldn't you like to fill up with graduate students?' And to a person they all said no, they didn't want to. We come along and we put in a taught M.A. and suddenly, the students knew, and the second the students knew LSE followed us within a year, and then everybody scrambled to get into the act. But it was a matter of somebody demonstrating that this was the way to go. The big thing was to demonstrate that a taught M.A. was the thing of the future.

TRIBE: You started off teaching in Wivenhoe House, did you?

LIPSEY: Yes, we started off in Wivenhoe House, that's right. And the Senate met, and it was like a Greek city–state; we had these great debates and things, and Donald Davie would give speeches, and we would all argue and then come to some kind of conclusion and it was very very exciting; and it wasn't until the first student explosion that we came into the real world.

TRIBE: What was your feeling about 1967–68? Did it seem to be somehow turning sour, the whole of what you had planned?

LIPSEY: No, I don't think that. I mean it was very, very upsetting because I was very close to Sloman, and was Dean and Chairman of the Disciplinary Committee, and Chairman of the Refectory Committee, there were so many jobs and so few people, and then I was away in the States and I came back the Monday after the students had upset this meeting. Some guy from Porton Down came, the chemical warfare establishment, to give a talk, and the students broke it up and that is what started it. We should have played it cool, but we were all so naïve then. And the chemists were screaming and yelling for blood, so Sloman asked me to be a one-man commission and to find out a set of people who were involved that he could use as an example; so I did a lot of sleuthing around and interviewed everybody and came to the conclusion that irrefutably there were at least three people involved and the evidence was pretty strong. There were others, but it was a bit harder to tell; so I reported this to Sloman. And after a lot of humming and hawing Sloman rusticated the three students without a hearing, and that is when the roof fell in. I can remember the meeting we had with the six professors. We used to meet once a week in Sloman's office, the founding professors and be his inner adviser cabinet. And Blondel was the only one who said, 'You guys are nuts.' He said, 'You shouldn't do this. This is no way to proceed.' And the chemists were howling for blood and everybody else, including me, went along with the chemists, and it was a real mistake. So the trouble is we started the first battle. There was going to be a battle anyway, but we started the battle on a very bad wicket because we were just wrong. We should not have rusticated these people, not at least without a hearing. So that went from bad to worse. But the economists by and large stuck by the University and they were a very good force. The economics graduate students were very active in trying to keep the thing under control and they did a lot of work. So by and large we were left with a pretty good feeling about our own students. Those that were out just to raise hell for its own sake were in other departments. And then there was a group who genuinely felt, quite rightly, that we had done wrong. I was involved in some very late night Machiavellian manoeuvres, but we finally extricated ourselves in the sense that we backed down and readmitted the three rusticated students. It got a lot nastier after. I never felt that our fundamental objectives were threatened until the UGC decided to give us such a small grant.

TRIBE: Surely, what you were doing would have chimed in very strongly with the then Labour Government's emphasis on education and technology?

LIPSEY: It was precisely what they wanted. I was fairly friendly with the Minister of Education, Tony Crosland.[23] He and I had known each other off and on for a long time, and the day he got to be Minister of Education he asked me to come down and tell him what I thought should be done about education. Oh yes, the government liked what we were doing, but there was the UGC, dominated by the old professors, and they had been shown up. The uncharitable thing is that they had been asked to expand and create graduate programmes, and their response was that it didn't need to be done; and we then did it and showed them to be wrong. When I went to Essex Brian Abel-Smith said to me, 'You know the establishment in this country doesn't want what you are trying to do. They don't want anything that is going to compete with Oxford or Cambridge. They just want a little second-rate Oxford college and that's all. If you succeed they'll get you!' And of course that is what happened. The first quinquennial review came up and the UGC[24] came around all stacked with the old people from the provincial universities and they spent a day listening to us. We were all naïve. We criticised their two-ninth's rules and various things, Young Turks that we were, and at the end of the day they raked us over the coals in front of our lay Council and said they had never heard such a bunch of upstarts in their life.

TRIBE: How did that relate then to the other new universities like Sussex, Kent, Warwick and York? I know that Sussex had a much more inter-disciplinary idea about the way they should set up. But do you see the Essex idea as the only one with an MIT-type graduate programme?

LIPSEY: No, we stood on our own at the beginning and then Warwick became the most obvious other one. But Sussex was the exact opposite. They used to say they were inter-disciplinary. They thought of themselves in terms of Oxford. That is where they looked for their model and they wanted to do some things better, and so on. But it was more an Oxford college and we were more MIT and I guess when Alan [Peacock] and Jack Wiseman went to York

---

[23] Tony Crosland was Secretary of State for Education and Science from 1965 to 1967.

[24] The University Grants Committee was at that time an independent body which allocated government funding to universities. It made its allocations on a quinquennial basis, renewal for the impending five-year period being associated with a formal visit by members of the Committee.

they certainly tried to do something similar to us. They specialised in their own areas, public finance, and they decided they were going to have a smaller centre of excellence; so I would say they were much in that.

TRIBE: But that would be all macro wouldn't it?

LIPSEY: Yes, oh yes. But they at least had the idea of 'Let's get something that is research-orientated that has a centre of excellence in some field, as opposed to trying to be inter-disciplinary and do a bit of everything.' I think in the first round we were certainly the leaders, and possibly alone in having a kind of professional MIT graduate training image.

TRIBE: So in 1970 you went back to Canada?

LIPSEY: Yes. And there were many reasons. I was very disappointed with the way we were treated at Essex. But also I had to make a fundamental decision. I spent five years in administration, and although I had published a bit because that's what was in the pipeline, I hadn't read much economics for five years at this time. It was full-time administration. It was very exciting. And I had to decide, am I going to go back to being an economist or do I see my future as a Vice-Chancellor? I was very tempted because I thought I was quite good at it, and it was not everybody who could create the atmosphere in which other people can work. If you can do it right, then that is very productive, big-scale economies. Anyway I was tempted, but then I finally decided that, no, I wanted to go back and fulfil my original ideas about wanting to understand more about the economy and stay being a professional economist. So that meant I had to cut all administration, and I decided there was no way I could cut the administration and stay at Essex. Even if the Vice-Chancellor said, 'OK, you can just go back to being a professor.' So I decided the only thing if I was going back to be a professional then I had to leave Essex. And that was with great misgivings, like a divorce, because it was a great dream, and we thought we had realised much of the dream. It was made easier by the fact that we were badly treated, I thought, by the UGC. And then I went to Canada, to Vancouver, for a year's leave just to kind of sort things out; back to my old university, UBC, as a visiting professor there. And in the course of that year, much to my surprise, because I was very attached to England, I decided that I would be better off to move to Canada. It was a big wrench for my family. Diana is English and the kids were all born in England, so it was emigration for them.

TRIBE: But in some respects you left at the right time didn't you? Because things got a lot worse after that.

LIPSEY: Well, when I want to boast – because I don't think this is altogether true – but when I am giving a talk, I say the best economic prediction I ever made in the world was in 1970! I took a hard look at this country, said this is no place to raise kids, and I left! I think there was a little bit of that, but not much. The remarkable thing is, three of the four kids have come back independently on their own as adults and make a good living in England. One of them is in television and one of them manages a very successful rock band that has been number one in the charts in Japan, and my daughter is a sculptress. So three of the four of them came back!

TRIBE: That must be very gratifying. So you see yourself now entirely based in Vancouver?

LIPSEY: Yes.

TRIBE: That is back where you started.

LIPSEY: I am right back where I started. It is home and it is one of the world's great cities, and for the last four years I have been with the Canadian Institute of Advanced Research, and I have a full research grant so I just work on this technology and growth field. I am now operating in the microeconomics of growth and technology, which I think is where the main explanation of growth lies, and one of the things that interests me is how growth got captured by macroeconomics, and macroeconomics has *nothing* to say about the details of technological change. There are just sterile models of optimal steady-state growth paths. But Schumpeter had growth right. It is all to do with technological change and entrepreneurs and micro. We have a group of fifteen international scholars from Canada, the States and Israel, and we meet and talk about growth and change, and it is fascinating. So I teach just one course based on what I am doing, one term a year. It is a very nice position, and I am staying on three years after retirement. I should have retired this year. But I am going to write this book on growth and change, a kind of Schumpeterian mixture of history and theory. Nobody will probably read it, but it takes me back full circle to my time as an undergraduate, when I started reading about Schumpeter and Robbins, and asked myself what is it we think we know, and why.

TRIBE: Isn't that rather curious, given the work you did in the late 1950s and 1960s, the contribution to the mathematisation of economics, the ideas of rigour and testability? Isn't that really a rather peculiar way to end up? I am not saying it is a bad way or a good way . . .

LIPSEY: No, I don't see that. I think that I was right in feeling that we needed a certain amount of mathematisation. That there was no point arguing in a literary manner about ideas that are essentially mathematical. I think it's a shame that the mathematics became an end in itself. But I think the rigour is needed in some areas. The problem is it just got out of hand, as an end in itself. I have been interested in trying to understand the ongoing in-time process of change and adjustment ever since I started, and I see this as a kind of coming back; and I guess to the acceptance that to understand growth you have to have a lot more history than I understood fifteen years ago. I think I am just a little older and wiser, that is all. I mean, I never believed that you could discover much about the world from contemplating pure models. At best a model is an aid to clear thinking, and it does or it doesn't help you to tell you what to look at in the world.

One of the things we did have with Robbins and all the old guard is that they were all anti-mathematics in economics. They had very good reasons, but we felt that one had to go to the step of being more formal, and that the world was going that way anyway. So at LSE I just slipped in this course called 'An Introduction to a Mathematical Treatment of Economics'. I didn't know any maths until I came to do my Ph.D. I had to teach myself calculus to do my own thesis. So I just gave this course and the idea, I don't know if you have ever looked at the book, was to teach maths in terms of economics you already know. Don't just teach pure maths, but take the demand and supply curves and then just mathematise them. And so we took each branch of economics and mathematised it that way. I went away after about a year or so. For some reason I couldn't give it, and Chris Archibald gave it. By the time I left LSE it had been put in the *Calendar*, I think I just asked Ann Bohm, the Graduate School Administrator, to put it in, but it was all still very much not part of the mainline. Then we made it a mainline course in Essex, and Chris and I wrote the book based on it. The book was very successful for fifteen years or so, but that was really the first exposure of the LSE students in 'Economics Analytic and Descriptive' to mathematics. The statistics people of course and some others got exposed to a heavy dose of maths, and that was the sort of maths that I thought they ought to learn which was in the context of doing some economics. You say, 'Now here are some places where it will help you to find implications you couldn't have found otherwise.' That was fun and a lot of people came to my lectures. It was four or five, six people at the beginning, and then it got to be about twenty or thirty by the time we finished. By the time we were done the graduate students who were beginning to come from the States, particularly, or India, were quite well trained in mathematics and they didn't need my course any longer. Because a lot of the graduates used to come to it at first although it was directed at undergraduates. But that was a kind of first sneaking of mathematics into Economics A and D at LSE. And sometimes you wonder, you know! The monster we untied! I don't have any regrets. I think one had to go that way; you couldn't pretend a set of reasoning that is basically mathematical, wasn't. One had to be willing to express the theory in mathematics. What has happened is that people have become mesmerised by the tool itself, and that is a mistake. I can only hope that it is a generational problem and you know, after a generation or so some people will take a look at it and say, 'Isn't this pretty silly?'

TRIBE: Well, the trouble is, as you said about the business schools taking over economics in the States, the problem is that already here in Britain the popularity of A level Economics is in sharp decline. That signals a loss of interest in the subject on the part of school-age students which will translate into the universities, squeezing courses. And with the expansion of a business school ethos . . . so the problem is, maybe a generation is too long.

LIPSEY: Too long, yes. There is path dependency in all this. It is easier to lose a position than it is to get it back. No, I think you may be right. Anyway it is sad.

TRIBE: It certainly is!

15

SIR ALBERT SLOMAN

Albert Sloman was the founding Vice-Chancellor of the University of Essex, retiring in 1987 after twenty-five years at Essex. Among the new British universities of the later 1950s and 1960s, Essex was distinguished by its focus upon graduate teaching and the development of an international research profile in a limited number of disciplines. This selective strategy included the Social Sciences, and within a few years of its first intake the University had established a reputation as a leading national institution for research and teaching in Government, Sociology and Economics. This was very much the consequence of Sloman's own selection of founding Professors, among whom Jean Blondel was Professor of Government, Peter Townsend Professor of Sociology, and Richard Lipsey Professor of Economics. Sloman himself came to Essex from a Chair in Spanish Literature in Liverpool, and he has left his personal mark on the University in its characteristic organisation of area studies and the approach to linguistics. Throughout the war he had served as a pilot in night fighter units, after which he was an Instructor in Spanish at Berkeley, California. As will be apparent from his remarks below, the Californian educational system left a deep impression upon him, and his thinking on the appropriate design of a modern university owed a great deal to the work of Clark Kerr in California. The following text is based upon an interview in the Savile Club, London, on 20 March 1995, with detailed additions and revisions made subsequently by Albert Sloman.

TRIBE: Could you begin by telling me something about your early career in Oxford, and the academic choices you made which eventually took you out to the United States?

SLOMAN: I went up to Oxford in 1939 intending to do PPE, but one of the colleges that I applied to, Wadham, happened to have a scholarship exhibition in Spanish. I was awarded it, so I switched from PPE to Spanish. But the war had broken out and I had decided that I was going to be a pilot. So I did two years at Oxford, but spent more and more time with the Air Squadron, and that led in turn to my being trained in Florida. Having survived the war I went back to Oxford, did a year on my doctoral thesis, and then was offered my first appointment as an instructor in Berkeley.

TRIBE: When was that?

SLOMAN: That was in 1946. I took a five-year appointment in Berkeley, a temporary appointment. But I had only been there about eight or nine months when the Professor of Spanish in Trinity College, Dublin resigned his chair. Trinity decided it couldn't afford to have a chair, and put the Headship down to Readership and offered it to me; so I came back to Europe and went to Dublin in 1947.

TRIBE: So what sort of students were you teaching there at that time?

SLOMAN: I would think that about 95 per cent of my students were English or Scottish, and about 90 per cent of them were girls. They were people who in the 1940s couldn't get into Oxford, Cambridge or a Scottish university, or possibly Durham; and thought that no other British university was the appropriate place for them. So they went to Dublin. The humanities in Trinity College, for about a decade, I suppose, really lived on girl students from this country.

TRIBE: And then you went to Liverpool?

SLOMAN: And then in 1952 the Professor of Spanish at Liverpool, which is the oldest Spanish Chair in the country, the Gilmour Chair . . .

TRIBE: Do you know when it was founded?

SLOMAN: It was founded in about 1908 by a person called Gilmour who was very much interested in the use of Spanish for commerce in Latin America. In 1952 Allison Peers died, and Liverpool invited me to come and take the Chair, a decision which I found very difficult, because in Trinity Fellows were there for life. You died in harness at about the age of 90. There was no retirement. But I took the chair in 1953 and stayed there until I was appointed to Essex in 1962.

TRIBE: Did you have much to do with the development of Liverpool at that time? My impression, simply from the buildings, is that they must have been expanding during that time.

SLOMAN: It was a period of rapid expansion in Liverpool. It went from something like 3,000 to 6,000, I suppose, in a very short time. It put up a great number of new buildings, and although I was pretty busy as Head of the Department – because it had a journal which I wanted as editor to make into a scholarly journal – I did get more and more involved with administration, in particular in relation to the students' halls of residence and other new buildings.

TRIBE: Did you form any ideas from that time about the purpose of a university?

SLOMAN: At the time I was appointed to the Chair in Liverpool at the age of 32 my thoughts were not about running a university. I was really interested in my own discipline, seeing if I could put Liverpool and, indeed, British Hispanism on the map. But I was very much involved in the development of the University, and in my final year I was appointed Dean of the Faculty of Arts, which at that time was half the university. It took in not only Humanities, it took in the Social Sciences, it took in Civic Design and Architecture and Education – and that of course made me think about how a university could be organised.

TRIBE: So what made you switch from the interest in your discipline to becoming a candidate for the Vice-Chancellorship at Essex?

SLOMAN: Well, it never occurred to me that I would become a Vice-Chancellor. In those days Vice-Chancellorships weren't advertised. The body appointing the Vice-Chancellor would consult a number of people, in partic-ular, of course, the Chairman of the University Grants Committee. They would write around to all other Vice-Chancellors and would collect a number of names. In the case of Essex, they collected about 120 names, I think, and reduced those names to about a dozen or fifteen, and then interviewed the people concerned. I simply found a letter in the post one day saying, 'Would you be prepared to come and be considered, with a number of other people, for the Vice-Chancellorship of the new University of Essex?'

TRIBE: Was this procedure the same with York and East Anglia?

SLOMAN: I would think exactly the same. My understanding is that Essex had a rather longer shortlist. I don't know the details, but I would guess that in Sussex it was simply said, 'John Fulton is the Principal at Swansea, perhaps he could be persuaded to come.' But in Essex they interviewed quite a number of people, then produced a short shortlist of three who were then re-inter-viewed some time later. They took about six months interviewing a number of people. There may have been more than fifteen, perhaps nearer twenty. Essex was established in May 1960. The Academic Planning Board, which was the body set up by the local Promotion Committee (but in effect by the University Grants Committee), was set up in October; and it spent the next eight months looking for a first Vice-Chancellor. So my appointment was in June 1962.

TRIBE: Did this Academic Planning Board play an important role, along with you as Vice-Chancellor, in then making the first appointments of chairs, or sketching out the plan?

SLOMAN: The Essex Planning Board, chaired by Noel (later Lord) Annan, drew up a plan for the University. At the same time they were looking for a first Vice-Chancellor. They then recommended my appointment, and in effect said to me, 'Look, here's what we have been thinking about, and broadly here is what we propose. But we accept that the first Vice-Chancellor will be the person who will actually shape the university; you have got our Report. It is now over to you.'

TRIBE: What were the specific peculiarities of the plan which you found? Did it distinguish itself in any particular way with respect to the institution, its aim, or the subjects it should cover?

SLOMAN: Underlying the plan which they came up with – one of the basic things about Essex – was that we offer only a limited number of subjects. That has been a fundamental principle which we have always followed. The case for new universities was that they would innovate, in addition to making their

own contribution to expansion. But innovation was for the most part innovation in the curriculum, in teaching. The prevailing view in the first new
universities was that departments were bad. Heads of Department, it was
argued, just looked at their own subject, they didn't look beyond their own
subjects and they didn't innovate. So the first three new universities, Sussex,
East Anglia and York, decided that the essential unit of organisation would be
a School of Study. It was also felt that universities were obsessed with research,
and that teaching was suffering as a result – that appointments were made on
the basis of research, that promotions were made on the basis of research. The
new universities should put the emphasis on the quality and nature of teaching. The Report of the Essex Planning Board was not quite as strong on this
point as the other new universities, but they said that they hoped that Essex,
like Sussex, and like East Anglia and York, put emphasis on teaching. It
thought that you should look to new sources for university staff, for example,
look to schools, in particular, for mathematicians. But of course, my own
background was in research institutions! My first post was in California, where
the department had about fifty or sixty staff, with a very strong graduate division. My own interest was in research. In Liverpool a lot of my time and effort
was in getting a research journal going. So I wanted to use the concentration
on a smaller number of subjects to see if, within a short time, the University
could be competitive with some of the leading departments, not just in this
country, but internationally. I put a lot of emphasis on this concentration
upon a small number of subjects, in fact, about half the number proposed by
the Planning Board, going for subjects, and areas of subjects, which on the
whole complemented what was happening in other universities. Looking carefully at the teaching programme, but concerned with graduate teaching as well
as undergraduate teaching. And taking the view that you had to make the
right appointments, that teaching at university depended crucially on the
excellence of the people you appointed. The international aspect was very
important for me; we should recruit staff as well as students from across the
Channel, from across the Atlantic. The most important thing for a new university is to have a clear idea of what kind of university you want; and to
appoint people who share that idea and will carry it out. I spent about six
months personally, in the eight disciplines that I had chosen, talking to leaders in those disciplines, and seeing if I couldn't lever out people who might
come and do this. And so the two things I would stress would be: first, having
a clear view of what kind of institution you want, and second, bringing people
who will share that view and carry it out. It was the Lipseys and the Townsends
and the Blondels who were going to give shape and form to what I wanted.

TRIBE: You mentioned earlier a four-week trip to the United States which
was very formative in the planning of the University.

SLOMAN: When I was in Berkeley I was impressed by the difference between
the Graduate Division in Berkeley in California and . . . well, there was no such
thing as a Graduate Division at Oxford – by their concern for graduate studies,

and the welfare of graduate students. There were other things that were new to me, for example the idea of a Dean of Students who would be concerned with the welfare of students. So that when, more than ten years later, I became Vice-Chancellor, I felt that I would like to go back and spend three or four weeks visiting half a dozen of the leading research universities in the States. The person that I spent most time with was Clark Kerr, who had just completed his Chancellorship of Berkeley, and become President of the University of California. He had decided to set up new campuses, for example at Santa Cruz, so I could discuss with him my own ideas and his ideas about a new institution. I was concerned about the distinctive place of a university within higher edu-cation, an idea which I suppose is not acceptable now in Britain. In California they took the view that, although the system should be large and comprehen-sive, only part of that system could be funded at the level where it could compete with the best universities in the world, in particular, compete with Stanford and with the private universities in the Eastern states. The University of California is only a small part of the Californian higher education system.[1] This led me into discussions with Clark Kerr about how you keep up standards, and what kind of things you can do to recruit staff and to retain staff. My own thinking after those important three or four weeks is reflected in some features of Essex that at that time were thought to be American, for example, that the chairmanship of a department rotated. In 1962 probably no other British uni-versity had that, except for a few departments. But more important than that, the visit clarified my own ideas on what a university was.

TRIBE: So, for example, in that respect departments were strong in Essex? You had Schools, but the departments had a different identity, and that ran counter to the prevailing wisdom of the time.

SLOMAN: Yes, I decided to start with eight departments, or centres. The Academic Planning Board was a bit unhappy about my using the word 'Department', so we used the word 'subject'. My concern was to find the first professors for these eight subjects, professors who shared my own view. In effect I said to them – to Dick Lipsey for example – I would like you to come, establish a Department of Economics, with your own vision of what a depart-ment of economics in the next ten years should look like. I shall give you freedom to appoint the staff for this department. I will give you the resources that I can, and would like you to establish a department which in five years or ten years can match the best departments in this country, and some of the strongest in the world. Of course, I could only attract people like Lipsey if I could provide them with the right conditions. You couldn't do much about the salary because salary scales were fixed nationally, although there was some dis-cretion with respect to professorial salaries. But it meant looking at such things

[1] See S. Rothblatt, 'Clark Kerr and the Pursuit of Excellence in the Modern University', *Minerva*, vol. 33 (1995), pp. 265–77 for an appreciation of Kerr's approach to higher education and the structure of the Californian system associated with *Master Plan for Higher Education in California: 1960 to 1975*, California State Department of Education, Sacramento, 1960.

as the time available to do research. Initially, of course, the first professors would have to spend a lot of time on administration to get the department off the ground. But I offered Lipsey and the others the hope that within three years, or five years, particularly if they made the right appointments, the chairmanship of the department could move to someone else. I made it a statutory condition, wrote it into the statutes, that they would have study leave, the first time, I suspect, that any British university had done that. I also thought that, by a pretty hard look at the university committee system – the number of committees that we had in civic universities like Liverpool, the size of those committees, the number of times that they met – it would be possible to reduce the administrative burden. I was anxious that staff should have the time and as far as possible the resources to do their own research.

TRIBE: When you were making those appointments you mentioned earlier a group of academics whom you consulted, among them two economists, you said. When was this group formed?

SLOMAN: That was the Academic Planning Board. After I was appointed in June 1962 I gave myself about four months to think through the kind of institution that I wanted, taking account, of course, of what the Academic Planning Board had recommended, and in particular their recommendation that initially we should be selective in the subjects we offered. I started looking for the first eight professors in October and my first decision was for the Chair in Government: Jean Blondel from the University of Keele. I sought the advice of people who had been used by other universities as advisers, and then two or three people who had just been appointed to chairs, young people in their late thirties or forties, taking their views, putting together a list and then making an approach to the person at the top of the list. In government I simply wrote to Blondel, who was only about 30 or 31, and asked him if he would come and meet me and talk about the possibility. With some the answer would be no. With others the answer would be yes, but in talking I wasn't convinced I had found the right person. But when I felt I had got the right person, I took that name to the Academic Planning Board. I am sure that on occasion, for example with Blondel, they were a bit surprised at my recommendation, but they accepted it. After all, the Vice-Chancellor must have the choice.

TRIBE: How would that differ from what was going on roughly at the same time in somewhere like Sussex, which did have this school-based system, where they didn't have departments?

SLOMAN: One reason for my preference for departments was that I wanted the person appointed to feel that he was himself wholly responsible for his discipline. I wanted Blondel to feel that he could determine the teaching and research in political science in Essex for five or ten years – the same for Dick Lipsey with Economics and Peter Townsend in Sociology – rather than being responsible to a School. But there was another reason. Had I first appointed Deans they would have been administrative appointments. Even if I had succeeded in making good appointments, it would then be the Deans who would recommend the appointment of the Heads of the different subjects. And I should myself be one remove from that appointment. I felt very strongly that, at least initially, I should make my own selection of the people who would come to Essex.

TRIBE: One of the attractions of Essex for the staff must have been the rapidity with which the resources built up. By the late 1960s there was a very good library.

SLOMAN: In order to attract the Lipseys I had to be able to assure them, not just that they had the chance of building up a department, but that their own professional life as a scholar would not be jeopardised. Being able to expand quickly was one part of this. Also, for an economist, or for a professor of literature, the library is extremely important. Essex in the first ten years put into its library as a proportion of its total income twice the national average. This was part of the research backing I promised to the people who were first appointed.

TRIBE: What was the timetable for the establishment and development of the University?

SLOMAN: I was appointed in 1962. The first eight professors – in fact six, because we were slower off the mark with two of them – the first six professors took up their appointment in 1963. A year later the students came. So the University was set up in May 1961, I was appointed in June 1962, the foundation professors by October 1963, the first students came October 1964.

TRIBE: So how many students were admitted then?

SLOMAN: Oh, it was a token number.

TRIBE: And you were in Wivenhoe House at that time?

SLOMAN: That's right. There was no time to get the permanent buildings built for October 1964. We had to make the decision as to whether we would start in temporary accommodation for a largish number, say 400–500, or make do in that first year in Wivenhoe House with something like 120 students, which is what we did.

TRIBE: Were the students equally distributed between the subjects?

SLOMAN: Broadly in the first two or three years a third in Comparative Studies, a third in Social Studies, a third in the sciences. But in that first year we didn't start Comparative Studies. We offered a preliminary language year teaching Russian and teaching Spanish, and started Comparative Studies a year later.

TRIBE: Did you have a plan for the three-year course before the students arrived, or did you build it up as you went along? At Keele it is very clear that the students came and they got through the Foundation Year and only during that did they give much thought to what happened next, so that the degree courses were constructed as the first cohort passed through. Did you have a syllabus for each subject?

SLOMAN: Once we had made the appointments of the foundation professors, the courses of study were determined by the Heads of Department and by a Dean who was co-ordinating the studies for the school of study; and so the details were really a matter for the Deans. They certainly were clear about the first year, and they gave some indication of the second and third year, so that students who chose to come to Essex had some idea of what they would be doing. The details of the second year and third year courses of study could wait for another year.

TRIBE: How far did you and the foundation professors co-operate on drafting the academic outline of the University? Obviously it was very much in the remit of the individual professors, but you wanted to be in on that too.

SLOMAN: There were certain general principles which we followed. For example, that the first year should be a broad year where a student would study three, possibly four subjects, and not be required to make his or her decision about specialisation until the end of that first year. We also agreed that at the graduate level we should as early as possible, in as many subjects as possible, put on one-year taught courses. But beyond that we didn't go very far centrally. We left it to the Dean of the School, as Chairman of the School Board (when it was formed), and the departments. My primary concern was that our teaching was research-based. The Academic Planning Board in its wish to innovate in the teaching programme, proposed that all science students should do an arts subject and all arts students should do a science subject. It was something which I personally didn't support, but in any case, I left the foundation professors to develop their disciplines as they felt best. I didn't say to Lipsey or to Townsend, 'You must produce some quite radical curriculum.' I said to them, 'You know your subject, get on with it.' Had the first appointment been a Dean of School, rather than a chairman of department, I think there would have been more curriculum innovation and more experiment. But you make a choice. And my choice – and you can't be surprised, given my background – my choice was to go for the best possible conditions for a research-led institution.

TRIBE: Nevertheless, in your area, in languages, there was quite a radical approach to the teaching . . .

SLOMAN: You are right. That was something which the Academic Planning Board had proposed: to provide a more contemporary and a more international approach to the humanities by making students study aspects both of their own society and of another. And the foreign 'areas' they suggested were, not France or Italy, nor Germany and Spain, but the Soviet Union and North America. Now you can imagine that, since my background is language and literature, I was very attracted by this. My contribution was to put in another area, which has turned out to be perhaps the most successful, Latin America. That reflects my own Spanish and Portuguese interests. The School of Comparative Studies provides an approach to humanities teaching which, thirty years later, is quite different from that of any other university that I know. Of course, it was conceived as a School of Study contribution. Given my decision on departments, I had to think out a way of developing it with departments. As you probably know, I came up with the idea, highly controversial at that time, of having a Department of Literature which took in, and still takes in, the 'areas' of Britain,

Soviet Union, United States and Latin America, and a separate Department of Language and Linguistics. Now, of course, virtually every university in the country has got a Department of Linguistics.

TRIBE: I have got a friend who is now in Toulouse, but who had a terrible time both in Manchester and UMIST – as a computational linguistics person, but French, she always ended up teaching French language to students.

SLOMAN: Well, I predicted that there would be difficulties of precisely the kind that you are talking about. Our first appointment in this area was a Professor of Applied Linguistics – I persuaded Professor Strevens from Leeds to move sideways to Essex – but I resisted his request to set up straightaway a Department of Languages and Linguistics. I thought that he would then not wish to provide the elementary teaching which was absolutely essential for the School of Comparative Studies, in Russian for example. We desperately needed people who would teach Russian in a preliminary year, and go on teaching Russian. And the same for Spanish. So we started with a Language Centre whose role was that of a service department, not a Department of Language and Linguistics. But it was clear that I would never attract or hold the quality of staff that I wanted if it didn't become a Department of Language and Linguistics. We made the change, I suppose, three or four years later.

TRIBE: But surely that would in turn presuppose students who were disposed to this kind of teaching, and not the conventional literature and language approach that they would have encountered through their A levels? Why should they (a) deliberately opt to come to Essex, why did that make that decision?; and (b) how do they get on once they are there, because it must run against the grain of their schooling?

SLOMAN: Without the literature and language approach they would probably find employment as schoolteachers more difficult. But it seemed to me that every department in the University should have access to a place in the university, a service centre, which would provide language teaching. Scientists might want Russian or German. I also wanted to be able to recruit people like Strevens, who was a leading scholar in applied linguistics. Now, why did a student want to come to Essex? Well it was certainly something you couldn't do elsewhere! When he read the prospectus he saw that he could learn Russian and study Russian literature, he could learn Russian and be a sociologist, he could learn Russian and be a political scientist. In the leading Latin American centres in this country at that time almost all students were either students of Language or History or Literature. Very few were Politics students. Very very few were Sociology students. I also wanted our political scientists and our sociologists who were teaching an aspect of Russian culture to be appointed by, and accepted by, scholars of their own discipline. That is a pretty severe test. In Essex, whether your interest is in Latin America or North America or in the Soviet Union, if you are a sociologist, you are in the department of sociology and your appointment and your promotion will depend on that. In my view this was the best way of ensuring the quality of people that we appointed and retained.

TRIBE: So this would apply to many of the other departments as well. Lipsey focused very much, when talking about Essex, on graduate studies, he presented it as what he wanted to do at the LSE; he couldn't do it at the LSE and so he came to Essex and he got graduate studies, in Economics and by extension the Social Sciences, off the ground in Britain. Was this something which was general across subjects? Did his ideas feed into the whole, or was this very much more just the social sciences?

SLOMAN: No, this goes back in part to my own experience in Berkeley. I was in the Graduate Division of Spanish and Portuguese in Berkeley, I took some elementary classes, but I also took a seminar in the Graduate Division. So the notion of graduate studies, of taught graduate courses, was something which I was experiencing back in 1946–47. There was absolutely nothing in Oxford! You would go to your supervisor and he would say, 'Yes, I accept you. Come back in a few weeks and tell me what you would like to do your thesis on, what your doctoral research will be about.' And once that had been decided, you would meet him perhaps once a month. That was graduate studies in 1945, in Oxford. So the idea of Graduate Divisions was something which I had experienced in Berkeley. You are absolutely right. One of the attractions of Essex, in addition to having a department which was viable in a very short time, was the opportunity to build up graduate divisions. Within a year or two – I think two years after we opened – with LSE, and perhaps one or two other universities, we had the largest graduate divisions in Britain in Economics, Sociology and Political Science, and received the largest number of awards from the newly-appointed Social Science Research Council. Certainly that was an attraction.

TRIBE: Lipsey also suggested that there were a large number of foreign students coming to do graduate work – Americans, Canadians, European students, apart from the Latin Americans, who were of course a significant group themselves.

SLOMAN: Yes. The foreign students began to build up within two or three years. Not in the first year, and not as I recall in the second, but I was very anxious to recruit foreign students at the graduate level, because so few other British universities were offering Masters' courses, and of course we were very competitive. It also made us very competitive for home students who had done their first degree in Oxford or Cambridge or elsewhere, and would move to Essex for a one-year course. I said earlier that I wanted the University to be international, international in the courses it offered – in fact, the only courses we offered in the humanities were international – and in both students and in staff. We went out of our way to get resources for visiting Lectureships and visiting Professorships. In, I think, the first year, perhaps in the second year, I persuaded a local industrialist to fund a seven years' Professorship in Economics – the Keynes Professorship in Economics – to bring people from abroad to Essex for one year. We had Bob Clower from Northwestern. We had Christ from Johns Hopkins. In their study leave we took staff off every committee in the University so there was no reason for them to stay in Essex, and we encouraged them, and to some extent helped them with modest resources, to go to other universities. They went off to the States, they went off to Australia. And there was hardly ever a time when there weren't at Essex a number of visiting staff. So from the point of view both of staff and students, we were international. And in the appointment of staff I had no hesitation about appointing assessors from France, or Germany, or America. For the Chair of Applied Linguistics we had, I recall, a professor from MIT.

TRIBE: You were very successful at Essex in achieving your immediate objectives. But when the UGC came for the first quinquennial review things took a turn for the worse. Why was that?

SLOMAN: Well, let me be clear. I am not claiming that Essex was a success. I am claiming that not only did I have a clear idea of the direction in which I wanted the University to go, but that the foundation professors were themselves absolutely clear. It was a highly cohesive group. The UGC visitation for the quinquennium 1967–72 was a disaster. The chairman of the UGC, Sir John Wolfenden, got into an argument with one of my junior members of staff about the purpose of a university. It was unwise of the member of staff to tackle the Chairman of the UGC in this way, but he was simply repeating what I had said and what the foundation professors had all said: namely, that we thought that universities had a distinctive role within higher education, which was to be research-led. I wasn't present, so this is just what a very angry chairman of the UGC said to me. Evidently the Chairman thought that we shouldn't be thinking about research – we were just in our second year. He had started life as a headmaster, so he perhaps felt that this particular member of staff, and others supporting him, were not putting sufficient emphasis on teaching. I told you earlier that innovation in the 1960s had been thought of primarily as innovation in teaching, new ideas about the curriculum, new ways of organising teaching. This was different from my idea of making a brand new university competitive, nationally and internationally.

The UGC in those days came to universities and met about four or five groups. They met the junior staff, lecturers and perhaps senior lecturers together, they met with the Senate, they met the administrative staff and technical staff, they met the Vice-Chancellor. And finally they met the Council. At the final meeting with the Council Wolfenden bluntly said that he had not been pleased by what he had heard. Now that could have been simply a bad day. But a year or so later, when the settlement for 1967–72 was announced, our funding was drastically cut. When we started, Keith Murray had given us targets for student numbers on which the whole building pro-gramme had been based. The minimum target was 3,000 students within ten years. The Grants Committee even talked about 4,000 students or 5,000 students. If we were to achieve the very minimum it meant something like 2,400 students in 1971–72. We were on our way there when the UGC based our grant on 1,700, not 2,400 students. We were the only new university treated in this way. The Chairman's explanation of this, which I didn't accept, was,

'Oh, but you have been so successful because you have concentrated on a few subjects that there is no reason why sociology or economics or government should get much bigger. They are already at a viable size. So you have no reason to expand them.' For me, I'm afraid the settlement was a criticism of Essex's idea of a university.

TRIBE: The curious thing about this is that it was almost a personal clash between two cultures, of what universities are for. Surely, in retrospect it should have been quite clear that it was the UGC which was quite out of step at this time, because the government of the day was all for exactly the kinds of things that you were promoting, and which the more successful of the other new universities were also . . .

SLOMAN: Twenty years later, of course. Selectivity, not trying to do everything and so forth. We were given no satisfactory reason. I went to see Sir John Wolfenden and, privately, saw other members of the UGC. I mustn't be too indiscreet now. We were given no reason, but in a sense worse than that, we were told, 'Well it doesn't really matter. This is a decision we have taken now, but over the quinquennium, there is always a chance for you to come back to us. Think about expanding into psychology, into engineering, into law, and it may work out that way.' In other words, don't take this as a final decision. It was clear it was a final decision.

TRIBE: It got worse, didn't it?

SLOMAN: It got much worse.

TRIBE: It got worse, because right through into the 1980s whenever they were listing universities for closure, Essex was always there in the top three; on strictly academic grounds, or on financial grounds, there could be no basis for that.

SLOMAN: Oh, absolutely. Because of the 1967–72 settlement and because of student disturbances we were vulnerable for the next twenty years. Politicians had a marvellous excuse for their criticisms. They would say, 'You have had all this student trouble, why should we support you?' So the chances of getting back on course with 3,000 to 5,000 or 6,000 students at that time was simply not on. A very large proportion of the funding for the first phase of the University went into the undercarriage of the University.[2] The podia, for example. All that was very expensive. The last of the squares, Square 5, has just been developed, thirty years later! Yes, the 1967–72 settlement was very damaging.

TRIBE: I used to spend a lot of time commuting to Cambridge because I had schoolfriends there, it was just two different worlds. What was very striking at that time at Essex was the ease with which students and staff and graduate students mingled, it was very easy to meet other people. The facilities for concerts or plays were excellent; and the design of the whole building was extremely

---

[2] The University was designed as in effect one building, but which was placed in a valley to diminish its impact on the park as a whole, all supported on a system of pillars together with a service area underneath. This 'undercarriage' was designed to carry a series of squares and their associated buildings, but after ten years only one and a half of these had been completed.

good. Was there any input into that from your side, or did you just get the architects to . . .?

SLOMAN: One of my six Reith lectures is about just that.[3] The first Vice-Chancellor has got a lot of decisions to take. One of the decisions is clearly the physical development of the site. We appointed, with a little committee, an architect to plan the University; and on 1 October 1962 the only two people on the site were myself – who had just taken up his appointment – and the architect, Kenneth Capon. For the first four months no one else was on the site. There was just the architect and myself. Kenneth wanted to find out what my own views of a university were, what I thought about the future and so forth. The concentration and the linking, not only of the different disciplines, but the social and the academic side, were Kenneth's attempt to express architecturally what my own views were. I wanted the library to be in an central dominant position, to be open all day, and on Sundays. I don't know whether it was in your days. It should have been! The fact that we built not on the parkland but in the valley was my reaction, and Kenneth's reaction, to the decision of the Grants Committee to put the University in one of the most beautiful parts of North Essex. It was not a sensible decision. You have a lovely park and then you put a university into it; and a university for some 10,000 students which would, unless you were extremely careful, totally destroy the park. So one of the basic decisions we took was to identify that part of the 200 acres which wasn't a park and say, 'We will put the university there!' And we left the park virtually unscathed.

TRIBE: There was this original plan to build something like twenty-one residential towers. I remember the model. And they only ever got as far as six.

SLOMAN: Yes. We had some argument with the architect about that! The model was intended to show that the whole of the University, the living side and the learning side, would be highly concentrated, that you could accommodate 10,000 or more, up to 15,000, in a small part of the site by going high; or if you can't go high, in a concentrated development. It was quite deliberately to safeguard what we thought of as one of our great assets: the park. We had two lakes; and the very first thing we did was to build a third! We took the existing park and extended it by putting in a third lake. But the plan also met needs we were talking about, for example, linking up the disciplines. It didn't work out exactly as we intended. We had intended originally for the teaching and research buildings to be one single building which, even with extensions, you could just walk through. I wanted the disciplines to mix; and one of the examples I gave in those days was for the linguists to meet up with the electrical engineers. In fact now they are the people who spend an awful lot of time together! So, yes, the physical plan was intended to reflect our academic ideals.

---

[3] A.E. Sloman, *A University in the Making*, BBC, London, 1964.

INDEX